# Temporarily Disconnected

Jeanette,

All of the prayers that you've
prayed for me have been received.
I thank you for all of your love
and support.

Love always,

Kelly Jua

# Temporarily Disconnected

*Kelly R. Jackson*

iUniverse, Inc.
New York Lincoln Shanghai

# Temporarily Disconnected

iUniverse books may be ordered through booksellers or by contacting:

iUniverse
2021 Pine Lake Road, Suite 100
Lincoln, NE 68512
www.iuniverse.com
1-800-Authors (1-800-288-4677)

ISBN-13: 978-0-595-41835-0 (pbk)
ISBN-13: 978-0-595-86178-1 (ebk)
ISBN-10: 0-595-41835-X (pbk)
ISBN-10: 0-595-86178-4 (ebk)

Printed in the United States of America

*For my brother, Paul*

*"...For unto whomsoever much is given, of him shall be much required..."*
*—Luke 12:48*

# Contents

# _Acknowledgements_

There are so many people that I could thank for their contributions to this book, that I couldn't possibly name them all. From my perspective, just about everyone that I've come in contact with throughout my life has shaped my opinions in one way or another, and therefore has contributed to this book. Although this book is a general commentary in nature, certain passages are about certain individuals. If you recognize yourself in the coming pages, I thank you. If you recognize yourself in some of the not-so flattering pages of this book (particularly Chapter 5), I apologize for me having to putting your story in print. But it was my story too and I felt that I had a right to tell it. And I thank you.

I'd like to thank my brothers and sisters. Were it not for certain family functions or special church services in which I was summoned to write by mama, you guys probably wouldn't even know that your baby brother could write. Having said that, if you had known, I'm sure you would've supported me just the same. In your own special and individual ways. All of those years up in my room all alone were spent attempting to perfect what you hold in your hands right now. We don't always understand each other because I'm special and you guys don't get that, but that's okay. I forgive you. All jokes aside, I love you all, even though I don't visit unless there's food.

To my nieces and nephews, thank you for the inspiration. This will be more than I've ever said to you guys all at one time about any particular thing. Hopefully, you can draw something from what I've written in this book. I wish I had written this when you all were a little bit younger, but Uncle Kelly had some growing to do on his own before he could receive all that God was trying to give him and even attempt to impart anything onto anyone else. Stay as close as you all seem to be and make sure that you're always there for one another. If you were all paying attention at the family reunion in '05, you'll remember what I wrote: there's nothing like family. Most of you are all grown up now and will soon be taking on leadership roles within the Flowers family. Be sure to take your roles seriously, but remember to respect your elders as such and remember where you come from so that you may have and an adequate understanding of where you should be going.

To my son Steffen, I thank you for being who you are: one of the best things that ever happened to me. Only God would've seen fit to create a carbon copy of me. I didn't think He'd do it to the world twice, but here you are. I'm doing my best to be a good role model for you and my hope is that whatever successes I achieve in life, you achieve 10 times as much. Don't put your faith in the world. Put your faith in God. Do these things and you'll not only be blessed for life, you'll continue to make your father proud. I know I seem a little hard on you sometimes, but it's only because I want the best for you. Someday you'll thank me for it. I love you, son.

And last, but certainly not least, I would like to thank my dear mother. The only thing that you've ever done for me is everything. I can truly say that you were my co-author on this journey. If I have expressed any wisdom within this body of work, it was the wisdom that you have given me. Most people that love their mom feel that she's special, and I'm no different. I've often told people that my mom is my best friend. But what made me feel special was what my mother told me that I represented in her life. My mom told me that after I was born, she took a long look at herself and her life and she decided that it was time to make a change. That change was for the better. She told me that I was the turning point in her life. Many people felt that I thought I was special because I was my mama's baby. That's only partially true. The fact that she felt that I was the representation of THE turning point in her life has made me feel more special than anything. The fact that she told me that I changed her life in such a dramatic fashion, made me feel that I was sent here to change lives.

You have always been my biggest supporter, no matter what career I may have been following at the time. I could never repay you for all of the many, many, many things that you've done for me, but I can try by being the best son that I can possibly be. You may feel that you were just doing what a mother should do for her son, but we both know that there are plenty of less-than mothers out there that wouldn't do half of what you've done for your children. You have always gone above and beyond, even when we didn't quite deserve it. You have been a blessing to me and my siblings and I love you from the bottom of my heart. In the words of Gladys Knight, "you're the best thing that ever happened to me".

Kelly

# *Introduction*

*"Just my thoughts ladies and gentlemen.*
*Just what I'm feeling at the time."—Taken from "The Ruler's Back" by Jay-Z, from*
*the album The Blueprint*

Though some of you may be afraid to read any further based on the artist that I chose to quote at the top of this page, fear not. Jay simply best summed up the basis of this project that I've elected to take on. And since I came up listening to hip hop, it seems only fitting that I would quote from it. Though I don't agree with all of Jay's views on *some* women (you'll find that out as you make your way through this journey with me), I respect him as an artist. At the same time, I probably haven't come in contact with the type of women that Jay has encountered in his life on a regular basis either. That could certainly change your points of view on the opposite sex. Those women will certainly be touched upon as we proceed. This book is not intend to suggest that my thoughts are the rules and regulations one must live by in order to succeed in life, but rather to express one man's opinion. The beauty of us as human beings is that everyone has an opinion. In the following chapters, you will know mine on a variety of subjects. It doesn't make me right and you wrong, or vice versa. It's just an opinion. That means you may agree or disagree, and that's fine with me. These are just my thoughts. Just what I was feeling at the time.

At the urging of some of my friends, I have decided to share my many, many points of view with the world. I have often sat around with them and given what they may construe as advice, but I simply see as how I feel about any particular subject. I don't claim to be some great philosopher or anything like that. I just speak my mind, sometimes with "brutal honesty", as an ex-girlfriend would often say. I feel that a lot of what I have to say makes sense, but most of the free world feels the same way about what *they* have to say. However, my friends seem to think that I make sense more times than not, and more times than most of the aforementioned free world.

For example, I used to argue with one of my friends about just how "right" I am all the time. He said that I was usually right about whatever I was talking about 90 percent of the time. I vehemently disagreed with him, and he promptly told me that I was wrong about that. Which, now that I think about it, made me right again. But, I digress. I often told him that no one is right all the time. Some of us just choose to speak at the most appropriate times. That's me. I've been wrong on many a day. But if I say nothing, no one knows. On the other side of that, you must be true to yourself, and thus others around you. What this means is that if I am wrong about something, I'm man enough to admit it right away. There's no need to argue if you know you're wrong. Though we don't have the ability to be right all of the time, we do have the ability to be righteous.

As you read through the chapters I've assembled here, you'll probably find yourself asking this question at one point or another: "What qualifies him to say that?" Well, I don't have degrees and such hanging on my wall, nor have I been to universities all over the world. My only real claim to writing is that I've been writing poetry and short stories since the age of 16. On the other hand, I'm 100% sure that this won't be the only book in libraries or bookstores that's written by someone with nothing more than life experience.

Most times, we learn more simply by living than we do in institutions of higher learning. I'm not anti-education, that's just a fact. Life experience will always be the best teacher. I did my "research" by simply interacting with people. We can learn a lot about life by simply communicating with one another. That's one of the main reasons we can't get along with one another today, be it between races, religions, genders or generations. We don't communicate anymore. Until we reacquire this lost art, we'll continue to struggle as a people. Not just black people, not just white people, but all people. Communication is the key to understanding.

Times have definitely changed since I was growing up. As I was nearing the end of my high school years, around '86 and '87, things were just starting to change. Each day it seemed that young men were becoming more and more brazen. Whether it was the way that they treated young ladies, the way they acted towards their parents, or just the way they acted towards one another, there was definitely a change in the air. I remember the first time I saw someone get shot. I was standing in the doorway of my high school. In fact, I was just about to walk out the door so that I could catch the bus home. Had I not forgotten some homework and had to go back to my locker a few minutes earlier, I surely would have been in the crossfire. That's another reason I will never forget it. God only knows whether or not I'd still be here.

As I approached the door, I saw a young man come running from around the corner of the building. I had no idea what he was running from, but something in me (as I got older I would come to understand that it was the voice of God) told me to wait before I opened the door and walked out. He was coming from about 50 feet away, so he had a little ways to run before he reached the building. Just then, another young man stepped from around the building and began to fire shots. He shot about 4 or 5 times, and then he ran off. Everything appeared to be okay as the young man kept running towards the school. But just as he reached the doors, he just fell down. As I went into the office to alert someone that a student had been shot in front of the school, I remember being shocked rather than scared.

Back then, that kind of thing was still considered somewhat of a shock. We had school fights and the like, but it was still a big thing to know of someone getting shot. As the high school rumor mill goes, the next day the other students had that young man everything from dead to in a wheelchair. I never really found out what the truth was, but all I know is that it changed my life. If I even had thoughts of straying off the path that my mother had set forth for me, they all fell down in front of my eyes in the form of a young man that may or may not have lost his life that day.

From times like that up until now, there has been a steady decline in society as a whole. This is especially prevalent in the black community. I *eventually* called this project "Temporarily Disconnected" for two reasons (I say "eventually" because it took as long to title it as it did to write it). First, I believe that we as blacks have become disconnected from the things that made us a strong people. We've gotten away from God (whichever God you may choose to serve), family and discipline. Though many may try to suggest otherwise, we were always a disciplined people. There's no way we survive slavery, lynchings, the 50's and the 60's, and all other forms of racial injustices without showing discipline and, above all, faith. The other reason is because I hope and pray each day that our condition truly is "temporary".

As soon as our babies started having babies, we witnessed a decline in all of the virtues that we once shared. This is no longer just a problem for blacks, though. This is a problem for our nation and for our world. How can our mothers teach when they haven't been properly taught themselves? How can they raise families, when they haven't been fully raised themselves? We have become so accepting of this Jerry Springer/Maury Povich-style life that's shown to us during our afternoons each day on TV, that we've forgotten what to be ashamed about. Believe it or not, sometimes shame can be a worthwhile emotion.

What I hope to accomplish with this book is to inspire those in need of inspiration, uplift those in need of uplifting, and enlighten those in need of enlightenment. If all of those things fail, then my hope is to create dialogue. Even if my points of view aren't what you seek, then maybe I can help some to open up themselves to what they really feel about these particular topics. My only mission is to help in whatever ways that I can. I have a voice, and I would like for it to be heard. We all have that right, whether we're right or wrong. Again, I don't propose to have the answer to all of the ills of society. My intent is not to come off arrogant or as though I am free from sin. In fact, some of my sins will be well documented in this piece, although I won't always point out exactly when and where (hey, this isn't a confessional).

As you go through these pages, you'll find my opinions on many different topics, with as much honesty as I can bring. You'll find a fair amount of slang as well, as I was taught that one should write like he or she talks. For example, if I have any white folks reading this or any blacks from the bourgeois set, you may find the word "brotha" instead of "brother", "sista" instead of "sister" and "playa" instead of "player". Do not be alarmed. I don't slip in and out of correct grammar and spelling, and there is a functioning spell check on my computer. But I am from the 'hood, which makes me bilingual. I can speak ghetto and job interview. We call it the "ghetto switch". They cheat you at the Coney Island? You gotta get black on 'em. You need a job? Talk like you just broke out of English class at the community college.

You'll find some very personal things about me as well. You, along with my family and some of my friends will find out the details of a bitter kind of break-up that I went through. It's not here for pity or for someone to feel sorry for me because what you'll read has happened to many before me, and will happen to many after me. It's here for that reason. It's here to show those of you that it has happened to that may still be dealing with it, and those that it will happen to, that there is a tomorrow.

Throughout this project, my love for music will be on display. Music has always been one of the biggest influences of my life. A lot of the memories that I have in my life have been surrounded by song. In fact, I used to joke with a friend of mine that I could tell her who I was dating based on which Prince album was out at the time (get used to that man; he's a recurring theme in this book).

Throughout these pages, you will read quotes from any number of songs that I've known or have been influenced by throughout my life (as you can see at the beginning of this intro). Chapter 5 should be an interesting one in that regard.

Music is a great form of expression. When done properly, it tells a story. All of us at one point or another have heard a song that told our story as if the song-writer had lived our lives. Sometimes it just best sums up what we may be feeling at any particular time. So, if I strike out and start quoting lyrics out of the blue to a song you've never heard before, just bear with me. However, if you do know it, feel free to sing along. That's what I was doing when I was writing.

I'll also talk about us as parents. I'm the father of a wonderful 14 year old boy and what's played out in front of him in our music, our movies, in our society and sometimes within our families, concerns me greatly. I'll give my opinions on how those things, along with shoddy parenting, are affecting our children. It's not something that we can afford to ignore any longer. We need to address the issues facing our children, what we're teaching them and what we aren't teaching them. This generation of young adults that's raising our children are missing some things that are very crucial to raising children. In fact, they're missing some things that are crucial in their own lives. They do a lot of things that don't make sense and are detrimental to their own well being.

Our young adults need to learn to move with a purpose. They need to under-stand that if there's no real benefit to what they're doing, then what they're doing needs to be questioned. It's not all their fault because there are some things that we failed to show them when they were coming up. We'll talk about some of those things. We can't give up on them. They appear to be in the dark. We as the older generation must be their light in darkness. This book isn't being written to look down on anyone while elevating myself. It's not to tell you how to raise your kids, serve your God or satisfy your mate. My intent is very simple. It's to share my opinion. These are just my thoughts. Just what I was feeling at the time. Enjoy.

KJ

# PART I
## Where's the love?

# 1

# *The Great Divide: Bridging the gap between beauty and the beast*

As a single man, I'm no stranger to all that goes into dating. There are so many more things to consider today than there were 10 or 12 years ago. When I was coming up, the one thing you had to worry about the most was whether a girl's parents were going to like you or not. That was a big deal to us. We all knew that if dad didn't like you, there was going to be trouble. On the other hand, if you could get mom to like you, then you were home free. Today, there's so much more to consider. Things like how many kids a person has, how they were raised, their sexual history, are there any crazy ex-lovers you have to worry about, and the all-important mental state. That's right, mental state must be considered these days. How many times have we watched the news and saw a report of some-one unknowingly dating a former mental patient, or someone that the whole neighborhood knows should have been put away, and the whole thing goes awry?

A lot of times, they didn't even know he or she had problems. You have to do a background check like you were selling the person a gun just to go out on a date and feel safe. It's nothing against mental patients. I understand that mental health is a fragile thing these days. However, you'd still want to know if a person has had some mental trouble in their past before you date them. It's just safer that way. Beyond that, there are so many factors that go into simply choosing the right date these days. Just finding the right person to spend two or three hours with can be a challenge. It takes a few weeks of conversation just to get to know a person, because we spend so much time these days misrepresenting who we really are. No one is really who they say they are anymore. The game has become full of games.

Just as most young people do around the age of 18, I considered myself ready for a "serious relationship". You would've had to shoot me dead to tell me that I wasn't: a) ready for love, and b) knew what love was. At that age, it's always a painful experience to find out just how wrong you are. A lot of nights spent alone in a dark room listening to sad New Edition songs. Songs that you've somehow convinced yourself will be classics one day in the mold of Sam Cooke, Al Green and Stevie Wonder songs. Well, I guess the guys served their purpose. But make no mistake about it, 18-year-olds fall in love all the time. In fact, so do 16 and 17-year-olds. But knowing what it is and how to handle it is a whole different story. At that time in my life, I felt that I was more mature than most young men my age. I was always aware of things that my friends just seemed to miss. Like the importance of actually listening to a woman when she's talking. You can learn a lot about them and even more about yourself.

I had a steady girlfriend at the time, and I loved her with all my heart. However, at that age, you're not ready for the responsibility that comes with a relationship, especially if you're a man. If you're 18 and you're a male, you've still got a few years of childhood left. As mature as I thought I was at 18, I wasn't as mature as a woman my age would've been. Back then, the credo of a woman being much more mature than a man her age was still in existence. It also didn't help that my girlfriend at the time was 2 ½ years younger than I was. So now you're talking about the blind leading the blind.

We had our ups and downs, as young people will do, but being naïve as we were, we still thought that we would somehow make it. But as I reached my 20's, and she grew into adulthood, some things became clear to me. She wasn't going to remain that same naïve little girl that I started out dating. She was developing her own opinions, her own thoughts and a sense of who she was. Plus, I had no idea who I was as a man. At that point, I had to ask myself: "How can I know what I want in a woman, if I have no idea who I am?"

Often I find myself in conversations with women who tell me all the things they want in a man. The list is longer than the list of personalities that Prince, Madonna *and* Michael Jackson have adopted in their *combined* careers. If you're not familiar with that, it's a lot. These women seem to want everything and more from a man. In a word, they want him to be wonderful. The question that I usually ask these women is, what do you plan to be for this wonderful man? So many times they'll tell me what they want their man to be, without ever telling me what they plan to offer him in return. What you plan to bring to the table is just as important as what you want your man to bring.

The reality is, if the man you seek is going to be wonderful, surely he will want a mate that is just as wonderful as he is. Otherwise, what's the point? Whether male or female, you never want to date someone that is beneath you. That may seem like a harsh statement, but it's a true statement. Let's analyze. It's not to suggest that some people are better than others are, because I firmly believe that in God's sight, we are all equal. However, the fact remains that here on earth we are all at different stages in life. Intellectually, financially and spiritually. Those things matter so much more than the ages that we often find ourselves caught up on. For those of you who are Bible students, you're aware of this Bible verse:

*Be ye not unequally yoked (joined) together with unbelievers: for what fellowship hath*
*righteousness with unrighteousness? And what communion hath light with darkness?*
—*II Corinthians 6:14*

Though it comes from the Bible, don't be confused and take that as simply a "religious thing". Don't ignore the full wisdom of that verse. It not only covers spirituality, but rather all phases of our lives. Simply put, we should all try and find someone that's compatible with us in these areas. If you date someone beneath your level, it's not impossible to bring them up, but more than likely, they'll bring you down. Sometimes, when we meet someone and we're into them, we automatically assume that they're the one for us and we're the one for them. We must be careful in these instances.

Sometimes we meet people that have needs that we can't fulfill. It doesn't mean that you're not good enough. You just may not be what that individual needs. You must remember to be honest with yourself. Sometimes, you're not the right person for the job. Don't be ashamed to admit that. Conversely, sometimes you can be too much for an individual. Again, don't settle for less. Without looking down on an individual, simply wait for them to raise their game. If they can't, then you have to move on. But these are things that you can't know until you take the time to get know a person. Make sure you do that before making assumptions on who you should be with.

At times, when situations such as this come about, we often figure that we can change a particular individual. In my opinion, nothing could be further from the truth. If you think you can change a person, you're fooling yourself. Though you can *inspire* a person to change, change is an individual thing. It's the same thing we tell the drug addict and the alcoholic all the time: "The first step in overcoming your addiction problem, is admitting that you have one".

We can talk, preach, pray and counsel all we want, but until that individual admits that there's a problem and decides to change for themselves, there's not a lot that we can do. They have to want to change. The same is true in love. Most times, people only change when they want to. Even if they change for the better, they make a conscious choice to change. Even if they change and reveal themselves to be exactly what you wanted them to be, that just means that somewhere along the way, you made sense to them, and they changed. But you didn't change them. They still made a conscious choice, and changed.

My fear has always been that if you change a person, or if they change for you, at some point, they may change back. You don't want that to happen after you've been married for 10 years and had 3 kids. It could be a mess. In order for change to be genuine, it must be just like salvation. A personal thing. I've known many a man to change in order to have a particular woman. But 9 times out of 10, he changed because she was right and he was wrong.

We shouldn't demand change out of a person for the sake of change. Make your point. State your case. If a change is needed, try to make it make sense to your partner. That's the best way to insure a genuine change. If your partner can realize that the change is for the best and will make him or her a better person, then it's more likely to be real. But if it's done just to appease you, then what do you think will happen when things aren't going so great? Your partner is sure to revert back to their old ways. However, in order to present your case, you must be secure in who you are. You must know who you are in order to get what you truly need.

## *ARE YOU STILL TRYING TO FIND YOURSELF?*

Before even attempting to find a mate, we must have a firm grip on who we are. If you're uncertain about that, then more than likely you will choose a mate you're not compatible with. Part of the problem is that we tend to choose our mate with our eyes and our bodies, as opposed to using our minds. How many times have you seen an attractive person in public and started planning the date before even saying hello? Happens all the time.

We tend to think in the physical most of the time, often thinking that if a person is attractive, then they must be otherwise okay. However, through my experiences, and I'm sure that some of you can identify, some of the most attractive people I've ever dated have had the most issues. Whether its conceit, arrogance, lack of class or lack of depth, they're subject to the same issues that befall us "ordinary" people. However, if you have some of those qualities inside of you, then maybe you'd be compatible with a person like that. There's nothing wrong with wanting an attractive mate, but wouldn't you rather have more than just a pretty face? Wouldn't you rather *be* more than just a pretty face?

When choosing a mate, we must also fully understand what we want out of life. Now for some of us, that's very simple. Money, cars, houses and jewelry. If that's the case, then maybe you should stop reading now. For those who want more out of life, you should look for more in a mate. We tend to underestimate things like spirituality, communication and compatibility. As we get older and our physical attributes fade away, and trust me they will fade away, these are the things you'll find yourself *needing*. If you can find someone to stimulate your mind as well as your body, you'll find that your relationship and your life will be much more fulfilling.

That *used to be* the benchmark for a good relationship. Today, it seems that somewhere along the way, sexual stimulation became the frontrunner. We've convinced ourselves that finding sexual compatibility is more difficult, and thus more important, than finding a soulmate. Nothing could be further from the truth. Though it is difficult to find sexual compatibility for both men and women these days, we mustn't be ruled by our libidos. Our priorities must be re-established to include our spiritual health as well as our physical desires. We must reach a point in our lives where we realize that if our souls are happy, then everything else will fall into place. An orgasm may bring good feelings, but it doesn't guarantee happiness. As my mother always says, it's a two-second pleasure. Though it may be pleasurable, what do you want for the part of your life that you'll spend *outside* of the bedroom? *Amen*

I once asked a woman I was dating what her mother taught her about finding a good man. She said her mother told her to marry a man with money. My initial thought was, "What the hell kind of message is that to give to your daughter?" I must admit that my thought hasn't really changed since I first had it. Women don't like to hear me talk about this. They immediately think that I want them to marry some man that'll have them living hand-to-mouth. That's not what I want. But in the case of this young lady and her mom's advice, I just wondered why she couldn't tell her daughter to marry a man that would take care of her. Someone that would take care of her mind and soul, as well as her body. First, let me say that there's nothing wrong with having a man with money. The question is, is he the *right man* and does that matter anymore? That just didn't seem as important to "mom" as it should have. Do you want his love or what he can buy you? Why wouldn't you want to share the mansion with the man you love? Do you want a husband, a provider, or both?

I've heard some women say that the right man is the man with the most money. So where do things like love and compatibility fit into the equation? Of course, some of you ladies feel that if he's got the dough, then you're compatible.

Whitney Houston's "My Love Is Your Love" comes to my mind, as she sings: *"If I lose my fame and fortune/And I'm homeless on the street/And I'm sleeping in Grand Central Station/It's okay, if you're sleeping with me."*

Now whether Whitney really feels that way or not isn't the point. The point is that the song is about unconditional love, something that's very, very rare these days. A woman should marry a man that she would stay with even if they went to the poor house. However, women today feel that if they admit that they love a man that deep, they're somehow suggesting that they *want* to be in the poor house. They feel as though they're willing to settle for less. It's that kind of shallow thinking that's helped ruined male-female relationships today. You're no longer in a love relationship as much as you are in a business relationship together. You're not marrying a man for who he is, but rather for what he can buy. A man's character is now judged by how much he earns.

You'll often hear a woman say that she has a good man based on how she's living, never realizing that it's only half the equation. If a man truly loves his woman, he wants nothing but the best for her and he'll do all that he can to keep a roof over her head, clothes on her back and food on the table. However, he should be able to do more for you than keep you shopping and keep you on your back. There must be a higher level of thinking when it comes to whether a woman has a good man or not. When you're on your deathbed, you won't reflect on all the things that were bought for you in your life, but rather the people in your life that meant something to you. It would be a shame if they all worked at malls, hair and nail shops, jewelry stores and car dealerships.

*"Diamonds ain't what I want out of a man. If I love him, he don't need a checkbook. And if I don't, then his checkbook won't do him no good."*
—Dorothy Dandridge, from the movie "Carmen Jones"

## *CALL 911, BLACK MAN DOWN...*

Now, let's move on to the men. I don't quite know where to start, considering the fact that we need so much work. We seemingly have lost all control of ourselves. There was a time when we would at least *pretend* to be civil and courteous for the first few months, before allowing women to find out what kind of idiots we can really be at times. However, those days are long, long, long gone. We have slipped into the abyss. We have unceremoniously returned to the days of cavemen. Alright, rather than dramatize it any further, we have simply fallen off. As boyfriends, as fathers, as husbands, as sons and, in some cases, as brothers.

Under the guise of "keepin' it real", we have lost our way. Why? Not only have we forgotten who we are, we don't even fully understand who we're *supposed* to be. We were once Kings, but now we're merely court jesters. We once ruled the land, now we simply corrupt it. To use an analogy, after we as blacks fought for the right to sit at the front of the bus, we as men have promptly taken a seat in the rear. Everyone knows that you can't lead from the rear, yet we have found some sort of comfort in being absent from our rightful place as leaders. It's past time for a change, but where do we start?

As I stated before, there are many different issues affecting men today. Many will be covered in the coming chapters, but for now, let's deal with our identity, or lack thereof. We have no idea who we're supposed to be. Part of the blame belongs to our women (we'll touch on that later), but we share some of the blame as well. We have developed some unforgivable character flaws. We have become a loud and boisterous bunch, lacking civility, charm, and class. A simple "hello" to an attractive woman we may want to date, has been replaced by derogatory cat-calls.

It may simply be a sign of the changing times, but all change isn't good, especially when we start *accepting* forms of disrespect. In our minds, dinner and a movie has become a down payment for sex. Again, the ladies aren't totally blameless in all of this, but bear with me. Now, if a woman dares refuses our advances, well, she must be either a lesbian, a "bitch" or a "hoe". It couldn't have anything to do with the way she was approached, oh no. "Damn, you look so good, you make me wanna hit that, can I get yo' number?" is a classic line. If she doesn't respond to that, there must be something wrong with the woman, right? How could she resist such chivalry? It's not us, guys, it's them. They just don't know a good one when they see him.

Of course, that's ridiculous. Deep down inside, women know the difference between a respectable man and an insensitive one. Yet, what's alarming to me, and yet becoming more common these days, is their willingness to date the latter. Men seem to have lost the ability to charm a woman. We seem to have lost the ability and the willingness to sweep them off their feet. We've come to associate such things with being "soft" or a "punk".

However, I've found that when looking beyond the façade that the so-called "hard" male puts on, it's the soft male that's afraid to show how he feels about his woman in the face of criticism from his supposedly stronger male friends. It's the punk that doesn't stick around to help raise his kids and teach his son some respect for the womb from which he came, rather than allowing the streets to shape and mold his opinions. But before I get ahead of myself, let me get back to the male identity. We too must become smarter about the women that we date. Also, just to make sure that I cover all the bases, we must become smarter about the women that we just "kick it" with as well. But in order to do that, we must take a long look at ourselves on the inside.

To take an honest look at today's male can sometimes be rather harsh, so the next few lines may be hard to swallow for both men and women. It all depends on where you see yourself in the picture I'm attempting to paint. Men have become the ultimate whoremongers (if this terminology is foreign to you, consult a Bible). We have *completely* given in to our bodies. It's all about our carnal desires. Though we have always had a strong appetite for sex, somewhere within us, we still wanted a *decent* woman to have that sex with. Today, both men and women are more giving than most local charities. Both men *and* women have begun to think only from between their legs, whether women are willing to admit it or not.

We men are so concerned with all the different ways and styles in which we handle our business, we could care less about who or what it is we're lying down with. We're so busy spreading falsehoods about our length, whether it is in inches or the time we intend to spend doing our thing, we don't even consider the consequences of our actions anymore. However, the old saying, "If you lie down with dogs, you get fleas", no longer applies to just women anymore. Men should also learn to take better precaution.

On the surface, that statement simply means contraception. But there's more to this than just sexually transmitted diseases. Keeping in mind that we must be aware that some STD's are fatal, we must also keep some of our thoughts based in the land of the living. Some of the consequences of our actions don't necessarily result in the loss of life or even just a burning sensation.

When a man chooses a woman, whether in anticipation of a long-term relationship or, to put it bluntly, just to screw around with, he must be careful. Like it or not, every time you have sex with a woman, there's a chance of creating a life. Acknowledging that accidents can and will happen, you must provide yourself with some sort of insurance. For example, we have auto insurance for a reason. Usually the reason, in most cases, isn't so that we can go around crashing into things purposely. The insurance is there *just in case* something like that happens. That's where our minds should be as men when choosing a woman for either of the reasons I mentioned above.

The same is true for women. I don't want to put a damper on your sex lives, but you have to be more careful these days. Every time you have sex, you're having sex with a potential parent to you child. There are only so many precautions we can take, and though I encourage taking those precautions, nothing is 100% safe. Condoms have broken before and birth control pills and shots have failed. These things happen. So, it seems to me, that we must learn to consider these things when making a choice. If it's just one date, then none of this applies. However, we all know when things are starting to get serious. Once they do, you should consider the person you're getting serious about. Be realistic. If you're thinking of having sex with that person, they become a potential parent.

## *THE COMPANY YOU KEEP*

*true*

With dating, just as it is with life, we must involve ourselves with people that are like us, or at least what we aspire to be. Most times, if you have a circle of friends, you share some similarities with them. You have some things in common. You're not exactly the same, but you're not total opposites either. Too often in life, when we make a choice in a partner that doesn't make sense, we tend to lean on the old "opposites attract" theory.

A woman I dated told it to me on a least one million occasions whenever I would wonder aloud what drug made me get involved with her. Though there is definite truth to the statement, at some point you'll have to have something in common in order to be successful. Otherwise, what will you ever do together? These days, you can't even rely on just sex. Sexual tastes have evolved to the point that you can even run into trouble there. In cases such as this, sexual compatibility is all you have left and if that goes, where does that leave you?

That's where we must become better at reading one another. We must become better judges of character. We must find people that *compliment* who we are, rather than take away from us or bring us down. Whether they're in your circle of friends, a potential partner for life, or just a potential partner, you must look for quality in an individual. This is not to condone sleeping around as a way of life, but the reality is that it happens. Not all who do it are whores, but it does happen. Those who do it don't necessarily do it on a weekly basis, but for a lot of us there have been times when we've had a sexual experience with someone that we weren't exclusive with. If we must fall prey to this behavior, we must at least make an attempt to do it with as decent a person as possible. It's not a justification, but rather the insurance I spoke of earlier.

Recognizing that it's sometimes difficult to nail down that special someone, sometimes it's best to date more than one person at a time. This has become increasingly necessary for women, as quality choices have become increasingly difficult to find. Again, this is not to condone sleeping around. I'm only talking about dating. You should simply give yourself some options. However, I reiterate, you must be wise in your choices. Though you may not be ready to commit full time to any of these individuals, do the best that you can to date quality individuals.

Understand that quality doesn't mean perfect. Quality means that though they're not *everything* you may want in a mate, they're still good people. We must realize that a person can still be a quality individual whether they're compatible with us or not. I understand that, once again, our physical desires will come into play. If you can't resist your urges, you must resist the urge to sleep with *all* of the people you're dating. If you must give into to your urges, pick the most qualified individual and go forward. And don't use that as an excuse to test-drive them all. Choose from the mental, not the physical. Once again, it's not a justification, simply insurance.

Going back to the old saying I referenced before about lying down with dogs, some people insist on getting involved with partners that they know are beneath them. Partners that they know are no good. You know he's got 4 or 5 women just like you. You know she's still sleeping with her ex. You know he's got two kids he's not supporting. You know she can't cook or clean a house. You know he's dealing drugs. You know all she cares about is what you put on her fingers, her back and in her hair. I firmly believe that there's someone for everyone, even for the types of people I just mentioned.

However, if you know that those aren't qualities you share or appreciate, then why even get started with someone like that? Why even give them one date? Why put yourself in the position to make a mistake? Remember: possible parents. Anything can happen. We have to learn to be careful of the company we keep at any level, friends or otherwise. Ask yourself, have you or someone you know ever wound up in bed with someone that was *supposed* to be just a friend? The answer is yes, no matter which category you fall under. The reason it happens is because we're human. We have desires and we have emotions. And we make mistakes.

Without getting into the many scenarios in which something like this can happen (as I'm sure we're all familiar with a few), this is why our surrounding friends of the opposite sex must also be chosen with the greatest of care. It's bad enough that we sometimes give in to our bodies this way, thus ruining a friendship in the process, but what do you do if the unthinkable happens? Have you made the mistake of creating a life with a person that would make a less than adequate parent?

Again, this is not written to make your life difficult. I know that most of us don't put that much thought into choosing associates. However, you know who you are as a person. You know if you're likely to wind up in a position such as this. You should take precaution. This is especially important for men. Rarely do we have female friends that we wouldn't at the very least consider sleeping with. That's not to suggest that every man wants to sleep with his female friends. It is to suggest that we *rarely* have female friends that we wouldn't at least *consider* sleeping with. I'm reminded of a line from the movie *When Harry Met Sally,* where Billy Crystal's character says, "Women need a reason to have sex, men just need a place". At the time, it was funny because it was true. With the way women are today, it's just funny now.

With character flaws at an all-time high these days, one would have to wonder why people wouldn't want to be more careful these days. Just take a look around you. If you take a serious look at some of the men and women that single people have to choose from these days, why would anyone want to have a child with some of these people? If I'm a female and I'm dating a guy who's constantly high or abusive to women, what would make me think that he would be a good father and role model? At the same time, what does it say of my character if I'm dating him in the first place? *( good questions )*

As a man, if I'm dating a woman that has five kids by three different men, never keeps her house clean, and has a mouth like Lil' Kim, why would I want to add to what's obviously becoming a baseball team of children, and have my child raised by a woman with some obvious self-esteem issues? These are questions you have to ask yourself as you date. Remembering that our children's first learning experiences come from us as parents, wouldn't you want to know that your partner has something enlightening to pass on to your seed? Like something more than how to roll a joint, how to drink beer or how to reproduce at an alarming rate?

Ultimately, who we choose to create life with tells us a lot about what's inside of us, like it or not. If you choose a whorish man or woman, then you probably have some whorish tendencies within yourself. If you choose someone that has a "little habit", then you'll develop that habit too. If you have nine broke friends, you're bound to be the tenth. You can add any other phrases or sayings here that suggest birds of a feather flock together. The bottom line is, this is a situation that we can control.

# LIBERATED, BUT ARE YOU FREE?

So, where does all of this leave us? How can we heal this situation? And most important, who's really at fault here? Well, there are many answers to all of those questions. No one is totally at fault. However, I feel that women have lost the most in all of this, and therefore stand to gain the most by leading the restoration of the male-female relationship. I feel that each individual is responsible for their own behavior, but I think we started to slide when women became more tolerant of men and their "ways". In my opinion, for the most part, men haven't changed too much. Some of the thoughts that we so freely boast these days were, quite honestly, always there. We always thought about sex first, we were always a tad insensitive and we always had a problem listening and understanding when it came to our women. We were a bit off from the beginning.

The difference is, as we grew older, we learned what life is like when you have a wonderful woman to love. We realized that we didn't want to spend our lives alone. Our thoughts turned from thinking of ways to get a woman into bed, to thinking of ways to keep her from running off with another man. We learned the shame of ever thinking of the mother of your child in derogatory terms. We learned just how special the right woman could be and just how happy she could make you. We were proud to be family men. We never threw money at our problems, but rather talked them out with our mate. We were never absent as fathers or husbands. Once we grew up, we became lovers, best friends and providers. But somewhere along the way, something changed. Our women changed.

There was a period where our women began to fight for their independence, and rightfully so. As a black man, there's nothing more beautiful for me to see than an independent woman. My mother, who is the most independent woman I've ever known, taught me that though it is important for a woman to be independent, she should not strive to be independent of her husband. Simply put, be *able* to stand on your own, as opposed to having the *desire* to stand on your own. Be proud that you can take care of yourself, but it doesn't mean you need to spend each and every day reminding your husband or your man of that fact. Though a man should be more secure within himself, this is an assault on his manhood.

Women must realize that they can be emasculating at times. There's a difference between not needing a man, and not needing a man to take care of you. To take that a step further, there's a difference between needing a man and needing to be loved. We all need to be loved. Women must realize that needing love doesn't mean that they need any particular man to be happy. There's having a man, and there's having the right man. Contrary to popular opinion, the right man isn't necessarily the man with the most money. It's the man with the most love for you. A man with the willingness to show that love for you.

Once again, men aren't totally blameless here. Due to the fact that we have become absent from our rightful place as father and husband, we have forced some of our women to become independent of us. Where their independence was once something to fall back on, it has become a necessity. As more and more fatherless children are born, some of our women have been *forced* to go out and earn a suitable living in order to take care of *our* children. This type of thing justifies their criticism of us. Men should be ashamed of this, but these days, a lot of them aren't.

As a product of a single parent home, raised by my mother, I could often understand why she said she didn't need a man, because she didn't. I saw it in how hard she was willing to work to feed her family. We as men have reduced ourselves to something that a woman only needs for physical pleasure. Women feel that they can't count on us for anything else, and in some cases, we fail there as well. Even in the bedroom, some of us are being replaced by machines. Men must re-assert themselves. They must show themselves to be worthy of a woman's love once again. Though they may seem cold at times, most women are still willing to warm to the right man. However, the fact remains that men have put women through quite a bit over years, and it's finally catching up with us. Some women have hardened their hearts to us because we left them no choice.

Our women have also changed in other ways. This is when I get into women's responsibility for the way that men have treated them. Somewhere along the way, women began to think that it was okay to be disrespected by their man, as long as he provided them in one way or another with money. If I remember this thing correctly, that's prostitution. Now, I've heard some men say that marriage is nothing but legalized prostitution. After all, there are certain financial responsibilities that a husband has to his wife. So in essence, he's paying for his sex, right? Well, here's the difference. A good woman won't stand for the disrespect that a john dishes out to a prostitute. A real man doesn't see taking care of his family as a license to cheat on and disrespect wife. There's a difference.

There are many reasons for the change of morals that women have gone through. The obvious reason is that they weren't raised properly. A product of babies having babies. Some of our mothers were so young when they had their children, that they were nothing but children themselves. Not fully raised themselves, how could they raise a young lady properly? How could they teach her virtue and respect for her body? How could she teach her daughter that sex should be something shared with someone that's special to you, and not something you do to pay rent or buy outfits, when she was nothing but a baby herself when she started?

On top of that, as opposed to telling our young ladies to say no, we've begun to teach them that if he *does* get it, make sure he's giving you something in return. Unfortunately, that something is never love. Now, I'm not naïve. I know that telling young ladies to "just say no" is unlikely these days, but I'd rather see that message sent out, rather than encouraging them to sell their bodies. Besides, in some cases, telling them to wait actually does work. We need to teach our young ladies not to live down to the "hoe" status that men are placing on them these days. But whether she's on the street corner or in the hallway at high school, whether it's money, jewels or a hairdo in exchange for sex, it's still prostitution.

Women have also started to behave like men. Rather than demand that we step up our game as men and become worthy of them, they have decided to wallow in the mud of infidelity with us. These days, a woman has just as many men on the side as a man has women. These men aren't just for show either. Women are in it for the sex, just like men are. They see it as some sort of liberation. This is where the independence took a turn for the worse.

Part of women's desire to be independent was based on the fact that men were held to a different standard than they were. Whether it was in the workplace or life in general, it was a man's world, and women didn't appreciate it anymore. Especially when you consider all that they were doing to help mold these men into who they were. For example, if women slept around, they were considered whores, while a man was considered a *playa*, when in fact, both are whores. So, in their quest to be equal to men in *every* way, they took on some of our behavior, as well as some of our roles.

However, some of our behavior wasn't even fit for us, so it's definitely unfit for a woman. I spoke earlier about the shame men should feel about women being forced to take on the role of mother and provider for the family. It's understandable to want equal pay for equal work. It's understandable to want to be respected as an intelligent human being. What I don't understand is a woman's desire to have multiple partners just because men are doing it.

For all the wrong that women see in us, and one of those wrongs is our inability to stay with just one woman, how have they come to think that it's somehow all good if they sleep with multiple partners? Just like men, you may think that it's okay and that it doesn't hurt you as well as the person that you're using, but if you have a soul at all, at some point, you'll be sick at the thought of what you've become. Once women sunk to the level of their male counterparts, that was the last straw. We were completely doomed.

Society has told our men and women that this type of behavior is acceptable. I could list a bunch or rappers, singers, movie stars, television shows and things of that nature that has contributed to all of this, but it's too many to name (and let's not kid ourselves, a lot of these influences come from within our own families). Besides, above any influences, the responsibility ultimately belongs to the individual, and not the entertainment industry that we try to blame for so many of society's ills. We mustn't be fooled by the entertainer's status in life, thinking that somehow they have morals, standards and common sense because they're successful. Some of them weren't raised properly either. Sure, they can influence us in many ways. Whether it's the songs we like, the clothes we wear, the way we wear our hair or how we talk and act. However, at some point we make a decision to follow them. It's all on the individual.

Our men and women have conditioned themselves to think that using each other is the way to go. These ways are what's destroying us as we speak. The women want to get all the money they can, while the men want to get all the sex they can, and from as many places as possible. We don't even recognize the viscous cycle that we've created. What happens when all of the money's gone and there's no one there for you? What happens when he goes out and finds someone younger, more fit, less of a hassle and willing to do things even you wouldn't do for his dough?

Women must come to recognize the power they have over this situation. You have the ability to inspire a man to change in ways that no one else can. Rather than just accepting his behavior, you must demand better of him. It was done in the past, and it can be done today. Men are no different than disobedient children. We'll only get away with what you allow us to get away with. You mustn't take pride in sharing a man. The idea that "he can do what he wants in the streets, as long as he takes care of home", must be done away with. Sooner or later, he will bring those streets home to you, one way or another. Whether it's disease or an illegitimate child, his deeds will soon find him.

Women have instead come to the defense of men like this, feeling that half a man is better than no man at all. They wear that feeling like a badge of honor. They even go so far as to call the other woman up and taunt her. Telling her things like "You may have had him for a night, but he came home to me". And you let him in after knowing where he's been? Bravo, girlfriend. The other woman's probably thinking, "At least I don't have to take care of his sorry ass. He served his purpose".

That's not to justify a mistress' behavior, but it always amazed me how the girlfriend or wife always perceived the mistress as her man's only fool. Ladies, if he's cheating, you're a link in his chain of fools, plain and simple. You can run down the list of things he does for you to try and justify it all you want. You can tell me about the car, the house, the wardrobe and all of that (and don't forget the STD he gave you that he promptly blamed on a hotel towel), none of that makes him right for cheating. If he's supposed to be committed to you, then you must demand that he show it. If he doesn't, you must show him the door.

If he's single and you're dating him, then other women come with the territory. You must understand the situation that you're in. If you want more from him, then let him know. If he can't provide it, then move on. If you choose to stay, then respect the fact that he's single and there will be others. Know your situation, and be realistic about it. There's nothing wrong with a man being single and dating a few women at a time, but he should at least have the decency to be up front with you about what's going on. He should want you to have all of the information you need, so that you can make a conscious choice as to whether to continue dating him, or move on. Other than having him to yourself, you can't ask for more than that.

However, if the two of you are supposed to be exclusive, then you should demand that he act like it. Contrary to popular belief, trust is more important to a relationship than love. Though love is extremely important, if you can't trust your mate whenever they're not in your sight, you'll always be wondering what they're doing and you'll never be happy. You must be able to trust your mate in order to succeed. Otherwise, you'll find yourself in a cycle that never ends. If the two of you are exclusive, then you must be exclusive all the time, and not just when you're with one another.

What women must also remember is, when you find that special someone that you've been looking for, make sure that you don't crowd him. Don't rush him and don't demand things prematurely in the relationship. First of all, you don't want to appear desperate, because that's makes you a prime target for someone to use you. Second, you don't want to scare a man off. If you appear desperate to the wrong man, he's liable to use you for whatever he can get out of you (usually sex), and dump you. If you appear desperate to "Mr. Right", you'll surely scare him off by trying to make him move too far, too fast. You can't be looking to move the man into your house after the first date. You don't wanna go Glenn Close (*Fatal Attraction*) on him.

You have to realize that not only do you have time, you need time. As I've already stated, a lot of times, what we see on the surface, isn't who they really are. Don't be dazzled by the first date. Look for consistency in his behavior. If he's the real deal, he won't change too much from what you originally saw. The same can be said for men. Don't be a stalker. Give her space. If she likes you, she'll let you know when it's time to come closer. We all just need to practice a little patience. Just because you're hot, doesn't mean the house is on fire. New Edition (again?) sang, "Cool it now. Slow it down". Trust me, you'll be glad you did.

## *"LOVE CAN MAKE YOU DO RIGHT...LOVE CAN MAKE YOU DO WRONG..."*

Getting back on track here, what I've learned is that it seems that whenever a man has made a significant change in his life, *most* times there was a woman involved. Whether it's mom, grandma or that special someone, women have always inspired change in men, one way or another. Women have brought out both the good and the bad in men. In some cases, they've made them better fathers, and in some cases, they've made them terrible husbands. In some cases, they've made them better role models, and in some cases, they've caused them to separate themselves from their families. Some have inspired men to remain gainfully employed, while others have caused them to lose a job or two. They've inspired men to cheat, as well as to remain faithful.

As research, go and listen to Al Green's "Love and Happiness". It'll tell you all the things that we can inspire one another to do. The key is, a woman can inspire a man to do many things. It depends on the woman as to what she'll inspire him to do. Some men don't do better because the women in their lives won't inspire them to do any better. It's not all their fault though, because a man has to want to do better for himself. But a woman can be just as much a part of the problem as she can be a part of the solution. If you have become so cunning that you're able to "trick" him out of his money, then why not use that same ability to help him become a better father? Why not try and help him become a better husband or son? Why not inspire him to become something that would be more beneficial to society, as opposed to just a means for you to go shopping? Why not inspire him to become a better man?

Women must raise their standards again, and if a man truly wants to be with you, he'll aspire to reach those standards. Women must also look for consistency in a man. Don't let him in after one or two kind acts. Make him prove himself over a period of time before you give in and give up everything for him. Remember, a man will do what it takes to get where he wants sometimes. But the question is, how will he act afterwards? Especially if he knows that you have a man or a significant other. Some men are just looking for a woman they can sleep with without having any commitment to. Let the other guy play the responsible role of taking care of you and being there for you, and he'll just come in and get the goods. And again, strangely enough, women allow it. You'll sacrifice a good man and relationship for a man that's not even willing to spend time with you if your legs aren't open. But if your standards are low, then you'll attract a lowlife.

Continuing on the theme of standards, another very important factor we must consider is our existing children. There are many of us that are single parents these days. We all must consider the types of people that we bring around our children. This is extremely important for women. When there are children born out of wedlock, more times than not, they're living with mom. The same can usually be said when divorce occurs. Women must be very careful of the types of men that they not only associate with as it pertains to this, but more importantly, the types that they bring around their children. Just like you want to protect your children from any unscrupulous types out in the street, we must avoid bringing those same types into our homes.

Men with nothing to offer your children shouldn't be allowed to associate with them. When I speak of things that they should offer your children, I don't mean in the monetary sense. Don't expect a man that you just started dating to take care of your children. If you can't make their father do it, then don't lay it at another man's feet because he seems more responsible. You should've thought of that before you laid down with "yo' baby daddy". But if you're unfortunately dating someone that has nothing positive from an intellectual standpoint to bring to your children, then you shouldn't bring him around them. If you insist on dating a man like this, there's no need to poison the children as well.

Also, you shouldn't date a man that doesn't accept your children. Mothers, especially the young ones, have to understand that your children are an extension of you. He can't really show you love if he doesn't have the ability to show that same love to your children. Too many times we put our desires (and they're mostly physical) ahead of our children. No matter how fine he is, no matter what he drives, no matter how much money he's got, no matter how good he is in bed, if he can't accept the fact that your children are part of the deal, then it's time for him to move on. There are no exceptions here. It's a shame that I have to say this at all, but it has become an issue. Our children should always come first. Once they were born, they moved to the head of the line, even ahead of us. Once things mature to relationship status, not only does he need to bring more than just his intellect, he needs to understand that he's in a relationship with you *and* your children. If he doesn't get it, then the train must keep moving along without him.

I don't want to put this completely on the women, however. I'm a single father, so I know how important this is to men as well. I sometimes find this hard to believe, but there are women out there that don't like children. However, what we men are usually dealing with in this situation is jealousy. If she can't accept the fact that you have a child or children and a responsibility to those children, then let her go. Too many times we let a woman come between our responsibilities and us as it pertains to our children. Usually because she don't like "yo' baby mama" or she's jealous because she didn't have your baby. Or maybe she's the type that would say derogatory things about your children's mother.

Just as men should respect the mother of their children, you shouldn't date someone that wouldn't show her that same respect. Our children have a way of hearing things that they shouldn't hear. It'd be a shame if they overheard some woman that they barely knew talking down about their mother. If you can't see in a woman the type of person that can love, nurture and be a good stepmother to your children, then the same thing I said to the women applies here. Don't poison your children. This type of woman shouldn't even be a strong candidate, but if you must continue to see someone like this, keep her away from your kids. However, truth be told, if she don't accept your kids, you should find the nearest curb, and kick real hard.

## FOR THE REST OF OUR LIVES OR FOR THE NEXT FEW YEARS?

We all need to re-evaluate where we're going in life. Instead of men choosing to throw money away on drugs, alcohol and the other woman, we need to help the mothers of *our* children take care of *our* children. Instead of women excusing their man's indiscretions in exchange for money and clothes, they need to demand his loyalty and respect. Families, especially black ones, don't stay together anymore, and this is a huge problem. We don't value family anymore. It's become more difficult to get married these days because you have to spend so much more time getting to know a person than you used to.

There was a time when people were more honest, more committed to working at marriage, and more willing to make sacrifices. Women were more willing to perform wifely duties, and it wasn't a stretch to suggest that a man was a good and *faithful* husband. These days, I hear people talk about getting married by saying things like, "If it doesn't work out, we'll just get a divorce". Already planning the escape before the ceremony. If you're already thinking of getting away from a person *before* you marry them, maybe you need to rethink your decision to get married. There's obviously something within your partner's personality that's got you thinking in terms of "if it doesn't work out". Marriage is supposed to be "'til death do us part". Understanding that divorce is a reality sometimes, it certainly shouldn't be on your mind before we even rent the tuxes.

Remember to choose for yourself as well. So many times I've met people, especially women, that choose based on what their friends say. If you're blessed enough to have wise parents and they're offering you advice, by all means consider their input. If they're wise, they want nothing but the best for you and will do all that they can to avoid steering you wrong. But in the case of those "friends", you must be careful. Some of them mean well, but sometimes, if they're single, misery loves company. I had a woman tell me once that I could only truly be hers, if her friends were okay with it. I then asked her, "Who am I going to be with, you or your friends?"

This is very important, ladies. Sometimes, your girlfriend may not necessarily like your man. That's not a reason to leave him. It sounds more like a reason for your man and your friend to never date one another. It's a personal problem for your friend. This is something that I run into quite often in my life. Often I'm dating someone whose friends don't like me. It's not because I'm not a nice guy, because most that know me say that I am. But I am very quite when first meeting someone, so I come off as anti-social. But once I get to know a person, you can't shut me up. However, it's a personality trait that's very hard for people to get used to initially. So, I've had a lot of these so-called friends tell women to leave me alone because they don't like me, totally disregarding how I may make this woman feel. To a true friend, that's what important. Not how they may feel about your man, but rather how your man treats you and makes you feel. After all, he's not hers, he's yours.

It's important for everyone to keep in mind who has to live with this man or woman that has been chosen. If you're the friend in this scenario, remember what should be important to you: Your friend's happiness. If you're in the relationship side of this equation, you must also remember what's important: Your happiness. Let your friends choose their own mates, not yours, especially if your friend is single. If they were such good judges of character, they probably wouldn't be single in the first place. You wouldn't take financial advice from a bum, would you? Of course you wouldn't. If you're gonna make a relationship mistake, let it be yours and yours alone. Don't let a "friend" run a good man or woman out of your life because they didn't like him or her, and now you're sitting there wondering how you let a good thing slip away.

Sometimes our friends can be jealous, sometimes they can just be wrong about the situation, and sometimes, sadly enough, they could want your partner for themselves. This is where good judgement on your part should come in. If you see that there's a problem, and you have a good man or woman, and a good friend, there's no reason to choose one or the other. Simply keep the two separate as much as possible. I personally feel that there should be a fair amount of separation between your relationship and your friends anyway. It keeps certain unfortunate incidents from happening, and I'm sure some of you know exactly what I mean.

However, if you're dealing with family, it's totally different. You don't ever want your relationship to destroy the relationship that you have with your family, because family is forever. Friends and significant others are a lot easier to replace than family. Your partner should be able, or at least make an effort, to get along with your family. There's no excuse for not trying, at the very least, when it comes to that. But true friends will look at the big picture and understand that the only time that their feelings are important, is when it pertains to you and how this individual is treating you, and never whether they particularly like or dislike your partner as a person. They understand that their feelings don't matter in that case. Choose based on who you want to see when you wake up each morning, and not what "Shaniqua and the girls" think.

I don't want the ladies to think that I'm laying all of this at their feet. As I said before, each individual is responsible for their behavior. However, women can turn this thing around by choosing a man from their heads as well as their hearts, as opposed to using other body parts. Think beyond the material things that you've become accustomed to. When choosing a man, think in terms of someone you want to spend the rest of you life with. Choose someone that nurtures the spirit as well as your physical being.

Wake up to the fact that if you choose an individual with morals, character and conviction, the last thing you'll have to worry about is who's going to provide for you. Choose someone that you can trust. Think in terms of someone that you want to father your children because he would make a good father, and not because the two of you would make cute babies. Truth is, a lot of these fools out here can give you beautiful children, but will he take care of them? Will he be there?

Don't believe the promises made to you in the bedroom. If you want to know the measure of a man, just watch him. If he's a good man, it will be on display, and in more ways than just financially. There are a lot of men out there that can provide for a woman, but very few are able to truly love a woman the way she deserves to be loved. There's only so much that money can buy you, but it never has and never will be able to buy you love. Once you've bought all of the material things your heart desires, your heart will desire love. It'd be a shame if you were sitting across the breakfast table from someone that has no idea about such things when that feeling hits you.

It's true that a lot of our men, especially the young ones, need more mentors and more role models to help them become better and more responsible men. I'm all in favor of men helping their own cause and inspiring our young, wayward souls to show more respect to our mothers, wives and sisters. But in the absence of such things, the challenge falls to the women to lead this particular revolution. Role models and mentors help to serve our young males better as it pertains to society as a whole. They make them better men in general and not just better dates. Women must understand that by demanding better of the men you date, you help in making society better, you marry a better man, you have children that have a better chance at becoming productive members of society, and, once again, you've inspired change. But this time, it's a change for the better.

# 2

## *"Let's Stay Together"*

After all that was said in the first chapter about finding the right mate, staying together can be, and most times is, harder than that. We have so many forces working against us in relationships these days. There was a time when it used to be just a matter of being faithful to one another. If you could do that, you'd stay together "forever and a day", as the love songs like to say. You could've worked through some of the other minor problems that may have come up. But now, you have so many other things that tear us apart.

There's money, drugs and dishonesty to go along with the infidelity that can break us up. There's also the opinions of friends, family and other outsiders, things that I spoke about at the end of the last chapter, that are also working against us. There's jealousy both within and outside of the relationship also at work. The questions is, with all that we have working against us, how can we draw on the things that we have working for us, and find a way to stay together? Again, it's just one man's opinion, but here it goes.

The first thing I want to mention is something that I think most people almost always forget: It's easy to fall in love, but incredibly hard to stay that way. When you first fall in love with someone, it's a feeling like no other. Everyday you miss them. Everyday you want to be with them. If you're not up under each other, you want to be on the phone with each other. All of your thoughts are of that special someone. All day and all night. What we don't understand or want to accept sometimes is that this feeling almost always will go away, unless you are one of the extremely lucky couples out there.

I don't think it's realistic to expect to feel that way forever about someone. When I speak of that, I don't speak of love or being in love. I'm speaking of that feeling of euphoria that occurs when you first get involved with someone. That feeling that makes you tell your parents to back off when they suggest that you should maybe slow down and really get to know that person before you fall too deep, too fast. We're not quite ready to understand that we can be in love with

25

someone without going absolutely insane at the mention of their names or the sound of their voice. But it's just that it's all so new to you that you feel like this feeling could last forever.

The reality is that the bump in the road is coming, and that's not always such a bad thing. It's all gravy when all you've had are good times and smiles. But that first uncomfortable disagreement is just around the corner. That first time we take off our masks. That first time you realize that he doesn't like all those Julia Roberts movies he's been willing to sit through. That first time that you let it be known that you don't like it when he plays rap *all the time*. That first time you suggest that maybe it's time he start spending less time with the boys, and more time with you. That time when he doesn't quite understand why he needs to continue bringing you flowers every week the way he did when you first started, because you guys are past that stage now. Again, this isn't true with all couples. For some of the lucky ones, they stay in that euphoria mode forever. But it must be noted that they are the truly lucky and blessed.

What I'd like to do in the next two chapters is to offer a few suggestions on how to maintain some of that glow that we inevitably lose as we go along in our relationships. Suggestions on how to accept the fact that though we may not always have that same brand new feeling, it's still worth it. It's almost like buying a new car. After a year or so, it's not the same brand new car that you purchased, but it's still serving its purpose. It still gets you to work, gets the kids to school and so on. It ain't what it used to be, but what in the world would you do without that car? However, we must treat our love and relationships like that car *purchase*, and not a 3 year lease, looking to trade it in once the mileage is up (forgive the analogy folks, that's just the car salesman in me; But it's perfect, don't you agree?).

# SPACE

First of all, this section isn't about NASA, nor is it about the "final frontier". It's about one of the more important words that we need to remember in relationships. Space. I know, when we're in love, we don't like to hear this word. It goes against everything that we're feeling. How can I give the man or woman I love space, when all I wanna do is spend time with them? Trust me, you must. It's so important for us to respect each other in this fashion, and it is a form of respect. The best thing to do is to recognize this fact early on. If you do that, you'll avoid one of the more uncomfortable situations that'll come along in a relationship.

Usually, one partner comes to the realization of needing space sooner than the other. Unfortunately for us guys, it's the men that feel it first. We start to feel crowded. We start to want to go back to the way things were before we met this "time burglar" (Bart Simpson reference) that we call our significant other. We start to miss that "quality time" with the fellas that we had so much of before we fell in love. So when it comes time to break the news to our women, we become the bearers of bad news.

How many times have some of you men out there dreaded having to tell your girl that you need a little space? The fear is that she'll misunderstand and think you're seeing other people (and I'm sorry ladies, but more times than not, that's the first thing that comes to your mind). Don't get me wrong ladies, a lot of times that's true, but let's not focus on the "playas" out there. For the sake of this chapter and making this point, let's focus on the real men out there that are in real relationships.

Both men and women need to understand the necessity for this space. Once we find that special someone, the first thing we want to do is to bring them into every facet of our world. Not just to make them a part of it, but to subconsciously force them into the things that we enjoy. It's not force in the negative sense, but from a place of love. We want them to love the things we love. Hate the things we hate. Listen to the music we listen to. Love the movies we love. We want them in our lives in every way. So we hope that they take to the things that we take to so that we never have a reason to be apart from them.

This also works in reverse order. Sometimes we're willing to take on everything that our partner is into, whether we like it or not, just to be near them. Though there are some things that we definitely need to share with our partners (I'll get into that later), it's not necessary to be into everything that your partner is into. In fact, in my opinion, it's not healthy to have everything in common. There needs to be some things that you don't share. It's an old cliché, but we must learn to celebrate our differences. There's only so much you really need to have in common and do together in order to make the relationship work. Find out what those necessities are for you and your partner, and make sure that you have them.

We must maintain some sort of separate lives so that we don't wear on one another. Again, that feeling of euphoria can make you think that such a thing could never happen, but it's happened to others and it can happen to you. There's nothing wrong with your partner having a life outside of you, but sometimes we can't handle it. We get a little jealous. I know that sounds strange, but bear with me as a lot of these things are subconscious, and we don't even know that we're feeling them.

Once we fall in love, we want to believe that we are the ultimate in our partner's pleasure, and if the love is true, we should be. But the fact that our partner can go and do anything without us and actually enjoy themselves kind of hurts our feelings initially. It's one of the ways in which our heart tricks us. It makes us believe that now that we've found the love of our lives, there's no need for outsiders or outside interests that don't involve us. You're all I need, I'm all you need and that's all that matters. It's the same thing that makes us cut off our friends and, in some unfortunate cases, our families, just to spend every day and night with that special someone. But trust in this, sometimes separation can be a good thing.

Separating from your partner and doing individual things can actually strengthen your relationship. If there is an exact opposite to the anxiety of missing the one that you love when you're apart from them, it has to be coming back together. But how can you ever miss someone if you're always with them? It's not all that possible unless you're obsessive, and that's never good. Your outside interests can actually help in enhancing the time that you do spend together. It helps you to appreciate your partner more and can actually give you more to talk about with one another, thus helping in the area of communication.

Don't get me wrong, just because you may not be as into what your partner is into, doesn't mean that it can't interest you. From my days as a television producer, I would often tell the events of my day to a woman I was dating. Though she had absolutely no interest in going into television, there were days she hung on my every word. Not because she wanted to produce television programs, invade my space or anything like that. She listened because she loved me and she had an interest in how my day went and what I did for a living. That's it. This way, she could share in my life, and yet I could do my TV thing whenever I wanted without her.

This type of separation is especially good for women. As I stated earlier, men are usually the first to feel that need for space. At the same time, women are usually the ones that shut themselves off from everyone in order to be with that special someone. Most times, this is usually a huge mistake. It's natural to spend less time with your girlfriends and such when you start to fall for that new man, but don't kick your girls to the curb completely. This is a little tricky as sometimes the girlfriends pull *the other way* a little too hard, especially the ones that don't have a man of their own (remember, misery loves company). It's also tricky in the sense that once your man starts to allow that love to really take over his heart, he can become a little jealous. I know that because I've been guilty of it myself. But you ladies must remember how important your friends are.

Understand that I mean *true* friends and not those relationship bandits that you girls sometimes call friends. Your "girl's night out" is just as important as his night out with the fellas. It can help you gain perspective on your relationship. You get to share stories with your girlfriends, whether bad or good. Some of your friends may be in good relationships, which can give you someone to relate to. Someone who may understand that whole "I'm in love" thing, and understand why you guys don't see each other as much anymore. And, though this may sound cruel, some of your friends may be in bad relationships, which can help you to realize how fortunate you are to have someone in your life that loves you. One final note on that, it can allow your friends to share in your life, without being all up in your man's face (it's never good to mix your friends and your man too often; it's a disaster waiting to happen). If your friends are true, they want to share in your happiness, and not take away from it.

Beyond maintaining friendships, it's also important for women to try to maintain hobbies and extracurricular activities that they may have had before they met "Mr. Right". Don't view the things you do without him as distractions or things that take away from your time with him. Sure, you may allow less time for these things, considering the fact that when love takes over, we tend to want to cling to one another. But try to keep your feet on the ground just a little bit and maintain some sort of normalcy in your life. Even if some of these things were things that you did alone, don't be afraid to continue them. Quiet time alone is so underrated. It can be a great form of therapy, even when there's nothing wrong with you. Remember that alone doesn't mean lonely. I know this will be hard advice to follow initially, but once the ether starts to wear off, hopefully some of these words will be helpful as you try to readjust to dealing with those of us you left here in the real world when you took off for Loveland.

For the men, well, you can just take every suggestion I gave to the ladies, and use it for yourself. Including the part about sharing your feelings with your friends, although I know I'm reaching there. Both men and women need to follow a few of these rules. It's really all about letting each other breathe. Letting the absence make your heart grow fonder. Knowing the difference between "I'll see ya later" and "Goodbye". It's not that drastic, people. Remember that you have family and friends that still love you too and would like to see you every once in a while without that Siamese twin attached to your hip. It's just like fine wine, sometimes you gotta let it breathe (imagine me saying that and I don't even drink; what do I know about fine wine?). If you keep in mind that you're giving space in order to enhance your relationship, though it may be hard, you'll find the strength to do it.

# *BOUNDARIES*

If the need to give space is difficult for you to understand or accept in your relationship, then knowing how much to give and how *not* to invade your partner's space can be just as trying. Knowing our boundaries in a relationship can be a tricky thing. I mean, it's a *relationship*, right? We share everything, right? I should be able to cross any line you draw in the sand and it should be okay with you because we're in love, right? If you answered "right" to those questions, stop reading here. Go back and read the section on space again. Either you didn't understand it or my explanation wasn't as clear as I intended.

Both space and boundaries aren't just important when getting to know someone, but they're also important after we've entered into the relationship. But I don't want to be redundant about any of this. We've already covered the need for space. What I want to talk about in the next few paragraphs is how much space to give. How to respect the boundaries that we've set up in our relationship once we've established the need for space and separate interests.

Okay ladies, let's start with you. Let's just assume that all is well and you've accepted the fact that he needs his space. He needs his time with the fellas. He needs his time to go play ball. He needs his time with his satellite dish so that he can *watch others* play ball (guilty as charged). He needs his time to just chill without you sometimes. You've accepted the fact that he doesn't love you any less when he needs his space. It's just what the man needs. (Now, don't get paranoid ladies; remember, I'm talking about the good ones, not the *playas*). What do you do when his need for space starts to interfere with your needs as his mate? What do you do when that 2 hour run at the court on Saturday morning starts to turn into 3 hours because he wanted to wait and get one last run in (you girls just don't know how hard it is to leave that court on a loss)?

What do you do when he wants to watch an east coast game *and* a west coast game on the dish, after you waited all day for him to get off work, hoping to spend some time with him? Are you just supposed to give up your time for Shaq and Kobe? What's a girl to do when all she want to do is to curl up under her man and, to quote Martin Lawrence from his stand-up comedy *You So Crazy*, he keeps telling you that "Craig and 'em wanted to hook up tonight. I'll see ya when

I see ya!" How can you respect his boundaries without allowing him to take you for granted and give all of your time to his other interests? I'll try to help.

The first thing I will suggest to the ladies is don't try the "tag along" method. This is usually one of the first things you guys try when you feel that he's spending too much time away from you. If you can't beat 'em, join 'em. As I stated earlier, when getting involved with one another, we try to force our significant others into the things that we're into. Conversely, we sometimes try to adapt to everything that our partner is into in order to spend more time with them. Sometimes this is good, sometimes it's bad. Again, you don't want to crowd your partner. You want them to feel that they still have an identity and life outside of you. There has to be room in the relationship for your partner to still feel like an individual, while within the confines of a relationship. This is especially true with men. Here's a solution, based on the scenario I presented above, and you can apply it to your particular situation.

Let's take the basketball example I used. Here's a way for you ladies to become more involved in his life, without making him feel invaded or crowded. As I said before, don't attempt the tag along. Maybe suggest to him that you'd like to come out every once in a while and watch him play. Now remember ladies, this isn't an excuse to clear out every Saturday morning to go to gym with him. I said every once in a while. This will help you to see what the fuss is about. Not only might you gain an appreciation for these grown men and the competitive spirit they display, you might even enjoy yourself.

Now in the very likely event that you *don't* understand what the fuss is about, don't put it down or make him feel like he's wasting his time. Realize that it means something to him and support it from the background. We don't always have to understand all the reasons our partners do what they do or are into what they're into in order to support it. As long as it's not a detriment to them or your relationship, then you should be able to support them.

Continuing to use the example of sports, it may be easier to close the gap in watching that satellite dish with him. It's been my experience that women tend not to like some sports because they don't understand everything that's going on. It's not to suggest that there aren't some hardcore sports fans out there among the women, but in most cases, they usually won't like a sport they can't follow. I never knew how complicated the game of football was until someone asked me to explain it to them. There's a lot to remember. But as men, we're usually taught this game from birth, so it's second nature to us. And since we're usually watching with other men, other than a rule here or there, we never have to explain this game from the ground up. But women don't want to spend all day watching something they can't follow or can barely understand. But they still want to be with you.

So women and men need to make the adjustment. We as men have to be willing to indulge those "silly" questions that women asks us about our passion and make it make sense to her so that she can, at the very least, follow the action. Having said that, I've never met a woman who, once she finally understood what was going on, didn't become more of a sports fan. As I said earlier, they just wanna know what all the fuss is about.

Understand what I'm saying ladies. This is just a way to better understand what he's doing or watching, and why he's so passionate about it. It's not, however, an excuse to watch every game with him. We as men still need that time away from you, so you still have to let him watch the game alone or with the fellas from time to time. It's also not an excuse for men to neglect you. He shouldn't teach you the rules to the games just so he can watch more games. It's just a way for you to share a little more in his life. You're gaining understanding. Now, whenever he tells you that you can come over if you want, but you need to understand that he's watching Allan Houston and the Knicks and that's that (this used to be my personal drug before Allan retired and ruined it all for me), you won't be completely bored out of your mind. Knowing boundaries doesn't mean that we won't cross them from time to time. We just need to know how to get in and get out without completely invading that space.

The sports analogy I used here is just an example. I'm well aware that all men aren't into sports. But since I am, it was a pretty good analogy for me to use. I have faith in the intelligence of those of you reading this that you can apply the logic of this explanation to whatever aspects of your life that it fits. Plus, we're all aware of the fact that high on that list of things that men and women more times than not disagree on is sports and how prevalent it should be in our respective lives. We can't get enough and you guys can't wait 'til it's over. For the umpteenth time, what's all the fuss about? But whether your man is into art, music, writing, his career, community or whatever, you can apply this logic to your life. Don't force your way into his life in that way. You may cause him to withdraw. Show an interest, learn a thing or two about what he's into, but in the end, let it be his. He'll let you in as he sees fit. But once the game's over, it's your time ladies.

Now it's time to talk about the men. My brothas, what can I say about us? Ours is a totally different situation. Our view on boundaries is different. Since we're usually the ones that ask for space first, thus making us the ones that want most for these boundaries to be respected, we tend to think that this is just something the women need to learn to do. Respect our boundaries. But don't be fooled. Women have boundaries as well and we're very capable of violating their space. Women's boundaries are more on the emotional side than ours are. Their need to spend time with their friends without us is usually coming from a place of emotion.

Now, I must ask the fellas not to get paranoid, as I'm talking about the good women and not the, uh, others (it's sad that I have to even make that distinction these days). It has less to do with getting away from the ball and chain and more to do with the genuine love that they feel for their friends. It's that whole *Waiting to Exhale* vibe. Their friends are important to their emotional well being. Ours are too, but we tend not to get in touch with that side of ourselves, so just pretend I didn't just tell everyone that.

Sometimes they need to get away from us and just be with other women, talking about and doing women things. So how should we adjust when we finally come down off of Mount NFL and have the desire to give our woman that last hour or so of the day before we nod off? When we've finally spent all of the time we want with the brothas, what are we to do when we hit her up on the cell phone and she says she's already out with her girls and she can't make it tonight? What should we do when *we* want quality time and our woman has gone out to have fun of her own, on her own?

As I stated earlier in the section on space, once that love takes over a man's heart, he can become a tad bit jealous. Sometimes women think that this is cute, but remember that jealousy is an unpredictable emotion. It can tear an individual and a relationship apart if not addressed properly. This is where we tend to invade our woman's space. It's all good when we're hanging with the fellas or doing our own thing, but as soon as she's out with her girls and we want some attention, we tend to start pouting.

As much as men complain about being crowded by women, we want that same woman at our beck and call sometimes. This isn't fair. Whether they're always aware of it or not, women need their space too. They need to establish boundaries and not only adhere to them for themselves, but make sure that their man does too. Relationships are about sacrifice and it's usually the woman that sacrifices the most for her man. Though this is an admirable trait to have, women must understand that there should be limits to the amount they're willing to sacrifice. Don't allow him to be the only one that demands space and makes you respect that. You have that same right.

Okay fellas, I'll use myself as an example. I've never been the type to go out clubbin' on a regular basis. Okay, never mind the "regular basis" comment. I never go. It serves no purpose to me, I don't see the point of doing it once a week and, since I don't drink or smoke, I can't stand the atmosphere. But, I digress. Somehow, some way, I always found myself dating women who liked to go out to the clubs. Obviously I never met them in the club, but I always seemed to wind up dating women like this. Now remember fellas, for the sake of this example, let's think about the good girls that go to the clubs just to dance and have a good time, and not the ones who unfortunately are looking for the one night stands just like some of the men you meet there.

Anyway, I would be lying if I said to you that I never tried to deter some of this behavior in the women I were dating. Some of it was the fact that I just didn't see the point in running out to the club every weekend. It just seemed like such a waste of time to me. But, at the same time, a lot of it was paranoia. The fear that she would meet one of these one night stand brothas with a smooth enough game to make her give in. But that's another story for another time.

Usually these women that I were dating were going to these clubs with their girlfriends. This was what they did together for fun. It was their girls night out. Now there were times where I was invited to go. Again, trying to subconsciously force your partner into your world. But I refused, as the club scene was just not something that I ever wanted to be a part of.

Trying to respect these boundaries proved to be a difficult thing for me, mostly because I didn't agree with the lifestyle. But I forced myself to do it. To me, there was never a need to go to the club with these women because, for the most part, it was what *they* did with their friends. The only thing that I asked them to do was to remember that they belonged to someone while they were out there, and to me, that was all I could do. As they tried to bring me into their world, I could have very easily tagged along. However, the only thing that would've resulted from that was me sitting at a table with a disappointed look on my face, constantly looking at my watch trying to figure out when we were leaving (those who know me are well aware of that look). Now, why should I go along and ruin her night like that? It wouldn't have been fair.

It was something that was a part of who they were at the time. It was what they enjoyed doing. And though they dreaded telling me when they were going out, knowing how I felt about it, I tried to let them have their fun. Though I wasn't always successful at it, I tried not to let my frustration show. As long as I got my time at some point, I tried not to let it become a problem. I never wanted to be neglected because of their desire to go clubbin'. But more important than that, I never wanted to be that guy that complained every time my woman went to do something without me that I didn't understand. This is how a man will tend to disrespect his woman's boundaries and space. Not only do we invade, if we don't like, agree or understand what we see, just like bullies on the beach, we want to tear down the sand castle.

Keeping in mind that this example is based on a good woman, no good woman would ever neglect her man in this situation. Nor would she forget that she belonged to somebody while she's on the dance floor with "club man". Having said that, and using the example that I gave, it would be important for a man in that situation to respect his woman's space. There was no reason for me to cross that boundary, especially since I had no interest in what they were doing. The only purpose it would've served would have been me ruining what was obviously something they enjoyed, just because I didn't understand or agree with it.

Though the women I dated didn't understand it sometimes, it was important for me to refuse to partake in what they were doing. I didn't need to be that guy that tagged along, never dancing with my girl, while at the same time getting angry and jealous if some other man wanted to. After all, what is she there for? Also, I never wanted to be that guy that waited outside the club for his woman to come out, just to try and "catch her" with another man. Respecting boundaries is also about trust. Believing that your partner can have an outside interest, even one that involves members of the opposite sex, without there being a reason to become paranoid. If you don't trust her, then leave her. Don't follow her around and make a scene.

Ladies, you must understand your partner as it pertains to things like this. Remember what I said about jealousy. There's nothing cute about it. If not addressed properly, it can turn into a destructive device in your relationship. Understand that we're all human and we're all capable of becoming jealous. If you know your partner, then you should know how serious it is. If you're dealing with someone that can control his emotions, then explain to him that your hobby or outside interest, whatever that may be, is not a way for you to slight him. It doesn't matter if you're going to the club once in a while, going to dinner once a week with your girls, involved in your career or whatever it may be. Make him feel like he's number one, despite the fact that you have other things on your mind besides him.

Men, you must understand the same things I asked the women to understand when explaining our boundaries. If the club example doesn't work for you, I know that somewhere in that example you can see your situation. If you wanna know what the fuss is all about, learn a thing or two about whatever it is she's into, if for no other reason, just so that you can share in it with her. But get in and get out, just like I told the ladies. Don't try to become a part of it unless it's what she wants.

Where this gets tricky is that more times than not, if you show an interest in what your woman is doing, she'll want you to be a part of it. Like I said earlier, women's ability to compromise exceeds ours as men. While we want to maintain those boundaries as long as we can, they're looking for ways to tear them down. But, to each his own. If she wants you that deep into her world, let her invite you first (and she will, so beware of what you take interest in).

The thing I've noticed is that women, when in relationships, tend to think more like wives than girlfriends, and that's why they're more willing to share their personal space than we are. Thinking like a husband is something we reserve for when we're about 2 to 3 years into the marriage. All jokes aside, though women don't like to think this way, they should look to maintain those boundaries in the same way that men do. It's okay to walk, and not run. Don't let him in too far, too fast, even if he is your "boo". Let's celebrate those differences, boundaries and space.

## *NEEDS VS. WANTS*

This is an area where I think most of us tend to have trouble within our lives. Identifying our needs, while not confusing them with our wants. Knowing what's really important in our lives, and knowing what's trivial. As usual, a lot of this is broken down among gender lines, as our needs and wants tend to differ depending on whether you're a man or a woman. The sad part about it is that we're both usually confused about which is which. As usual, women have a better grasp on these things than men do. Unfortunately, as it is with a lot of things that I've spoken about thus far, the gap has closed considerably over the years. A woman's wants are just as much of a hindrance to her growth these days as a man's has been throughout existence.

Again, instead of leading us men out, or at the very least dangling the carrot of a virtuous woman to lure us out, women have decided to fall with us instead of demanding that we focus on what's really important. Both men and women need to accurately identify what's really important to our successes in life as individuals and as couples. This is not said to diminish the importance of *wanting* certain things out of life because it is important to do so. It's more about putting our wants in their proper perspective. The importance of meeting our needs in life can't be understated. You can't properly assess these two things without knowing which is which. The line can sometimes be blurred, but with a little common sense and a little honesty, both within our ourselves and with our partners, distinguishing one from another can be achieved.

First, let's do a quick examination of these two words. Webster's defines a need as "a lack of something necessary, useful or desirable". For the sake of what we're doing here, we're going to focus on the necessary and useful end of the definition. Webster's definition of a want is "to desire greatly or to wish". It also says to want is "to <u>need</u> or to require". So, as you can see, these words are very similar in definition, but make no mistake about it, they are definitely not the same. It's like Democrats and Republicans. They share similarities because they're both politicians and can't be fully trusted. But because of some differences in philosophy and intent, they're very different.

You can look at the words 'want' and 'need' in that same way. The philosophy and intent of these words are different. There's a sense of urgency when we hear the word 'need'. That same sense of urgency is not there when we hear the word 'want'. The word 'want' is almost like the selfish cousin of the word 'need'. It seems to be all about the individual using it. Although Webster's eventually uses the word 'need' in its definition of this word, it's not until after stating first and foremost that it's primary definition is "to desire greatly or to wish". Now, how many of us, if we had three "wishes", wouldn't be selfish with the first two? If you're being honest, not very many of you.

How many times have any of you reading this, arbitrarily used the word 'need' in an inappropriate fashion? It happens all the time. "I *need* to get that outfit I saw at the mall", knowing full well that you have a closet full of clothes that you don't even wear anymore. "I *need* to get those new Jordans", knowing all too well that they don't translate into more ability on the court. "I *need* to go to this party Saturday night", knowing that all it's gonna do is make you late for church Sunday morning. "I *need* to go and see this girl tonight", knowing damn well that she ain't your woman and what you need to do is stay home. "I *need* a man!" "I *need* a woman!" You see? We use it all the time in the place of things that we really just want. I know I used some rather simple examples and these are common mistakes that most people, including myself, make on a day to day basis with that word.

No one really means any harm, it's just one of those human flaws that we all have. However, some of the most seemingly harmless habits that we have can eventually become the most harmful at times. Maybe by starting with correcting some of the little habits that we have in life, we can prevent them from becoming big habits and bigger problems. Is it possible that with just a simple correction in vocabulary and better use of the English language, we can change some things in our lives? The answer is yes. In my opinion, by simply putting into practice *not* using the word 'need' where 'want' should go, you will eventually apply that same philosophy to your life.

My mother taught me this a long time ago. I, like so many others, would often state that I was starving when I was simply very hungry. Anytime my mother heard this she would remind me that not only was I not starving, but that I had no idea what it was like to starve. To me, there were two messages there: Be thankful for what you have because you *could* be starving somewhere, and don't just randomly use words without considering what you're saying. The same can be said with us in relationships. So many times we want something so badly, that we overstate its importance by using the word 'need' in order to get our way. We feel that if we put the urgency of the word 'need' in there, we're sure to get what we 'want'.

A lot of times, this works. Usually because we've misplaced and misused this word so often in our everyday lives, that no one seems to be able to tell where it does or doesn't belong anymore. What we fail to understand, however, is that this misuse of the word has crept into our subconscious and contributed to the blurring of the line between wants and needs.

For example, me telling my son that I *need* him to go to the store and get me a pop carries a little more weight than me telling him that I *want* him to go to the store and get me a pop. Now, I'm his father and he'll do it either way, regardless of the way I tell him (or else), but that's beside the point. By simply misusing the word, I've place greater importance on this pop (something that's really not good for me therefore I can't really need it) than necessary. We do this all the time in our relationships. By misusing words, we place greater importance on the things we want out of our partners, rather than focusing on what we actually need from them.

Now that I've beaten these definitions to death, let's move on. As I've stated so many times early on in this project, we must learn to identify what's really important. We've already discussed this from the standpoint of choosing a partner, but it mustn't stop once we've found that special someone. We can cause great confusion in a relationship by not knowing what we need and what we actually just want. You can place undue pressure on your partner over something that's really not that important by overstating its importance.

The reality is that most of the time, when we just want something, we're usually being selfish. It's usually something that serves our individual purposes. If our partner somehow benefits from our wants, that's usually just a bonus. To explain it a little clearer, if I decide that I wanted my girlfriend or wife to do something for me and it actually benefits her as well, then that's just gravy. All it does is increase the likelihood that she'll do it because it benefits her as well. Having said that, I shouldn't increase its importance by presenting it as a need as opposed to a want.

From my perspective, most of what we do in a relationship for our partners is what our partner wants us to do. It's part of the compromise. I had a friend tell me once that she wants her partner to have her back whether she's right, wrong or otherwise. I told her that if she ever had a partner that supported everything she did, "no matter what", he would be doing her a great disservice. No matter how much you love a person, no one needs to be supported on every issue, no matter what. If someone really loves you, they will love you enough to tell you when you're wrong. That's what love is. Sometimes, when we're in the middle of a situation, we can't really see the whole picture. Though we may want someone in our lives that will back us no matter what we do, it's not always a good thing. What's needed is someone that will give us perspective. Someone that can show us another direction in which to go if needed.

Don't be confused by what I'm saying though. I'm not suggesting that we don't support one another when we make mistakes. I'm not suggesting that we don't support our partners in accomplishing individual goals that we sometimes don't understand. What I'm suggesting is that we use our support with some discretion. Some things in life are a matter of opinion, and some things in life are a matter of right and wrong. What I'm speaking of is support from a behavioral standpoint. I'm speaking of your partner's well being.

There are some things that we don't need to be involved in. I'm not going to list anything here, as you can determine that based on your own values system. What I'm suggesting is that we remain honest with one another. That's what's needed in a relationship, but not always wanted. If you can see your partner is on the wrong path, whether it be as an individual or as it pertains to your relationship, you should speak up. That's what's needed. You should never blindly follow someone. If I'm on the wrong path, I need someone in my life that's not afraid to tell me. I don't need someone in my life that's going to follow me even though she can see that I'm wrong.

In this day and age of making sure that somebody "has your back", we must remember that support doesn't mean unconditional agreement. Though I may support you, I may not agree with you at times. Herein lies one of the dilemmas of wants and needs. In some situations where we may need support but want agreement, we may switch the two and place the emphasis in the wrong place. For example, a man could have a wife, a family and a good job. One day, he could develop the desire to switch jobs. Not a career switch, because that's a little more serious, and after a certain age, a little more complicated. But, maybe for no other reason, he may feel the need for some new challenges in his particular line of work. Though his wife may not fully understand or see the need for him to switch jobs, she can still support his move.

In this example, the husband must realize that her support is what's most important. As long as she doesn't let the fact that she doesn't fully agree or understand the need for the switch affect her support of her husband, he shouldn't have a problem. His need is her support, not necessarily her agreement. The agreement is his want. Although it's nice to come to an agreement, sometimes it's not always possible. Continuing with this example, the only thing that they need to come to an agreement on is that the family will not suffer and will still be taken care of. On that particular issue, he does need her agreement. (For the sake of clarifying any lingering thoughts on my example, it's my feeling that in that situation, if a man doesn't have his wife's support, he should strongly consider not making the move.)

The moral of that parable is the line between a need and a want is so blurred that they sometimes seem like the same thing. However, as I stated earlier, don't mistake the importance of our wants. In the example that I used above, achieving agreement is important and should be attempted. But it's not as important as the wife's support of her husband's desire to challenge himself within his career, but not to the detriment of his family or his relationship with his wife. She can support his upward mobility, though she may not fully understand his path or his timing. We must respect our partner's opinion on things that affect them as well as us. Respecting your partner's opinion is needed. Again, it doesn't mean that you have to do what they tell you, as long as you hear them out and respect their point of view. That leads me to my next point.

So many times I've heard people say that they want to be respected in their perspective relationships. Again, the word want is used where need should be. None of us should simply want to be respected in a relationship. Respect is something that we need in a relationship. In fact, it's something that we should demand. Not angrily, but we should be firm in this demand. This is going back to something that I touched on in Chapter 1. Both men and women have systematically traded in our need for respect for various wants. Women have traded in their need for respect in their relationships for the emptiness of material things. Not fully recognizing that if men indeed respected them and the sanctity of their relationship with them, the last thing they'd have to worry about is getting anything of a material nature out of him.

Women have forgotten that they truly can have it all, they just need to stop settling for less. Men have got to get back to a place where they realize that they need a wife and mother to their children, or at the very least, a good girlfriend. Otherwise, if she's only there to cook for you, keep the kids and have sex with you, she's just a glorified babysitter with fringe benefits. I don't wanna go over Chapter 1 all over again, but men have to trade that want (the ability to come and go as we please without being questioned) for the need (a good woman that loves and supports us and ain't having all of that running the streets).

Wants and needs in relationships tend to differ depending on whether you're talking to a man or a woman. What a woman wants tends to be much more complicated than what she actually needs. This is also true with men, but not to the same extent. We're actually quite simple. In Chris Rock's HBO stand-up special *Bigger and Blacker*, he said men need three things from women: Food, sex and silence. As funny as that is, especially when coming out of Chris' mouth, he's actually not that far off. Men can be that basic in a relationship sometimes.

I've heard so many women throughout my life talk about how hard men are to figure out. That notion is hilarious to me. The only reason a man is hard to figure out to a woman is because she's trying to hard. You guys are literally making a mountain out of a molehill. The food and sex thing that Rock is talking about is on the money. You can't ever go wrong with that. We also need love just like women do. Though we don't always know how to express this, or even how to ask for it, we definitely need the love of a good woman. The other thing we need is an extension of that love, and that's the support that I've already touched on. This is especially true with black men. It's the most complicated need that we have, and thus it's sometimes the hardest to come by. The reason being, this need of ours sometimes collides with a woman's wants.

Now don't take this as a sign to start taking care of your man financially. I'm not talking about that kind of support. We need a woman that supports what we're trying to do. We need a woman to be our backbone. A woman that can hold us together when the world is trying to tear us down. We need a woman that, as long as we're trying to do something positive with our lives, will be there for us, and not abandon us because our car isn't hot enough or our money isn't long enough or we're not buying her enough things. This is where our need collides with a woman's wants. If she wants all of the material things that life has to offer, she'll have to develop the patience to stand by her man until he's reached a level in life where he can provide her with such things without strain.

Believe it or not ladies, stretching his dollars until they become thin is not only a detriment to him, it's a detriment to you. How can he adequately take care of you if all his finances are used addressing your wants, rather than your needs? As far as the silence that Chris was talking about, well, you can chalk that up as a want. Maybe even a wish. All jokes aside ladies, though we may want you to shut up sometimes, more times than not, it's usually when you should be talking and telling us a thing or two about a thing or two. The only thing you girls need to learn is when enough is enough. Know when to say when shouldn't just apply to drinking. Don't beat your man up. Though you may <u>want</u> to, we don't <u>need</u> that.

Having said all of that, let me summarize our needs as men. The support I spoke of is the most important to men, whether we realize and admit it or not. Without the support of a good woman, we are more likely to fail than to succeed. That's true whether she's your wife, girlfriend, mother, grandmother, etc. The need for food is obvious to all humans, but it is rather important to men. For those of you ladies out there who weren't taught well by mama, you'd be surprised how far a good, home cooked meal can get you. As for the sex, the "need" of this by men is usually overstated.

Yes, we love sex, and don't get me wrong fellas, I love sex just as much as any one of you out there. But the old adage about not letting the little head control the big head is just as true today as it ever was. The only difference today is that the advice is much more pertinent these days. And, if deprived too often by women, men will often began to view sex as an actual need, rather than a want. But unlike food and the support of a good woman, this "need" can be controlled. I'll die, or at the very least suffer from malnutrition if I don't eat properly. And I'll surely feel like I'm dying without a good woman by my side to inspire me to greatness. But just because it can be controlled is not a reason for women to deprive their men of sex. Sex is important to a relationship. We just have to keep it in its proper perspective. This applies to women as well.

However, sex is simply a carnal desire and, as far as I'm concerned, all carnal desires can be controlled. That goes for all the cars that we wanna drop ungodly amounts of money on to attract more women, while we argue with our baby's mama about how much child support is coming out of the check. And the strip clubs we wanna frequent, giving twenty dollar bill after twenty dollar bill to a woman (probably named Amber or Mercedes or Bambi or Champagne or Misty or whatever other stripper stage names you wanna insert here) that could care less about us, as long as after the next three songs, she's got half of her rent money. Or all the money we want to spend on bud or beer or whatever else we do for "entertainment". All the things we feel that we "need" to do to be a real man.

If this is what some of you men do for relaxation or entertainment, more power to you. I'd be lying if I said I wasn't knocking it. Though I've never drank or smoked anything, I'd also be lying if I said I'd never been in a strip club or had a lap dance. I'm not judging anyone, and if it's coming off that way, it's not my intent. All I'm saying is don't confuse what you want to do with what you need to do. If this is what you want to do with your time and money, then you've earned it, live it up. But don't try to convince your woman that this is a part of being a man and what you need to do. It's not an integral part of being a man, it's just what men do. There is a difference.

Now that I've angered the men out there, women have similar issues in regards to their wants and needs. Their needs are based more on the emotional end rather than the physical end. Whereas the only need I discussed for men that deals with their emotions was the issue of support, women's needs generally tend to start in their emotions. While it takes a man quite a while to move mentally from having sex to making love, for women, even if they don't love a guy, they'll probably still refer to having sex with him as making love.

More times than not, there is an emotional attachment to most of what they do. The support that I suggested that was so important to men is doubly important to women. They like to feel that their man is there for them emotionally and physically, and in that order. Quite simply, they need love. Any other need that a woman has stems from this. Even though things have changed over the last 10 or 15 years, women have never been completely hung up on the physical aspects of relationships. There's more emphasis than ever put on a man's performance in the bed, but at the end of the day, no matter what they may say in movies, on television, in songs or in romance novels, women will take real love over an orgasm any day of the week.

Stemming from the need of the love of a good man, women need a strong man in their lives as well. More often than we ever do, women need a shoulder to cry on. Because they're naturally more emotional than we are, they tend to take things a little more to heart than we do. Now, when I say shoulder to cry on, I don't mean in the literal sense. There are plenty of strong women out there, and they don't all just cry at the drop of a hat. When I suggest that they need a shoulder to cry on, I mean that women like to talk it out. They like to talk about their feelings. They don't internalize like we do.

If you want to make your woman happy, you need to develop the ability to listen. I know to some of the men out there it seems that I'm asking a lot. We don't always wanna hear about some little fight they had with their mother or girlfriend, or how their boss doesn't appreciate them or how they don't feel pretty today. But this is not a want, though it may seem that way. It's a need. Our women need us to listen to them. They need us to know how they feel. To take that a step further, they need us to know that they have feelings. And it doesn't need to be just a token ear that you're lending. They need you to care about what they're saying. You don't necessarily have to have the same passion that they do about whatever it is that they're talking about. You just need to love and care about her enough to listen to her.

To elaborate further on the notion of strength, women need a take charge man. I used to tell a male friend of mine that a woman wants to be with a man that's both sensitive and manly. She doesn't want him so rough and tough that he's afraid to show his love for her, but at the same time, she wants to know that she's always safe with him. That he would defend her at all cost. In short, she needs a real man.

There are a lot of women out there that like the roughneck types, and there's nothing wrong with that. However, I don't think any of them are reading this book. No matter how hard a man is and no matter how attracted a woman may find herself to this man, every woman wants flowers every now and then. What's happened over time is that men who are willing to display that combination of strength, courage and sensitivity toward his woman, have disappeared. That has forced a shift in a woman's thinking as it pertains to what she really needs in a man. That's where the emphasis on sex and material things came in. We weren't bringing anything of substance to the table, so it forced women to focus on other things.

Over the last few years, I've heard more horror stories from women about the performance, or lack there of, of men in the bedroom than I'd ever thought I would hear. I was surprised to hear it, but at the same time, I wondered why all of a sudden I was hearing it. Surely this couldn't be something that happened over night. But I came to certain conclusions after hearing all of this, the first of which I already knew. A more attentive man is a better lover to begin with. Any woman that's ever been with one will tell you that. Men have forgotten that this attentiveness starts outside of the bedroom and can't be faked inside of it. Unlike us, they're actually aware when we're faking it or going through the motions, if you will. Just because she says nothing about it, doesn't mean she doesn't know.

The other conclusion that I came to is something that I've already mentioned in short. Women will sacrifice a certain level of sexual satisfaction for a man that truly loves and respects her. That's because, again, unlike us, they realize that although sex is good and enjoyable when engaging in it with the right person, they won't die without it and it won't last forever (no matter what the makers of Viagra or any other male enhancement drugs want you to believe). They want a great sexual experience, but they're willing to trade a little of it for true love.

"So what's the problem, KJ?" you ask. Once we stopped bringing said true love and respect to the table, sex and the "need" for it to be performed at a high level came to the forefront. Once they started doing it like we were, simply for the sheer thrill of it without any emotion attached to it, they started grading our performances. Thus, they found out just how inadequate some of us are.

The other by-product of our emotional inadequacies as men was women's increased emphasis on material things. Though it's obvious to anyone that material goods are simply wants and not needs or integral to the success of a real relationship, they became necessities in women's eyes because we weren't giving them anything else of substance. As I stated in my first chapter, these things took the place of what's really needed by a woman. It's the equivalent of hush money paid to witnesses by the Mafia. Conversely, just because you give a woman all the love she needs, doesn't mean that she won't hit you up for the occasional pair of shoes, dress or jewelry. It just won't be her priority to bleed you dry if she really loves you. If you give her what she really needs, which is love and attention, material things will always be secondary. That's right fellas, you can dictate her wants by providing her with her needs.

Now in the last few paragraphs, I've commented on any number of things that a woman both wants and needs. As you can see by how intertwined they've become, there's a lot of confusion as to which is which. They're all so close. It's not just about saying "I love you" all the time. Although a woman may want that, that's not necessarily what she needs. She needs you to show it. She needs your attention, which is an extension of the love she needs you to feel for her.

I mentioned the fact that no matter how "hard" her man may be, a woman still wants flowers every now and then. It's not so much about the flowers, as much as it is about you showing her some form of appreciation. You may be with a woman that doesn't necessarily go for flowers, but if you follow the advice that I gave about listening and caring about her feelings, you'd know her well enough to know exactly how to show her that you love her. Because it's all so tangled up, if you simply take care of your woman's needs, you'll no doubt be giving her what she wants.

# 3

## *The Work Pt. 2: Respect for Your Relationship; Are you willing to work for what you have?*

*"U see I'm willing/Willing 2 do the work/Willing 2 do what I gotta do/I'm willing/ Willing 2 do the work/Tell me now…what about U?"*
—*From "The Work Pt. 1" by Prince, taken from the album The Rainbow Children*

That's not actually a love song that I quoted, but the chorus sums up what this chapter, and also the last one, is about. The work. How hard are we willing to work to maintain what we have? Because work is what it will take, along with respect for what we have, in order to maintain and be successful in this game of love. There's a lot to learn and if both aren't committed to doing what it takes, there will be no success. These are areas in which we could all learn a thing or two. Once we've achieved a level of respect for our partner, and ourselves, we must remember to respect our relationship as a whole. We must remember that it mustn't be taken for granted. However, there are some things that attack our relationships that we ourselves either invite or bring in. In order to hold on to what we have, we must learn to respect and appreciate it.

In the last chapter, I started by talking about the many forces that exist that can tear a relationship apart. Sometimes these things just come about, and as a couple, we have to fight them off. Things like families, friends, work, and unfortunately, members of the opposite sex can all contribute to the downfall of a good relationship. This usually happens when we don't properly respect the relationship that we have. Allowing others or their opinions of how we should run our relationship is usually one of the more common ways in which we disrespect what we have. Whether its family or friends, someone else always seems to know what's best for us. Although it's important to have friends that are there for you and that you can count on, it's important to make sure that they keep a safe distance from your relationship. Not only is it a show of respect to your partner, but respect to the relationship as a whole. There's you the individual, there's your partner as an individual and then there's the two of you together that make up the whole.

These opinions are also quite common as it pertains to our families. Parents and siblings alike are also prominent when it comes to relationship advice. The same can be said for them as can be said for our friends. It's great to have family that's there for you, but make sure you keep them at a safe distance. A lot of these things can be accomplished by simply respecting your mate. But the idea of the relationship itself has to mean something to you just as your partner does. We must respect what it stands for. If you've built a solid relationship, you stand to lose a lot more than just a partner if you're not careful. If you've done it properly, you stand to lose a friend. By limiting other's access to the inner workings of your relationship, you can protect it. Sure there are times, especially when things aren't going that well, when it's necessary to lean on a friend or a family member for support. But there must be a limit to how much info you're willing to share with someone outside the relationship.

Some things need to remain sacred during the time that you and your partner are together. Friends and family can sometimes poison your relationship, both intentionally and unintentionally. Usually, it's just because they care. That's why we must be careful of how far we let others into our business. Though they may be well intended, they may lead us in unwise directions simply by not knowing all of the facts.

We should remember that when we're crying on a loved one's shoulder, they're just hearing our version of the events. What if you're the one who's in the wrong? We tend to slant things toward our point of view, which could lead to some unintentional bad advice. This is not to suggest that we keep our friends and family in the dark. It's important that someone has at least an idea of what's going on in case we're in a situation where we're being mistreated. It's good to have someone that can advise us in wise directions as well. I'm just suggesting that we use discretion in how much of our personal business we share with others.

Another very important area in which we must maintain respect for our relationships is in the area of friends of the opposite sex. This is one that always seems to get out of hand. If you've ever had to deal with this is your relationship, you know what I'm talking about, even if I don't write another word about it. I know that on the surface it seems like just a case of respecting your partner, but as I stated earlier, you not only need to respect your partner, but your relationship as a whole. Recognize that it's not just about hurting someone, it's about losing the whole thing. Knowing the importance of holding on to something that should be dear to us is paramount.

We have to be careful when we're in relationships and we befriend members of the opposite sex. Some of these friendships are born out of bad intentions. However, some of them are actually harmless. But if not handled properly, they can each do the same amount of damage. As I pointed out in the earlier sections on space and boundaries, it's important to maintain outside friendships, even if they are of the opposite sex. But not only do those friends need to respect your relationship, you should as well.

Remember that jealousy can be a factor in all of this, especially if you share a level of friendship with that member of the opposite sex that you don't with your partner. Understanding that this is always possible, as sometimes we don't always share some of the same interests as our partners, we need to be respectful of our partner's feelings. However, if there's any damage done by our friends, it's usually because we let our concentration lapse somewhere.

In this regard, it's important to maintain communication and honesty with your partner. Don't be hush-hush about your friendships with members of the opposite sex. Secrets are only necessary if you have something to hide. Don't blame it all on your partner as to why you kept that friendship a secret. So many times we suggest that we kept that type of thing a secret because we felt our significant other wouldn't understand. I understand that it's true in some cases, but there's never a good time to be secretive in a relationship. The more we let the other person know, the more secure they usually feel. There are those of us that are strong enough to handle our partners having members of the opposite sex as friends. Conversely, there are those of us that can't. But I'm a firm believer that if you were to sit your partner down and disclose all information, they're sure to feel better about the situation. Sometimes not right away, but over time you'll find that honesty is always best.

Now there are some harder cases out there where no matter what you tell them, they don't want anyone else around you. In the event that we're talking about a friend that's truly platonic, then it's time to work this out with your partner. If the paranoia and jealousy continues, then there are some deeper problems that need to be worked out. But if you've given them no reason to mistrust you, then you must stand your ground, reassure your partner that you have the utmost respect for the relationship that you share and that you'd never put it in jeopardy. But don't just convince them of that for the sake of convincing them, try to live by it as well.

You and your friends of the opposite sex also need to realize that the amount of time you spend together must be limited. Together meaning physically together *and* on the phone. Again, you must both respect the fact that you're in a relationship. You can't continue on like you're single when you're in a relationship. Put yourself in your partner's shoes. You wouldn't want someone of the opposite sex calling them at all times of the day and night, and spending all sorts of time with them, even if it is just a friend. Respect what you have. Realize that sometimes appearances can be just as destructive as your actually doing something wrong. I've made this mistake in a past relationship, and I couldn't have been more wrong and insensitive.

It's like a mind game. I have a saying that I use: The imagination can be worse than reality. Sometimes, it looks worse than it is. Left to our own devices, we always come up with a worse case scenario. If he or she is just a friend, then it's harmless. But if it looks like more to your partner, then it can tear them apart. Sometimes that's a matter of sitting your partner down and talking to them, and sometimes it's a matter checking yourself, and limiting your friend's access to you. Not eliminating, but limiting. There's enough time in the week for you to talk to and spend a little time with your friend of the opposite sex without it interfering with your relationship. But it should be limited out of respect for your partner. If they're true friends, then they'll understand.

Now let's talk about those "other friends". You know the ones I'm talking about. The ones with the not-so-innocent intentions. The ones that have every intention of changing your emotional address. The ones that Biz Markie was "singing" about on that classic hip-hop track "Just A Friend". You remember that, don't you? Okay, how 'bout this: *"You, you got what neeeeeed/But you say he's just a friend/But you say he's just a friend/OH BAAABY YOU...*See Biz at that piano with that white Beethoven-like wig on? See Biz doin' that water wave right before the video fades to black? Remember now? I thought so. Biz warned us: *"So please listen to the message that I send/Don't ever talk to a girl who says she just has a friend (has a friend/has a friend/has a friend/has a friend)"*. Sorry about the echo.

Anyway, we all know the types of "friends" that I'm talking about. I've been that friend before once or twice in my life, as I'm sure some of you have either had or been that friend as well. These are the types of friends that, no matter what you may tell them, or how platonic you may want things to remain, they still want something else. No matter how committed you are, they're looking to change that. This is not a problem that's specific to men or women. We both face this type of pressure when in relationships. At the same time, as I stated earlier, it can only become a problem if we let it. It can't come in if we don't bring it or invite it. Problem is, too many of us come to the party B.Y.O.P. (Bring Your Own Problem) or we're sending out the aforementioned invites.

For those of you who don't know the obvious answer to this type of problem, that's why I'm writing this book. As a matter of fact, for those of you that *do* know the answer and choose to look the other way, I'm writing it for you as well. If you have a relationship that you want to hold on to, it would be foolish and irresponsible to maintain a relationship with anyone that intends to damage what you have. And don't let the smooth taste fool ya. No matter what they say, if they know you're in a relationship and they still want to be that "special friend" to you, they intend to damage your relationship.

Sometimes these characters will tell you that they don't mean any harm and don't wanna break up anything, they just wanna be friends. Like I said, I've been that friend once or twice. Whether we secretly harbor thoughts of ruining what you have or whether we just wanna be that "special friend", the end result will be the same for you if you're not careful. Remember, from the perspective of said "friend", if anything goes wrong, it's your problem, not theirs. They may not completely run your partner off, as some of us tend to hold on too long sometimes (Chapter 5), but they may do irreparable damage. At which point, it may as well be over.

It's also foolish to think that you can simply sit a "friend" like this down, explain the situation to them and have things automatically go platonic. It's a disaster waiting to happen. Going back to a question I asked in Chapter 1, How many times have you heard someone tell a story of winding up in bed with a "friend" because they just got caught up in the heat of the moment? Here's an idea: When it gets too hot, turn down the heat. Isn't that what we do in our homes when the heat's up too high? We don't turn on a fan, we turn down the heat.

Or better yet, how many times have you heard someone tell a story of winding up in bed with a "friend" and telling you that "it just happened"? Well, KJ's here to tell you that nothing "just happens", unless it's an act of God, and nothing like that is an act of God, no matter what God you believe in. A series of events always leads to something like that. We lose relationships over stuff like this because we're not responsible enough to do the right thing.

Our lives are about risk and reward. Weighing out your options before you make decisions. If you find yourself in a situation like this and something in you tells you that it's okay to maintain that "friendship", then you don't value your relationship as much as you may think. You've also set a course for failure. Often we'll take on unnecessary challenges just to prove that we can handle certain things. Drug addicts start out this way a lot of times. My only question is, why take the risk?

Usually, the only reason we hold on to a friendship of this nature is simply because we want to. We all like the attention of the opposite sex, but we shouldn't accept it to the detriment of our current relationship. Accept it for what it is and move on. We need not gamble with our relationships, and in some cases our futures, over some fleeting fancy. If you're in this situation, you have to decide what's more important to you, doing what you want or holding on to what you have. I don't know about you, but decisions that will affect my life deserve a little more consideration from me. Whether we believe it or not, sometimes we're making the decision of a lifetime. You could be deciding between what will amount to a roll in the hay and the love of a lifetime. It'd be a shame if that decision were made in the "heat of the moment".

Another way we take for granted what we have is allowing work to interfere with our relationship with that special someone. Again, I'm familiar with this, as some of the women in my past have accused me of being a workaholic. In fact, during the writing of this book I was accused of neglect, while simply trying to give all of you something to read. How selfish were they? Seriously though, a lot of us, at one point or another, are guilty of this. In the name of trying to provide for our families or simply having that drive to be the best at whatever it is that we do, we sometimes neglect that special person in our lives that's always supporting us to begin with. Those of us with said drive, especially us creative types, are always looking for a little understanding from our significant other as to why we have to work so hard. Those of us who just have to work hard to support our families are also looking for that same understanding.

We must try to keep in mind that sometimes our better half isn't just nagging. They just love us and want to spend time with us. Remember that other than God, too much of anything can eventually be bad for you, and this is especially true with work. There has to be some sort of balance that you can find as it relates to your relationship and your work. While your partner needs to understand that your work is important, no matter which side of the fence you fall on, we also must understand the importance of remembering that someone loves us and wants us home some of the time. And that's a love that we usually need after a hard day's work. Without even noticing, you can make your work a mistress. Don't just assume that the only way that you can make your partner jealous or cheat on them is with a member of the opposite sex. Neglect is neglect.

Whether it's the job or someone else, you can still leave your partner lonely and bitter. If you have love, your relationship should mean more to you than the job, but keep it in perspective. I'm not suggesting that you quit your job over something that can be talked out. Conversely, those of us on the neglect end of that shouldn't play both sides against the middle. Respect the fact that your man or woman has to work, whether it be to provide for the family or for personal and professional fulfillment. If you feel neglected, let it be known in a mature manner and work it out. Again, there has to be a happy medium somewhere. You should be able to find it with a little work and communication. Which leads me to the last, but probably most important section in my chapters on maintaining relationships.

## HONESTY, TRUST AND COMMUNICATION

Whew! Where do I begin on this one? Anyone reading this book that knows me personally, will no doubt read a lot of stuff they've already heard me say a million times. Some of it will go back to the "brutal honesty" comment that was attributed to me back in the intro. Some of it, those same people have experienced with me on a personal level. Either way, I hope I can offer a perspective that will help you in your current situation.

(Redundancy alert!) Again, it's just my opinion, but the three things you see in that heading are sometimes more important elements to a relationship than love. And some of you will be surprised to find out that they're even more important than money. For, how would someone know that you loved them if you never communicated it in one form or another? Exactly. I don't expect to say anything in the following paragraphs that any of you have never heard before. Some of you will actually understand and agree with what I say. But once again, it raises an interesting question. Why it is that we understand some things, but still refuse to live them out in our daily lives?

Let's start with honesty. First off, let me start by saying that, for me, there's nothing worse than a liar. I'm sure that a lot of you feel the same as I do, but I hate being lied to. Finding out that you've been lied to can be the worst feeling in the world, depending on who told you the lie. For example, as I stated in the last chapter, politicians can't fully be trusted. Now, if I have any politicians reading this, I don't mean to offend you, but, let's be real. I don't have to tell you about yourselves, you already know. But, I digress. If a politician is revealed to be a liar, it's almost expected. You don't feel as bad sometimes, depending on what he or she lied about. However, if someone you love and trusted lies to you, it can be one of the most devastating things in the world, depending on what they're lying about. And since we're talking about relationships, you know how you're gonna feel when you hear a lie in this context.

When it comes to honesty in relationships, many different people have told me a number of things about why it's not only okay in their eyes to lie sometimes, but necessary. The most prominent excuse given to me is to protect someone's feelings. Let's examine that for a minute. When we lie, how are we really protecting the feelings of the one we're lying to? You're keeping them from finding out something that they probably *should* know, but won't want to know when they find out. You're avoiding hurting them over something that you did to them or behind their back. If you've done something wrong, you've already created a bad situation, so you don't wanna make it worse by confessing. A lie will most certainly smooth things over. After all, what a person doesn't know about won't hurt 'em. I mean, things are going well, and you don't wanna mess it up. Does any of this sound familiar to any of you? If you said no, guess what? You're lying.

This all reminds me of an episode of *The Simpsons*. When Homer Simpson's wife Marge found out he'd lied to her about something, his response was "I'm sorry I lied to you, but I swear, I never thought you'd find out". That's how most of us feel when we tell a lie. Other than the reasons (excuses) that I gave above, most of us lie because we think we'll get away with it. We think our partners will never find out. Now, there are those of us who are smart enough to know that we'll eventually be caught. Those are the ones that lie to buy some time until they can find a proper justification for the truth that will eventually surface. I give those people partial credit simply because they're smart enough to know that a lie, more times than not, will not hold up. Sooner or later it all comes out in the wash.

For any Bible students reading this, you're familiar with the phrase "Everything done in the dark is soon brought to light." That's not only true with that late night creepin' you find yourself doing from time to time (although that's another form of lying), it's true with the things we say. However, at the same time, too much credit can't be given. After all, these people that I speak of have lied.

The idea that one lies to protect another's feelings is (guess what) another lie. I can't stand it when people use this excuse. What are you really protecting? Other than your own interests, nothing. We like to mask it underneath the guise of protecting our partner's feelings, and on the surface I can see where that seems to be true, but in reality, lying is a selfish move. It's our own pride and position in the relationship that we're seeking to protect. I can't believe that I've actually had arguments with people over this. The only purposes lies serve are prolonging the inevitable and creating a separate problem. Because once the lie is found out (and if you stay with a person long enough, it will be found out), not only do you have to deal with what you initially lied about, you've got to deal with the fact that you lied about it. So now your partner's pissed about two things.

I understand the thinking behind it all. If I can keep you from something that will surely hurt you, then a lie is okay. However, if you've ever been caught in a lie, whether on the spot or the always worse down the road version, you know how damaging it is to your relationship. You wind up looking like a liar, which isn't good because telling one lie doesn't make one a liar. It's constant lying that does that. Plus, now your partner doesn't trust you and has to call into question not only everything you say from here on out, but also everything you've said in the past. This can be devastating to you habitual liars out there.

If you don't know already, then I just let you know. There's no way of getting around it. No matter what we may want to believe, lies always have and always will do more damage than good. Simply because one lie leads to another lie. The hole will get deeper and deeper. At that point, you're struggling to keep up with all of the lies. Soon, you've told so many lies, that you don't even know what the truth is anymore. To quote from LL Cool J's classic "That's A Lie", *"You lied about the lies that you lied about"*. The fact of the matter is it's so much easier to tell the truth. It's twice as easy as that to keep up with the truth. You know why? Because the truth never changes. It is what it is. You don't have to make up anything or remember what story you told. The facts remain the same and as long as you remember those facts, you'll be okay.

Sure, if you've done something wrong in the relationship, your partner will be hurt in the interim, but in the end, you'll be respected for your honesty. That's important. Believe it or not, that honesty will keep you together much longer than any lie will. There are enough insecure people out there for us to come in contact with without creating that situation for ourselves. You don't want to be in a relationship where every time you're out of your partner's sight, they have to wonder if you're where you say you're gonna be. But that's exactly what we create when we make a habit of lying. There's a lot that can be said for an honest person.

We usually lie out of fear. Fear of being found out and fear of losing something that means something to us. If we make a habit of telling the truth in our everyday lives, then it won't be so hard to live by once we find ourselves in a relationship. Also, if we learn to make sound judgements when in relationships, the truth will be easier to come by because we won't have anything to lie about. This is probably the biggest key in all of this. If people would just practice doing things that they wouldn't be ashamed of if someone found out, they're lives won't be engulfed in secrecy and lies. As far as what we should and shouldn't be ashamed of, that's a long story that I'm not really willing to tell. It's really an individual thing anyway. But the advice still applies. Do things in your life that you're not ashamed of, and you'll find that the lies, and the desire to lie, will disappear.

Honesty does not guarantee success in the relationship. The truth hurts, and I guess that's where most of the fear is. We feel that if we tell the truth, our partner is liable to get so angry, that they'll walk away from us. This is a very real possibility. However, I must reiterate, it's the choices that we make prior to the lie that starts it all. If you've done something wrong to your significant other, depending on what it is and how it affects them, they have every right to walk away. Being honest in situations such as this is simply about accountability. We have to learn to be accountable for the things that we do. My feeling is you've already caused a problem by doing whatever it is that you did. You've already done something to hurt someone that you love. Be a man or a woman, and stand up and face the music.

Whatever the repercussions are, you just have to accept them. Don't punish you partner twice by lying. In effect, that's what we're doing. In a situation where *we* should be punished, we're punishing someone else for our mistakes. Make better choices in your relationships (which means consider how your partner will feel about what you're doing before you do something stupid) and you can eliminate the need for any dishonesty. As I said, the truth hurts, but a lie hurts twice, because it comes accompanied with that truth we were initially hiding. None of us like to be lied to, so if we can remember that, and treat others as we want to be treated, then we should be able to maintain an acceptable level of honesty in our lives, and thus our relationships.

Now, let's move on to trust. In my eyes, there's no more important element to a relationship. None. Not love, not money, and not communication. Although the honesty I just covered is almost as important, as honesty is an element of trust, trust to me is most important. I'm not with you right now, but I get the sense that some of you have just looked at your book with that same confused look that a dog gets when he hears a strange sound. You're asking yourself "What is this clown talking about? Both the late and great Luther Vandross and Gregory Hines told us on that song that "There's Nothing Better Than Love". KJ obviously didn't hear that song." Well I did, and I loved it, but it was just a good song. And although I can make you laugh, I've never been to Clown College and I know nothing about balloon animals, so watch the clown comments. It's just a belief that I've always had, and I'll spell it out for you in the coming paragraphs.

On the surface, we all have the sense that love is the most important element of any relationship. We've been taught from the beginning that love conquers all. Family, friends, movies and music have hammered it into us. I'm here to tell you that love doesn't always conquer all. You could love someone all day and all night, but if you don't trust them, it will tear your relationship apart. People that love each other without trust break up all the time. The reason for that is the fact that it's the trust that keeps you from worrying all the time. Worrying about whether or not your partner's being faithful. Worrying about whether your partner's being honest or not. It keeps you from being insecure about your relationship. If you have the ability to trust your partner, it puts your mind at ease. If you don't, then it becomes a very difficult thing for all involved. The insecurity that comes with not being able to trust within the relationship can cause great stress on you and your partner.

If there's anything more difficult than having the ability or feeling comfortable enough to trust someone, it's knowing exactly when to trust someone. We must remember not to blindly trust people, regardless of how we feel about them. Trust is something that's earned. No matter how much we may love another, no matter how cute they may be, no matter how much money they may have, everyone's not trustworthy. One of the things that make the issue of trust so tricky is the fact that we tie it in with so many other things.

Now, I'm not suggesting that keeping all of these things separate is an easy thing. All the things that we feel and experience in relationships wind up getting tangled up. Love, trust, communication and all that. Although these things need to work in concert with one another in order for us to have successful relationships, we need to remember to check them all individually as well. We need to allow people to earn our trust over time, rather than just giving it to them. It's all about keeping all of the various emotions we feel in check.

Chances are you'll probably fall in love with someone sooner than they actually prove themselves worthy of your complete trust. That's not to suggest that it won't all still come together, it's just to say that we shouldn't put the cart before the horse. You can't control the way these things happen, but you can at least try to slow them down. Going back to what I said in the last paragraph, we should allow someone to gain our trust. Give them a chance. Don't completely turn yourselves over to them, but at the same time, give them a chance to prove themselves. Don't fall into the "all men are the same" or "all women are the same" mode. Though men and women share similarities, we're all not the same. I don't know very many men that would've have written what I've written about men in the first two chapters of this book, let alone what's coming in the next chapters. Just because you're in love with someone and everything's all good in the beginning, doesn't mean that they should be trusted.

My philosophy is you never know a person until you've had some trouble with them. That's usually when you can tell the make-up of a person. That's when you can tell whether or not you're dealing with a quality individual, whether or not you're dealing with an individual with character or whether or not they'll really be there for you. How they respond to adversity will not only tell you whether or not you should even be involved with a person, but also how much trust you should attribute to them. Before you put a lot of trust into an individual, there are some tests that they should pass. Trust in a relationship goes so much further these days than just asking yourself whether or not someone is going to break your heart. Because of the way that things have changed over the last twenty years, you have to be able to trust people with more than just your heart.

A lot of us are single parents these days, and you have to be careful who you trust your children with. This is where the heart, the libido and the mind all need to separate. Just because you're in love with someone doesn't mean that they can be trusted with your children. Child molesters aside, sometimes some of us single parents foolishly fall in love with people that don't care for children. This is something we touched on in Chapter 1. It's something that should be settled when choosing a mate, but we sometimes lead with the aforementioned libido and wind up choosing people that don't make sense. Without rehashing all of Chapter 1, it's just one more thing to think about before we just blindly trust someone.

There's also the issue of finance. A lot of times when we fall in love or call ourselves loving someone, money gets all mixed up. On top of "shackin' up", we have the nerve to go out and get joint bank accounts. This is just KJ being old fashioned, but I don't feel either of these things should happen until you've said "I do" to one another. It's bad enough that we've begun to share bank accounts *without* living together, but if you must share living spaces, at the very least, keep your money separate. We've somehow become stupid enough to think that as long as we don't make it legal, if things don't work out, we can just go our separate ways without the law getting involved. But all you need to do is look at the endless parade of idiots going through Judge Judy, Judge Joe Brown and Judge Mathis' courtrooms to know how uninformed a decision that is.

Anytime money is involved, it doesn't matter how much love we have for one another. If there's a breakup, it will get legal. Everything from who paid what bills to who gets the CD and DVD collection (I can see myself going to court over said items). A wise thing to do in that regard would be to have a joint bank account for bills only, but keep your personal bank account separate from the relationship. This isn't only true in the sense that we sometimes get involved with people that intend to use us for our money, but sometimes we're involved with people that just aren't good with money. Letting these people at your finances is a huge mistake.

I know it seems that I'm off track to some, but this is still along the lines of trust and how much we should have with our partners. For example, from my time as a car salesman, you'd be surprised at how letting someone with bad credit get mixed up with your finances can change your life. It only takes a few short months to ruin one's credit, but it takes a long time to build it back up. It'd be a shame if someone ruined your credit other than yourself. It's bad enough when someone steals your identity to do it. It's worse when someone you trusted does it. (One more note on that: Be careful who you co-sign for. If they need a co-signer, there's a reason, and that reason is usually that they don't pay their bills on time. Don't let 'em drag you down too.)

Obviously, trust is extremely paramount as it relates to fidelity in the relationship. While losing money to someone that has betrayed your trust can be devastating, nothing is seemingly more devastating than to have your heart broken. In the game of love, nothing is worse than having someone you love cheat on you. This is the ultimate in betrayal of trust as far as relationships are concerned. When this happens to us in a relationship, those of us who are in love begin to convince ourselves that we'll never be able to continue on with life.

Basically, the reason that it hurts so much is because someone we loved has betrayed our trust. That leads to feelings of being violated. When you've put your heart on the line and your trust in an individual and they respond by cheating on you, it can, and most times will, turn your world upside down (we'll talk about bouncing back from that in the Chapter 5). Once you find yourself alone, you begin to question how you could ever trust such an individual. But mind you, the love hasn't left you. Only the trust has.

This is why it's important to allow someone to earn your trust. This is also why it's important to keep our emotions in check. Don't allow the fact that you're in love cloud your judgement as to whether or not you should trust someone. As it pertains to fidelity, cheaters usually show some signs of who they are before they commit that emotional assault on you. Sometimes when we're in love and we see some of these signs, we tend to look the other way. Sometimes in hopes that we can change an individual, and sometimes in hopes that we didn't see what we just saw.

If you see some of these signs, don't be afraid to slow down and look around. Don't be afraid to look for, and maybe even demand more proof of why this individual deserves your trust. And, most importantly, don't be afraid to pull the plug if it's proven that they don't. Again, these are some things that should be addressed before entering into a relationship, but life ain't perfect and sometimes the chicken comes before the egg. But don't be afraid to slow down. We sometimes tend to think that once we're in a relationship, that there's no room to slow down. Nothing could be further from the truth. If you don't like what you see at any point in your involvement with someone else, there's always time to slow down and take a look around.

To bottom line all of this, without trust, the relationship is lost. Once someone has broken your heart through infidelity, and thus violated your trust, it's not like you immediately stop loving them. The love still remains, and that's why it hurts so much. You find yourself wondering how someone that you love so much could do this to you. That's why trust is more important than love. Because no matter how much you love someone, once they violate your trust, things are never the same, especially when it comes to infidelity. Once that occurs, most times your relationship is damaged beyond repair. You find yourself questioning everything your partner says to you, and with good reason. For all of the hopeless romantics out there, sometimes love can conquer this. I don't want it to sound like I don't believe in love, because I do. Sometimes problems like this can be solved, but it takes a lot of work on both ends.

It's just that without trust, your love by itself won't be strong enough to hold your relationship together and keep you happy. It's not that we don't get fooled sometimes. Sometimes one can be worthy of our trust, and then change on us. Sometimes we come across one so good that they make us *feel* as though they're trustworthy when they're not. There are many different reasons why things like this happen. The moral here is to make sure it's not your own fault. Don't let it happen because you turned a blind eye to some things you should have paid attention to. There are enough surprises in our relationships without us adding to the fun. Keep in mind how valuable trust is, and how your partner must be worthy of it. Without it, you'll just be in love with someone who's probably not worth it.

Lastly, I wanna talk about that old stand by, communication. This, to me, should be the easiest to come by. Although I've stated over and over again how trust is the most important element to a relationship, and honesty is a very necessary component, it's communication that leads to both of these things. This is usually something that we as men have much more trouble with than women. If anything, for us, women talk *too* much. But that's okay because we never have to guess about what's on their minds. The only time women seem to have trouble expressing themselves is usually when they realize that we're not listening as much as we should. This leads to them keeping their feelings bottled up inside, which is more of a problem for men than we think, because once they explode on you, it's only then that you know real trouble.

There are a lot of ways in which we as men need to be much more attentive, and this is the most important. Listening to our women is a skill that must be re-acquired by men if we intend to truly make them happy. Most times, they're telling us what they really need from us. They're much better communicators than we are, so it always baffles me when men say that they don't know what their women want. If we spent less time trying to stifle (Archie Bunker) our women and more time listening to what she's saying, you could easily kill two birds with one stone. You can find out what she needs *and* she'll stop talking. Women need acknowledgment. Acknowledge that you've heard her rather than brushing her off or ignoring her altogether. It'd be great if there were results to go along with that acknowledgement, but let's take one step at a time, ladies.

We as men not only need to learn to listen to our women, but we must learn to express ourselves as well. We fail here sometimes because some of us don't quite know how to put into words exactly what we feel. We've always had trouble dealing with emotions, as evident by our inability sometimes to say, "I love you" to our women in public or in front of our friends. Sometimes, unfortunately, we fail in this sense because we don't know how to communicate from above the waist. This type of thinking, or lack thereof, has to stop. I still believe that having the ability to stimulate a woman mentally will lead to more physical stimulation. No matter how much they've changed in terms of their aggression and, in some ways, their lack of respect for themselves, women at *some* point in their lives will always want stimulating conversation with their sex.

Sometimes our women don't respect our feelings because we aren't letting our feelings be known. Don't be afraid to say that you hurt sometimes too. To quote Michael McCary of Boyz II Men in the song "End Of The Road", don't be afraid to say, "I feel pain too". And if you use the bass that brotha has in his voice, you might yet again kill two birds with one stone. You've let her know how you feel *and* it might lead to some of that physical stimulation we just talked about.

Seriously though, talking about your feelings within the relationship, whether good or bad, is the key to it all. So many problems are caused simply due to lack of understanding. The only way that we can understand each other completely or understand each other's position during times in which we disagree is through communication. I feel that communication is the easiest thing to accomplish in the relationship because it's something that doesn't hinge completely on emotion. It's just a matter of talking to each other. It's something that we can do long before we officially become a couple. It can be started during the dating process. Things as simple as what time you're going to meet up, what types of activities one likes to do, what you expect out of a mate or anything of that nature. These are all forms of communication. If we start out communicating from the beginning, starting with the little things, once the relationship graduates to the next level, it shouldn't be that difficult a transition.

Communication at the beginning of the relationship can also tell you whether or not you and an individual have a future. Often times we get involved with people and start thinking too far ahead. Way too far ahead. We start thinking about the alter (ladies, I'm talking to you). But before you got too far, you better talk to that man or woman. Make sure you know who you're dealing with and that you're on the same page before you start rehearsing nuptials.

Introducing KJ's Rule of 3. One man's opinion here, but it's been my feeling that if you don't come together on 3 critical elements, either your relationship will fail, or, if you do make it to the alter, your marriage will fail. If you don't come together on God, money and child rearing, you won't make it. Outside of obvious issues like the fidelity and trust and all that other stuff that we've covered, these three things will ruin you. If you don't serve the same God (and some of us are crazy enough to marry people that don't worship any God, much less ours), how will you agree on spiritual issues?

Most times, people who believe in a higher power are led by that higher power, especially in times of trouble. If you and your partner don't share this belief, it will cause division in your house or relationship. Simply put, when you pray, your partner should pray with you. In the event that you don't believe in a higher power, you should probably be with someone that feels the same way. Otherwise, if you're with someone that does, they won't make any sense to you, and all of that will come to a head sooner or later. Every religion is different, and though I'm not here to suggest that one is better than the other, whatever religion you choose to practice, your partner should as well.

Go back to the Bible verse that I referenced in Chapter 1: *II Corinthians 6:14*. Whether you believe in the Bible or not, it's a verse of wisdom and can be applied to any life. Again, don't try to change an individual, just find someone that shares the same spiritual beliefs as you. If you communicate and refuse to be afraid to ask questions in the beginning, you'll have the answers you need before the love bug bites.

On the issue of money, it's quite simple. There should be one philosophy on money in your household. It can't change from month to month. This is especially true when your income is limited. Money, or the lack thereof, can put an incredible strain on a relationship, particularly a marriage. You can't have one person that spends like there's no tomorrow, and another that saves and plans for a rainy day. It doesn't fit and will lead to conflict. You should tailor your lifestyle to what you make and not what you wished you made (and to my African-American brothers and sisters out there, please, let's stop living above our means; Credit is a crucial thing and must be protected).

If you and your partner are going in different directions trying to run a household, how will anything ever get done? It won't without an argument. Sure, we're all different in how we spend our money and how cautious we may be, if at all. No two people are the same on this. But you need to find someone that you can at least reach some common ground with. Again, how will you know that without communicating with them?

And lastly, child rearing. This wasn't always a problem, but these days, with so many different styles of child rearing, this is something that definitely should be discussed when dating. Especially before we began a physical relationship with someone. Remember the possible parent from Chapter 1? Anytime you engage in sexual activity, you're engaging with a possible parent to your child. This is important for men and women. All of us weren't raised the same way, so all of us don't see child rearing the same.

There was a time way back when, when pretty much everybody raised their kids the same, especially in the black community. But now, things are different. We have "time outs" now. In my house, the only "time outs" we saw occurred on the TV during sporting events. There were no "time outs", only "knockouts", provided by my mother. Nowadays, things are different. Everybody sees raising kids a different way and you need to be on one accord in this area with a potential parent to your child. If you believe in raising kids one way, and you partner believes in another, you'll no doubt confuse your child. This goes for everything from whether or not to spank to whether or not we go to church. That's why being involved with someone of the same faith is so important.

I know some of the flower children out there will want to know from me why the kids can't experience the differences in mom and dad's philosophies and learn from them both, but we all have an idea of how we want our children raised. And in the unfortunate event that they're being raised from two different households, we'd all prefer that it still be done with some consistency. We don't want to deliver two different messages to our children. If they want to branch out and blaze different trails, they can, and will, do it when they're older.

We'd all like to instill certain morals and values in our children. When you consider someone as a partner through marriage or just in a relationship, you need to assess what their morals and values are, and even if they have any. You need to be confident that they match up in most ways with yours. That way, again, in the unfortunate event that they're being raised in two homes, you can feel confident that good things are being instilled in your child when they're away from you.

Again, by simply talking to the people that we're dating long before any seeds are planted, you can find out exactly where a person stands on issues like this. These are very important things to consider when dating someone, but they can only be learned through that initial communication. By not allowing ourselves to get so caught up in physical attributes and feelings, and slowing down and taking the time to get to know someone, we can avoid some of the mistakes that come from not communicating and expressing what we want. You can also find out what another person has to offer, where they are in life and where they're going. By communicating with your partner and being open to their communicating with you, you open the door to the honesty and trust that I've already talked about.

By maintaining communication with your partner, it becomes easier to determine when and how much trust should be invested in your relationship. Not only does it help you get to know a person, if you're communicating with your partner on a regular, it's easier to maintain honesty in the relationship. As I stated earlier, we lie out of fear. Sometimes, that fear is the fear of not knowing how our partner will react to the truth. Through communication, you have a better understanding of your partner and how they will react to certain things. This information shouldn't be used as a barometer on whether or not to actually tell the truth, but rather how we should go about telling the truth.

Since women are more prone to communicating and being open about things, they must continue to push the envelope on this issue. Continue to speak your mind and communicate with your man. If he doesn't hear you, then make him hear you through persistence. Don't nag, because there is a fine line between nagging and persistence, but don't give up. If you eventually find that you're fighting a losing battle and you're with a man that won't open up to you, then it may be time to seek shelter from that particular storm. However, be sure that you're worthy of him opening up to.

Don't have a man open up to you, only for you to crush him. Opening up and sharing his feelings is a very difficult thing for a man to do. Having a man fall in love with you is not a license to use him. If you have the love of a good man in your life, be wise with it. His heart can break just like yours. Be careful how you treat a man in love with you. This is not the way in which you want equality. We shouldn't use women and they shouldn't use us. If your heart's been broken before, don't seek your revenge on a man that loves you. If his love is real, then this is a brand new day for you.

As for the men, it's time to stop being afraid to tell that woman how you feel. We need to kill off this notion that a man can't talk about his feelings or he's soft. You ain't a man if you can't talk about your feelings. That's what real men do. That's what real women appreciate. We have to understand that relationships are about working. Everyday. It never ends. As soon as you get lazy or fall into a routine where you're not working very hard to hold on to what you have, you lose.

It's not easy, but if you love one another, it's worth it. Going back to the open of this chapter, you must be willing. Willing to do the work. Men, open up to your woman. I'm not asking you to be wimp, because if you are, she might be out the door regardless. What I am saying is that we need to be more expressive. Bottling up only leads to anger, frustration, misunderstanding and sometimes the end of a relationship. Now if it means that much to men out there to appear "hard" to your friends, then go right ahead. Just know that sometimes the price of being hard is being alone, and who needs that (double-entendre free of charge)?

To conclude the first three chapters of this book, I chose to include a piece that I wrote 2 years before even attempting to write the book. It's actually a precursor, if you will. This was the inspiration to what I spoke about in the first three chapters. I feel that I summed it up best when this piece was first conceived. I shared it with friends and some family, and most who read it enjoyed it, so I've decided to include it here.

It's just an interesting perspective on something that men and women have seemingly been going through since the beginning of time. But it wasn't always that way. It all started in Eden. We were in paradise. We can get back there if we try. But we have to want it. Our desire to succeed has to be stronger than our desire to do wrong. Hopefully this fictitious letter can inspire some to go in the right direction. Hopefully it will inspire us to mend the fences that remain torn between the sexes. Hopefully, it will help to lead us back to Eden. Read on…

## *AN OPEN LETTER FROM ADAM TO EVE*

Dear Eve,

It's all coming clear to me. I understand it now. I've been trying to figure out why we continue to be two, rather than one. I can tell you now. In fact, I will tell you. I will tell you in the next lines. It's my fault. It's your fault. It's our fault. There have been too many wrongs committed by me. I've failed you as a man. I haven't done what I was supposed to do. What I promised I would do. I promised to be faithful. I failed. I promised to respect. I failed. I promised to be a good father. I failed. All of these things I promised, and yet I never came through. Instead of showing you love, I pretended to be hard and acted as if I didn't care. Instead of being a father, I left you to raise the kids all alone. Instead of coming home at night, I went to bars and strip clubs. Instead of making love to you and only you, I slept with other women and put you at risk. My excuse? "I don't love her, but I love you and you should understand that". Somehow, that was supposed to keep you from hurting.

Instead of spending quality time with you and the kids, I chose to throw material things at the situation. Money, hairdos, jewelry, clothes and toys for the kids were supposed to take the place of an absent boyfriend, husband and father. To put it plainly, I treated you like a whore, and my kids like bastards. What kind of a role model am I for my son? What kind of man am I presenting to my daughter? Will she see this as normal, and go out and find a man just like me? Will she find a man that shows her love, respect and treats her like a lady, and dismiss him because she thinks he's "soft"? Will my son grow up and make babies, only to neglect them? Will he grow up and disrespect women in the way of his father? I don't know. The only thing I do know is that if I don't change, they'll be worse for it. But it's not all my fault. I'm not the only one to blame. You've failed as well. There are some things I need from you. Yes, you've failed too. The question is, how have you failed?

There have been too many wrongs committed by you. You've failed me as a woman. You haven't done what you were supposed to do. What you promised to do. You promised to be faithful. You failed. You promised respect. You failed. You promised to be a good mother. You failed. All of these things you promised, yet you never came through. Instead of raising the kids, you left them with grandma all of the time. Instead of staying home and being a good mother, you chose to run the streets with your girlfriends and party all night. Instead of making love to me and only me, you slept with other men and put me at risk, just to get revenge on me for my actions. Somehow, that was supposed to keep you from hurting over what I did. Somehow, that was supposed to hurt me and make me act right. Instead, it only continued a vicious cycle.

Instead of spending quality time with me and trying to work through our differences, you accepted material things from me instead. Money, hairdos, jewelry, clothes and toys for the kids were payment enough for you, instead of demanding that I be a better boyfriend, husband and father. To put it plainly, you acted like a whore, and allowed me to treat my kids like bastards. As long as you were living in a luxurious house and had lots of money to spend, it didn't matter to you what I did in the streets. Just bring home the paper. What kind of a role model are you for my daughter? What kind of woman are you presenting to my son? Will he see this as normal and think that the only way that he can gain the love of a woman is to buy it? Will my daughter grow up and become the same woman as you? Will she think that a man doesn't really love her if he's not emptying out his pockets for her? I don't know. The only thing that I do know is that if you don't change, they'll be worse for it. But it's not all your fault. You're not the only one to blame. We've both failed. There are some things we need to do individually, as well as together. But where do we start?

I can start by showing you the love and respect you deserve. I must learn to love you again. You should mean more to me than anything on this earth. I must return to a place in my mind where you are my life partner. Where I feel that I can't do without you. Because the reality is that I can't. I need you in my life. I can't let my pride interfere with that. I must be man enough to show you what you mean to me every day. No matter what my friends say. I must return to a place where you mean more to me than just a place to lay my head.

You must become more to me than just a sexual conquest. You must become more to me than just the carrier of my children. You must become more to me than just someone that I take out my problems on, rather than talk out my problems with. I must return to a place in time when you were my Queen and I was you King. I must return to a place where I provided for you because I loved you, as opposed to giving you material things to cover up for my indiscretions and inadequacies. You should be my reason for living. Everything else should be secondary. I must regain my focus. One woman for one man. Two souls with one focus. To create heaven on earth for one another. I must return to that place. Again, the question is, what do I need from you?

If I prove myself worthy, you can start by showing me the respect that I deserve. You need to learn to love me again. I should mean more to you than anything on this earth. You must return to a place in your mind where I am your life partner. Where you feel that you can't do without me. Because the reality is that you can't. You need me in your life. You can't let your pride interfere with that. You must be woman enough to show me what I mean to you every day. No matter what your friends say. You must return to a place where I am more than just a bank account to you. I must be more to you than just someone to put down to your friends when we have disagreements. You must return to a place in your mind where I am your man, and you are my woman.

You must return to a place in your mind where a man's bank account isn't the measure of the man. You must return to a place in your mind where you know the difference between a man who provides for you out of love, and a man who gives you whatever you want, just to keep you quiet while he sleeps around. You need to return to a place where it's not <u>as important</u> the size of the house you're living in, but rather with whom you're living. You need to return to a place where the size of your engagement ring doesn't matter <u>as much as</u> the character of the man that gave it to you. I should be your reason for living. Everything else should be secondary. You must regain your focus. One woman for one man. Two souls with one focus. To create heaven on earth for one another. You must return to that place. But we must do it together.

Since the beginning of time, we were meant to be together. From the moment God took one of my ribs and made you whole. So, after all this time, why have we decided to go away from one another? Why is there a great divide between us? I can tell you. There was a time when I had to adapt to your way of life in order to have you. It was that way because your way was, and still is, the best way. It's a way of peace. A way of love. A way of family. It's God's way. To adapt to my way of life would surely be self-destructive for you, and thus family as a whole. Unfortunately, that's where we are today. You have adapted to my way of life. And we have self-destructed. Instead of being my reward for turning away from my foul ways, you have become as promiscuous as I am. Instead of demanding that I respect you, you have allowed me to call you "bitch" and "hoe" without reprimand.

You've only required that I increase your bankroll and your wardrobe in order to continue to behave in this manner. I have thus become more aggressive in my behavior. I show no remorse for the loss of your love. I've completely taken you for granted. You've taken what used to be a part of just being a man, which was taking care of his woman, and made it a license to abuse you. In turn, I've taught my seeds to disrespect the very womb from which they came. And you've allowed me to do it. Instead of condemning my whorish ways as you have in days past, you've chosen to wallow in this shame with me. Instead of leading me into the light, you've followed me into the darkness. But our fate has not been sealed yet. We can still be saved.

If you could turn your eyes from the dollar, and view love as the ultimate gift. If I could turn my eyes from my carnal desires, alcohol and drugs, and view love as the ultimate high. Because love is the ultimate. It's the greatest emotion that God has enabled us to feel. And we've turned away from it. But we can be saved. Because our Creator is still alive, we can be saved. We just have to be willing to work. We must work with renewed faith. We must rededicate ourselves. The Garden of Eden should have been the last time we went against God's wishes. But it wasn't. Surely you and I as adversaries is not what He envisioned when He placed us in the paradise that we eventually ruined. Let's create a new paradise. Let's return to the thrones from which we have fallen. You are my Queen. And I am your King.

Adam

# 4

## *Sex: Things Done Changed…*

Well, I bet I've got your attention now. This was a chapter that came about after a lot of debate between me and some friends of mine. I didn't necessarily want to write a chapter on sex because I didn't think it would fit into what I was trying to convey in this book. I've spent so much time trying to downplay sex and put it in its proper place in the relationship that I was trying to figure out whether or not I could place a chapter on sex in this book, without bringing down the overall message. I didn't want it to seem like I was sending mixed messages, saying on one hand that the emphasis on sex needs to be lessened, while glorifying it in another chapter. I didn't want to write a "how to" on sex, but rather expound on what it's supposed to be used for and where it belongs in our lives. Every time I would wonder aloud to one of my friends about whether or not I should write the chapter and how tasteful it would be, it would lead to a discussion of my views on the topic. My fears that I would sound like a typical male when writing it were soon put to rest as a lot of my views were in complete correspondence with what I was writing in this book. With that, my decision was made and here we are.

In this chapter we're going to take a little detour from what we've done so far in the book. We've talked a lot about the relationship as a whole up to this point, and we will get back to that. But for now we're going to discuss that relationship double-edged sword known as sex. However, we won't be discussing it from a relationship standpoint, but rather in a general sense. A lot of the problems that we have in relationships nowadays are caused by sex. There's either not enough sex, too much sex, too many requests for sex or it's being made too important to the success of the relationship. Truth is, a lot of times when we get into trouble, if you break the situation all the way down, we're misled at some point by our desire to have sex in either the wrong situation or with wrong people. It's a battle that man has been fighting since the beginning of time.

How much better off do you think Samson would've been had his desire for Delilah been quelled a bit (16th Chapter of Judges)? Even King David fell victim to his lust in the Bible. Read the 11<sup>th</sup> Chapter of II Samuel in your Bible and you'll see King David carry out what would be considered today the equivalent of a Mafia killing. All due to his inability to control his lust. And this was a man chosen by God. If he can't control his urges, what chance do we have? However, as you can see, even when we're chosen by God, we're still human, and we all can be susceptible to the flesh. Though he was blessed by God and ruled over many, David was just a man, and his lust for another man's wife caused him to abuse his power. And God is not amused when his chosen stray from the path that He's set. After Chapter 11, you can read the 12<sup>th</sup> Chapter to see what that lust got David in the end. Talk about reaping what you've sewn.

I won't be discussing sex from just an infidelity standpoint. I'm also talking about lust. That lust is just as prevalent in us when we're considering cheating as it is when we're considering doing our thing with someone that's not attached to anyone. I'm talking about what happens when we let our bodies take over our minds and we do things that somewhere in our subconscious we know are wrong. I'm talking about all the ways in which we use sex as an excuse for or to justify some of the poor decisions that we make in our lives. I'm talking about those situations where a little restraint would have done us some good, and a little courage to do the right thing is necessary, even though our bodies are crying out to do the wrong thing.

However, sex isn't just a negative thing. There are many positives to sex. A lot of people don't really realize it, especially some of the extreme religious types, but God intended for us to have sex. And believe it or not, it wasn't just in the name of reproduction. Sex is a good thing. However, God did intend for us to do it the right way. Man should take his wife before he just runs off and does his thing. Of course, that's where the confusion comes in. But we've got a whole chapter here to sort it all out. It's not my intent to tear down sex, but rather put it all in perspective.

We'll talk about the good, the bad and the ugly. The do's and the don'ts. Even us single folk should be able to get something out of this. But before the letter writing campaign gets going, I want everyone reading this to know that I'm in no way trying to suggest that I'm an innocent man. I've confessed a lot of my sins in this book so far, and I'm not afraid to do it again. Bottom line, as of the writing of this book, I have a 14 year old son, and I've never been married. Do we understand each other? Good. Some of the things that I write here, whether good or bad, will be from experience. A lot will be written from things that I've learned from other's experiences over the years. We ain't gon' be all night with this one, but let's get down to business.

For many years, both men and women have used sex as a weapon. Women have used it to get men to behave the way that they want them to, and men have used it to keep a woman where he wants her to be. In both cases, sometimes that's a good thing, and sometimes that's a bad thing. Just like in comic books and stories about heroes, we have to learn to use our powers for good, and never evil. Whether it's being used in this context in a good way or bad, we have to come back to the understanding that sex was never meant to be "used" at all. It was never meant to be used to gain an advantage on any particular individual.

Even if you feel that what you're using it for is for the good of whatever kind of relationship that you find yourself in, that's not what it was for. Sex was meant to be shared between a man and his wife, two people that love one another. It was supposed to be an expression of that love. Now once again, KJ's not naive. I understand that there are many of us out here that are engaged in sexual activity with people that we're not married to. While not condoning that, I must empha-size the importance of this act being performed between two people that love one another. Note the number of people that I said that should be involved in that love: Two. If only one of you is doing the lovin', then you have a problem. But I don't wanna get ahead of myself.

In the case of the men, we've always been disillusioned about sex. It was always something that we made way too big of a deal out of. If we're not actually having sex, we wanna be somewhere having it. And if we can't do that, then we're talking about it. If we're not just talking about it, we're lying about how much we actually get. It goes on and on. We've always made it seem that we'd die without it. On top of pretending that we can't do without it, we've always made the assumption that women can't do without getting it from us as well. I've always wondered how all of us could be the best ever at doin' it. Again, women have helped in some of these misconceptions that men have, but we'll discuss that shortly. If there was ever a time where a man was chaste, it was either because his woman wouldn't give it up or he was really influenced by a good woman while growing up.

For the most part, men never viewed sex as something special between a man and a woman. It was just something that we did. We saw it as nature. We never saw it as that expression of love that I spoke of. We never saw it as something that could be gentle and even beautiful. Of course that changes just a little when we fall in love, but that was never the way we saw it from the beginning. We usually saw it through the eyes of an animal. It was something that was aggressive. Just like animals, we hunted our prey, and then we attacked. We did our business, usually at a furious and *brisk* pace, and then we were off to sleep. The only real preparation that we'd do for the moment was possibly music selection to set the mood and alcohol for all you drinkers out there (I've been told that getting her drunk is also known as "seduction"; I wish you could see my eyes rolling).

Sex was simply something that was talked about in the locker rooms and barbershops as a rite of passage. Becoming a man. You were supposed to have sex with as many as you could in your youth, and once you've worn yourself out, then you go and get married. Now, in this scenario, a man is considered a *"playa"*. He's considered experienced. However, a woman in this scenario is considered a tramp and damaged goods. Women have long since felt that this was unfair. However, though the double standard is unfair, that doesn't mean that half of that statement isn't true. But I'm still on your side ladies. I'm just painting a picture. Just be patient.

Again, women perpetuate some of this madness that's carried on by men, but we're just as responsible for our own twisted views. When we're not throwing money at our woman problems, we're not afraid to throw our sexual organ at the problem as well. How many times have some of you out there heard of a man having problems with his woman, suggesting that she just needs a little to set her straight? Happens all the time, I know. I've been guilty of thinking those things about women that I've dated myself. If we're not blaming a woman's attitude on her menstrual cycle, then we're blaming it on her lack of "activity". I can hear women saying "Amen" to what I just wrote. I'm sure all of you reading this have heard it all before. But, that's just how men are in their thinking sometimes. We're very simplistic. If that woman's got a problem, then we've got the answer and it's either our wallet or our penis, but make no mistake about it, it's somewhere in our pants. Again ladies, you're feeding this monster, and I promise, for those of you that don't already know, I'm gonna explain very shortly.

## THE BIG 'O'

I'm reminded of Eddie Murphy's 1987 stand-up comedy film *Raw*. During his performance, Eddie suggested that if you bring a woman to an intense orgasm, you can pretty much do whatever you want in the relationship after that and get away with it. Now, Eddie didn't suggest that your woman wouldn't notice all of your wrongdoings, but he rather suggested that after that intense orgasm, she'd become incredibly forgiving. One more time ladies, not necessarily untrue. This wasn't some new and fantastic revelation that was just known by Eddie Murphy, however. This was something that men had always known about women. The unfortunate part of that was the fact that not only was it true with a lot of women out there, it helped to further cloud the vision of man. If it were already hard enough to get us to understand and appreciate the beauty of sex in its proper context, our goal shifted to bringing our women to that ultimate orgasm so that we can run wild.

Now mind you, we never wanted to bring her to that orgasm for the sake of making her feel good like we were supposed to, oh no. We couldn't just do it for her, we had to do it for *us*. We wanted to do it just so that we could run wild. And I'm sure that some of you ladies that have experienced this will agree that once you receive said orgasm, it's hard to get another one after that. Simply put, a brotha will just stop trying on ya. That's why women make such a big deal out of the orgasm. They never know when they'll get one from their man in the first place, and once they do get it, it's like "loaning" money to your kids, you never know when or if you'll ever see it again.

What this usually leads to are a couple of unfortunate situations for women. At this point, women began to place the improper emphasis on sex. As I stated above, Mr. Murphy isn't completely wrong in his assessment. After the "great sex", women fall into that notion of believing any and everything her man says simply because he's good in bed. Because he can make you feel like you have "never felt before", all of his lies start to sound true to you. In some unfortunate cases, women have even been known to endure physical abuse as well, all because of the way a man may make her feel in bed. It's a sad reality, but a reality none the less.

All of us have known a woman at one time or another in our lives that has stayed with an abusive man for much too long. Usually, when asked why they stay with such a man, if the answer isn't flat out money, you usually hear something along the lines of, "It's just the way he makes me feel". Translation: The sex is good. I mentioned earlier in this book that due to the lack of qualities that men seem to possess these days, women have begun to judge men solely on their performance in bed. In the process, they've ceased looking for more meaningful qualities in their men and placed all of the emphasis on sex.

Without even noticing, women blurred the line between "He's so good to me" and "He makes me feel so good". It's not that there's anything wrong with having good sex with someone. We all know that it's something that's a little more difficult to find these days on either side, but it can't be a reason to allow someone to make a fool of you. It can't be a reason we turn a blind eye to some behavior that's detrimental to us.

Women have to re-learn the fact that sex is not a cure-all to some of the problems that exist in relationships. It doesn't make up for any inadequacies a man may have. If he doesn't possess all of the qualities that you feel that a good man should possess, you can't be of the mindset that he "makes up for it in bed". In addition to that, the good qualities that you feel a man should possess shouldn't start with his performance in bed. Though it is good to have sexual gratification in our lives, in terms of its importance, it can't run along side fidelity, the ability to love you for you and the ability to take care of you and any potential children you may have. What good does it do you to have a man that's good in bed if he's sharing the goods with everyone?

Men have always been in a rush to get women into the bed. That's just the way it's always been. The only thing that used to slow us down was the women. But what has happened over the years is that women have now begun to do the same thing to men. With all of the sex horror stories that they share between each other at the hair and nail shops, women have decided that the last thing that they wanna do is wind up with a man that can't satisfy them sexually.

No matter how well he treats them, no matter how much he respects them, no matter how good he is to his mama, no matter what kind of character he may have, if he can't put it down properly, she don't want him. The only exception that they *are* willing to make is in the area of bank account. They'll trade a little of that sexual gratification for a few extra zeros (sad as that may be). Again, though it's nice to have all of that, where does it stop? Women have to get back to that point in their lives when they draw that line. They have to decide how much they're willing to sacrifice just to have good sex. Sometimes, the trade off is just too much.

There are a lot of less than desirable men out there that are very capable of having you walking on air from a sexual experience (less than desirable meaning in terms of character, and not in terms of looks). Women have allowed their physical desires to override their mental and spiritual well being. In their haste to satisfy the flesh, they've neglected those parts of themselves that will remain much longer than their desire to roll around in the bed with another human being: The mind and the spirit.

Though the attraction is physical when we first meet one another, any man that's serious about you will be attracted to these two things more so than the physical. And if he isn't, why do you need him? What's always forgotten in this search for a sexual nirvana is the fact that the sexual part of our lives will surely fade. What will you do when he can't make you feel the way Mr. Murphy says he will anymore and you're forced to deal with the person that he is? Aren't the chances of you being happy forever with him a lot better if you've first checked above his shoulders for the man that he is, rather than below his waist?

Now, I know there are some women reading this that are saying, "You're right, Kelly". There are women reading this that are swearing that they will do better as it pertains to this. There are women reading this that swear that the last time that they foolishly laid down with a man that they know they had no business being with will be the last time that they foolishly lie down with a man that they have no business being with. They understand now that sleeping with that man that you know is sleeping with 10 other women, just because he's good in bed, is going to stop right now. You guys see now that just because he put you in more positions than you even knew were possible and had you doing things that you didn't even know the human body was capable of, isn't reason enough to continue on seeing him.

You get the fact that just because he's better than your ex-boyfriend in the sack, doesn't mean that you should keep trying to convince yourself that if you could just stop all the physical and mental abuse and his calling you out of your name, whether he's drunk *or* sober, he'd be the perfect man, a good mate and a role model to any children you may someday slip up and have. From this moment on, things will be different. If he ain't right, you won't be bothered with him. No matter how good it feels to you, you're telling yourself right now that you're giving it up because you want more. Some of you that are saying these things are telling the truth. Some of you are lying. In fact, out of those of you that are lying, some of you already know that you're lying. Sad, but true.

## *HEY YOUNG WORLD*

However, what's worse than that is the fact that some of you, especially some of you younger people, are looking at the words that I'm writing and saying, "Whatever, Kelly. I'm young and this is the time for exploration. Besides, men do it all the time. I may as well explore my body now and find out what I like before I settle down". Ah, the ignorance of youth. I remember when I was that way. For some reason though, the ignorance is a much more vivid memory than the youth. Maybe it's because the ignorance was around much longer than the youth. But, I digress.

Young ladies are much more aggressive sexually than they used to be. However, this new sexual revolution that we're under is also a lot more costly than it used to be, both in the financial and the mortal sense of the word. Not only can being so free with your bodies lead to premature parenting, it can also lead to premature death. If the young ladies of today aren't more careful, in more ways than one some of these men out here can give you something that will last forever.

Of course there's always protection, but we've already talked earlier in this book about what can happen in "the heat of the moment". It's bad enough that even when you *think* you've gotten to know someone, you could still be at risk. It'd be foolish to put yourself at that same risk through not even trying to get to know a person. Through all of the partying, drinking, drugs, self exploration and whatever else young people do to cloud their judgment these days, they need to remember one very real fact: AIDS is real, and it doesn't discriminate.

Sadly, having sex has become a part of the dating process, as opposed to something reserved for someone special. It's become as much a part of the date as deciding which movie you should see or where you'll be dining. Sometimes, it's considered a given before the first date even takes place. In fact, in some cases, there is no restaurant or movie. The "date" has been reduced to a man going to a woman's house, watching a little television and then *she's* leading *him* to the bedroom. Wow! It's gotten to the point these days where women *expect* to have sex at the end of the date. Isn't that the same thing that over the years, men have been vilified for? I'm ashamed to admit this in print, but if girls were that easy when I was growing up, I'd have a house full of children and I'd need three jobs just to take care of all of them.

Though young people shouldn't rush into relationships or marriage, if you got a real one staring you in the face, don't be stupid. Don't fool yourselves into thinking that there's some sort of fun being had in the dating world. Don't lie to yourself by suggesting that you date because you "enjoy your freedom". Though there's nothing wrong with being by yourself and taking your time, in my opinion, there are three types of people that date: People that are looking for someone, people that wanna sleep around and people that have no choice due to a break-up. But believe me, with the current landscape in dating, no one really *wants* to be out there, no matter what they may say.

Deep down inside, we'd all like to have one special somebody that we can call our own. If you're fortunate enough to find that someone at a young age, don't throw it away all in the name of being free and too young to settle down. This isn't a call to marriage, as I feel that young people should wait a little longer than our parents and grandparents did to get married. But rather, don't throw the baby out with the bathwater. If you've got someone in your life that's good for you, don't just give them up because you're not ready to go all the way to the altar. And definitely don't give them up because of your desire to run the streets and lay with anybody with a cute smile and a willingness to oblige you in your hedonistic quests. When you slow down and those desires are replaced by a desire to be loved by someone that loves you for you and not your abilities in the bedroom, it would be a shame to know that you had it and gave it up for a few memories that in time you'll do your best to try and forget.

As for the older folks that have adopted some of this behavior that we've discussed thus far, it's astonishing that you don't know any better by now. Sooner or later, we have to get back to the understanding that sex doesn't equal love. Love equals love. That will never change. I wish I could say that it's simply a lack of understanding between men and women as it is with relationships, but it's really just a matter of us controlling our bodies with our minds, instead of the other way around.

I hate to keep bringing it back to the ladies, but I'm afraid that's the only way this will get turned around. Men have been this way since the beginning of time. While a lot of us have made progress in becoming more aware of a woman's feelings and her need to be respected, we'll probably never be where we ought to be on our own. It goes back to the basic fact that we can only get away with what women allow us to. If you guys are gonna lift up the skirt for us, this thing will never get fixed. In the name of repetition, if we don't have any incentive to do better, we never will. Left to our own devices, not only will we never change, we'll raise a new generation of horny toads, much more chauvinistic than we could ever be. After all, isn't that what we're seeing right now?

## *"I HEAR THIS GIRL AT THE OFFICE GOT YOU...WHIPPED..."*

With all of this talk about women and their behavior, I'm sure that the men are all feeling neglected. As though I've forgotten about us and all that's wrong with us. Conversely, I'm sure some of the guys reading this are asking themselves, "What about us? What about what we go through?" Actually, I've been talking about us all along. All of the things I'm telling women to watch out for are perpetuated by us. At the same time, there are some good brothas out there that are victimized by some of these same overly aggressive women that I've been trying to calm down in the earlier paragraphs of this chapter.

While there are instances where we have abused women through sex and our misuse of our reproductive organs, we have also begun to find ourselves on the other side of this coin a lot more than we did in the past. All in the name of equality, women have begun to use our overwhelming desire for sex against us. We've been so driven by our carnal desires for so long, that women flipped this whole thing on us. It's not that women haven't used sex in the past to get certain things out of us, but it was usually within the confines of the relationship. Surely there were always exceptions, as sex has been used throughout time by women to change the tide in their favor, but they have become increasingly malicious over the years.

While men have been ruled by our desires for sex for a long time now, as good as it feels, it hasn't always brought a pleasant aftertaste to our mouths. Although the act itself is good, there are sometimes some unpleasant consequences to what we have done. Even though it sometimes doesn't seem like it to us, there are consequences to lying down with the wrong woman that go beyond disease and unexpected pregnancies.

For those of you that are aware, you'll remember a certain scene from the movie *Boomerang*. A certain scene featuring actor John Witherspoon. A certain scene where Eddie Murphy's (again?) character "Marcus" was told he was, uh, whipped (I can't write what he said; my mom is reading this book). If you've never seen that particular scene, you've cheated yourself for way too long. Go rent or buy that movie and you'll enjoy it. Now, a lot of men will try and tell you that they've never been where Marcus was in that movie. A lot of men will be lying to you. At one point or another, we've all been where poor Marcus was. And we've usually been in the exact same situation as Marcus. Whipped by a woman that couldn't care less about us, while something that's real in our lives is right in front of us and slipping away.

The old folks use to call it "chasin' tail". That's what men find themselves doing on a regular basis. Forgive me if this gets vulgar, but men also have a saying: "The only thing better than some (tail), is some new (tail)". Now, I was paraphrasing there, but as I mentioned, my mom is reading this book. The problem is, men sometimes feel that way whether they're in a relationship or not. For years we operated on this premise and the *good* women in our lives suffered. It was all good to us as long as our women never gave us any trouble about it. Even after they found out what we were doing, we still didn't wanna hear anything about what we were doing or the way we were treating these women. It was all good until it started to go the other way.

As I stated earlier, women have used sex to get their way over the years, mostly because that's all that we as men responded to, but also usually within the confines of their particular relationships. But over time, it became a way for them to use men. It became a way for them to gain financially. As they say, they would make use of the world's oldest profession. They began to use it to control men in ways that benefited them and only them. In their minds, they began to take their revenge on us. The old folks had another saying as well: "She got yo' nose wide open".

Through our undying lust and the assumption that we ruled everything, men at some point began to lose this sexual war that we'd often found ourselves winning. While thinking that the sun rose and set in our underwear, we lost sight of the fact that women were getting fed up with us using them to live out whatever little fantasies we may have had about sleeping with as many women as we can before we die (or before it kills us). We were so arrogant about what we were doing, that we never thought for one second that women would ever rise up and do the same thing to us that we were doing to them.

We never paid attention to the power that women actually possess with *their* sexual organs. We never saw a day where we would be on the other side of this thing. For the life of me, I don't know how it is that we couldn't see this coming. I mean, when you sit down and think about it, when we were out there doing our dirt, who were we doing it with? That's right, women (well, *most* of us were with women). It was only a matter of time. After so many years of having the game played on them, there were bound to *learn* the game. Of course, we men never had as much of a problem with them learning the game as we did with them using their new found knowledge against us.

Realizing that we were suckers for sex, some women began to take us for all we were worth just by simply giving us what they should've been making us earn. They began to embrace something that we had been trying to force them to accept for the longest. The idea that not only was traditional commitment in a sexual sense old fashioned, it was unnatural. They began to share the belief of men that there was nothing wrong with having a few sexual partners. I mean, what's everybody so uptight about? By trading their bodies for worldly possessions, they began to embrace the notion of getting something in return if you're going to give up your body. As I've stated a few times already in this book, unfortunately, they stopped wanting love in return. Respect was no longer good enough. Commitment was the furthest thing from their minds.

On the flip side, we men never thought it could be this easy. All we had to do was take her out here and there, buy her a gift or two, and we can have all the sex we could stand. Women felt that they were finally getting their revenge, and we were none the wiser. Men felt that we were finally getting our sex, and all it was costing us was a few bucks here and there, but without the commitment. How sweet is this arrangement? But, like so many arrangements between men and women, this honeymoon would be short lived. What appeared to be balanced would soon become unbalanced. By the end of this chapter, I'll explain how stupid we all are in the midst of all this confusion.

As I've stated so many times in this book, KJ is not naïve to the fact that sex never has, and never will be something strictly shared between a man and his wife. We'll never be there as a society. My wish is that we as a society can get back to a point in this life where it is at the very least shared by two people that really care about one another. Maybe if we start there, we may even get back to a point where the words "makin' love" can actually be a proper description of the act. For those of us raised in the church, you'd often hear the preacher suggest that we put on the full armor of God. In doing that, we first need to remove the armor of the whoremonger.

Whether you were raised in the church or not, I'm sure we can all understand what's been written in this chapter. This is a call to our men to wake up to the changing climate that we're in. No longer are we the only ones viewing the opposite sex as a personal conquest. Women are just as promiscuous, conniving and abusive as we have been in the past as it pertains to sex. In the name of equality, they've take on characteristics that were usually attributed to men. We have to be just as careful of them as they've had to be of us.

They're not about having sex with us for financial gain only anymore. They go back and hi-five their friends the same way that we have. And also like us, they'll put you down to raise their own self-esteem as well. Don't be fooled. You'll look just like Maaarrrrrcus (remember Lady Eloise?) in *Boomerang*. Ask a woman that's been burned, and she'll tell you. The only thing worse than being whipped by a man that don't care nothing about you, is being in love with that same man. It hurts like hell.

If you're a good man out there and you think that these women won't use their bodies to take you for your money, time *and* your heart, you are in for a rude awakening. They're very aware of what they're doing while they're doing it as well. If you're not careful, they'll empty your bank account, alienate you from your family and friends *and* break your heart. You wanna hear the worse part? If you're not stronger in your spirit (if she hasn't broken it already), all she has to do is tell you that she was at Victoria's Secret today, and you'll go running back for more. Because we as men don't have proper balance sometimes, there are times when we think we're in love when it's just sex, and vice versa. You *think* she loves you, but it's just sex. That's right guys, it used to be our game, but now they're playing. If you're not in touch with yourself, these types of women will notice your weakness and exploit it.

I once had a woman tell me that the reason that I've had trouble with women in the past is because I know things that women don't want men to know. She told me that in order for a woman to have the control that she wants with a man, whether she's playing a guy or in a relationship with him, there's a certain amount of stupid that she needs him to have. She said that my problem is that I ask too many questions, but that's the only way I know to get answers. Anyway, it's not that women want a dumb man, but she needs him to be oblivious to certain things. Because we naturally don't understand women, though it can be frustrating to them at times, they actually use that to their advantage.

However, just as I've stated with sex, if a woman loves and respects you, she'll use this advantage within the confines of the relationship. In essence, she may use it to get you to go somewhere you really don't wanna go or buy something that you can't really understand what the need is for it in the first place. You're a little dumb about some things, but as long as it's done to make her happy, in the end, it's to your benefit. If she's a good woman, not only will she make it up to you, she's worth it anyway. But if she's looking to use you and you're a little smarter than the average bear, she'll move on, just like a no good man would do in the same situation with a woman. But if you let one get their hooks in you, no matter how hard you may pretend to be, when it comes crashing down on you, it'll be a while before you get up again. But I wanna be fair about this. If the ladies aren't careful, they can suffer that same fate. Unfortunately, men aren't above taking money from a woman anymore. Don't just watch your body ladies, watch your purse too.

## *WHAT UNIFORM ARE YOU WEARING?*

There was a time when women used to withhold sex from men to get them to behave the way that they wanted them to. There was a time when women would withhold sex from a man when they felt that he didn't deserve it. Things are different now. So very, very different. Women have decided that instead of withholding sex to get what they want, they will *have* sex to get their way. They've decide that they would "use what they've got, to get what they want".

This used to mean maybe dressing a little more provocatively so that a man would notice you. Nowadays, it means dressing like a tramp in order to get noticed. These days, the word virtuous is only used to describe the Virgin Mary. These days a woman loses respect for you if you're *not* trying to sleep with her. Gentlemen are considered soft by today's standards. If you respect her as a woman she may appreciate that quality in you, but she's still more likely to gravitate towards that guy across the room that plans to have her undressed by the end of the night. Once a temple, their bodies have now become weapons.

After years of abuse at the hands of men, women began to find empowerment in sex. As I stated earlier, while they once found it empowering to show some restraint as it pertains to sex, they now see actually having sex as a way to gain an advantage on a man. While they once saw an advantage to making a man get to know them and show them some respect before they felt the need to show him all that God has given them, they now feel that it's okay to audition a man, even though they've never met anyone in his family (though not always foolproof, it's usually a sign that a man really likes you if he's willing to take you to meet his family).

Also, as I stated earlier, the motive behind their actions are completely different as well. While sex was once an expression of love to women, they began to use it to get material things and money from a man. Again, the oldest profession in the world. However, for some strange reason, when doing these things for the reasons that they're doing them, if you called one of them a whore (or "hoe" if you're from the 'hood), they have the nerve to get indignant and claim that they're being disrespected. How's that for a double standard?

If you know a woman that's guilty of this kind of behavior, ask her why she's doing it. I can almost guarantee you that at some point during her "explanation" she'll tell you that it's okay because men do it all the time. Somehow, when we were doing it to women it was wrong, but when women do it in the name of revenge, it becomes alright. The saddest part of all of that is that these women really believe in the words they're saying. However, it doesn't stop there. If you thought that men could come up with some really bad explanations to why they did what they did, you should hear some of the ones I've heard from women.

Overall, they may not be as bad, but they can get pretty lame. Outside of the shamefulness of sleeping with a man because he has money, some of the best explanations I've heard have included: "he was there and I was horny", "I'm grown and I can do what I wanna do", "I was curious", "I wanted to see if he could back up what he said he would do to me" (and in most cases, he can't and he already knows it, so who's the fool there?), "we left the club, went to his house, and one thing just led to another", and the list goes on and on. Though a lot of those "explanations" are true in most cases, are they really proper justifications for selling yourself out?

Now, I dare not move on without giving you my all-time most lame excuses that I've ever heard from women as it pertains to having meaningless sex with a man: "he just kept asking me, so I finally said yes just to get him off (or on) my back" and "he was a really good dresser". I kid you not on that last one. A female actually told me that she slept with a guy because he looked good in his clothes. And, to make matters worse, that wasn't something that was far down on her list of reasons as to why she did it. It was the first thing out of her mouth when I asked why she did it. Isn't that sad?

You wanna hear (or read) something worse? Do you wanna know why she said she wouldn't sleep with him again? Because once he took off his clothes, he wasn't as attractive with them off as he was with them on. Not because she behaved like a tramp and realized the error of her ways, oh no. If this brotha that she had nothing in common with and no other attraction to other than his penchant for fine clothing had been just a little more attractive in the buff, he might have gotten another go-round. If women like this are going to be raising our daughters, I weep for the future and the choice of women that my son will have when he becomes of age.

The problem with focusing on the physical rather than other aspects of an individual is that if the physical doesn't measure up to what you think it should be, you'll lose interest. To put it a little more bluntly, if he doesn't perform up to expectations, then you have no other use for him and almost immediately you want nothing else to do with him. If we haven't reversed our roles here, I don't know what else to call it.

This is mostly a woman's issue as men are different. For the most part, as long as we're *having* sex, it's a good experience. This is the problem with the scenario that I presented in the last paragraph. When the relationship is based on sex and nothing but sex, it has to be good or the relationship will end after one night of intercourse. The other problem with that scenario, the problem not seen by this young lady, is that one night of foolish acts can last a lifetime. This was a dilemma that women used to *face*, and now it's one that they cause. When operating under these pretenses, you also run the risk of missing out on a quality individual. By not getting to know someone and using them for your own selfish and carnal desires, you could be ruining a good thing before it even begins.

I know there are a lot of women reading this that have no sympathy for a man in this situation. After all, men have been doing this to women for years. Never getting to know them, simply using them for their bodies and then running off with someone else. Never even getting to know the woman that she is or even the woman that she wants to be. She may have even been his wife. But he couldn't see past his physical desires and he used her. But remember how it felt ladies. It was wrong when men did it to you, and it's wrong when you do it to us. In fact, you guys are actually twice as wrong. You're wrong for your act and you're wrong for seeking revenge.

The only thing worse for a woman in this situation is if it backfires. If he actually lives up to expectations, then you have a real situation because now you want more. However, the problem you may run into is the fact that considering you gave him your body so quickly and with little resistance, you now have a man on your hands that sees your relationship as nothing more than physical. Even if he wanted something more initially, because of your willingness to move to the bedroom at the speed of light, you've more than likely changed his perception of you. He now sees you as just another notch in his belt. Oh, and one more thing ladies, once he feels that way about you, it's nearly impossible to change it.

If you ask for more of a relationship, he sees you as pressuring him and we don't respond well to relationship pressure. Plus, he has an opinion of you that's not favorable and no man willingly takes on a woman when he has a less than favorable opinion of her. Conversely, if you begin to resist his advances in an attempt to change the tide of the relationship, you become a tease in his eyes. You see, ladies, giving it up too soon is never a good idea, no matter how you slice it. Even if you made a mistake and gave it up in the infamous "heat of the moment" and you're a good, clean and wholesome girl and he's a quality guy, chances are, in the back of his mind, he's wondering if you *really* made a mistake or if that's who you really are. And though there are exceptions to this, more times than not, he's gonna keep looking and you'll be left out in the cold. Make no mistake about it ladies, we'll take what you give us, but we always stay with ones that make us wait.

In essence, we both do the same thing. If a woman goes to bed with a man right from the start, then it's merely physical. In this scenario, if a man doesn't perform to her expectations, she's usually done with him. At the same time, if a woman goes to bed with a man sooner than she should, his opinion of her is forever affected. Even if you were to somehow forge some sort of relationship out of this, what do you think will happen the first time you tell him that you have a male friend? He'll get paranoid, and rightfully so. After all, that's how you guys started and before there was any kind of commitment, you guys were in the love sack. Who's to say that it won't happen again? Now you've got trust issues. I bet you didn't think that just a little sex could be so complicated.

In the end, both men and women have become completely foolish with sex over the years. We've both placed unnecessary importance on something that should never be the sole reason that we choose to, and in some cases choose not to be involved with someone. How we've come to allow a decision as important as who we spend the rest of our lives with to be made from between our legs is completely beyond me.

More than likely, most of you reading this book have had sex with someone that was in no way, shape or form capable or even worthy of being your mate for life. Some have even made the unfortunate mistake of making children with these people. All in the name of sex, we'll make some of the biggest mistakes of our lives. In some cases, we'll actually make the same mistakes over and over again. For some, once they've realized that they've made the mistake, instead of taking steps to correct the situation, they'll try to make a wrong situation right. In essence, to quote my dear mother, they'll try to make God a liar.

I talked in the opening chapter of this book about being unequally yoked. By not recognizing when we are unequally yoked with another individual, we sometimes wind up in situations where we're being ruled by our desires rather than common sense. We're listening to our bodies rather than our consciences, which is actually the voice of God speaking to us and trying to guide us in the right direction. We've told ourselves that even though we can see that we don't belong in a relationship with a particular person, it's okay to have a sexual relationship with them. Again, we've told ourselves in these situations not to throw the baby out with the bathwater.

We've told ourselves that though this individual lacks what it takes for us to feel comfortable in a relationship with them, because of a physical attraction that we share, we can't pass up on the opportunity to experience the sexual fruit of this particular tree. Did we learn nothing from Eden and forbidden fruit? For the ladies out there, how many times has a man told you, or at least insinuated, that he's not trying to marry you, he's just trying to "make you feel good"? I'm sure you've all heard that before. The sad thing is that a statement like that used to offend women. Now, they accept it as justification for getting in the bed with that man. They've begun to bristle at the thought of commitment *before* sex just as we have for years.

I know this is becoming repetitious, but instead of demanding that we stand up and be men, women have decided that they're willing to get down in the gutter with us. All in the name of "just havin' a little fun" and "livin' a little", a lot of us have willingly mortgaged our futures. A lot of us, some of us young and immature, some of us old and foolish, have ruined relationships with quality people in our lives, all in the name of being "free". But how free are you really if you're a slave to your genitals?

Young people have always foolishly assumed that they have time to fool around before they get serious. Though half of that statement is true *sometimes*, it shouldn't be a license to whore yourself out. Your youth should be a time of exploration and experimentation only to a certain degree. It should be time to date and experience other people, sure. What I can't understand is why all of a sudden has that experimentation broadened to include a sexual relationship with everyone that you date. I know women personally that have slept with just about every man that they've ever dated.

One young lady in particular comes to mind. She slept with four different men in a 12 month period. Though I've never tested this theory, I'm 100% sure that she would become enraged if someone were to refer to her as a whore, even though she was exhibiting some pretty whorish behavior. Now, I understand that some of our young ladies are confused and just looking for some love that went missing somewhere in their lives and they don't quite understand that it can't be found in the bedroom. I'm aware of the fact that some of our young ladies don't really understand that a man's willingness to have sex with them doesn't translate into acceptance. He's just doing his thing.

I understand that some of our women have some issues and those issues sometimes manifest themselves in the way of them disrespecting themselves and laying down with Tom, Dick *and* Harry, all within a 3 month period. However, being a whore with excuses doesn't change the reality of the situation. Some women are in a place like this right now, while at the same time feeling that they're the furthest thing from a whore. If a woman in this situation doesn't feel that she's a whore, she must at least be willing to admit that though she may not be a whore, she's engaging in some whorish behavior. To quote comedian Dave Chappelle from his HBO stand-up special *Killing Them Softly*, "You may not be a whore, but you're wearing a whore's uniform".

# *WE NEED A RESOLUTION*

In the interest of full disclosure, I'm aware of a lot of this behavior because I've been a part of a lot of it. Some of it you can chalk up to a young man that was immature and thought he was much more intelligent and aware than he actually was. Some of it you can chalk up to an older and more selfish version of that young man that should've, and most times did know better. A man that, although he respected women in a way that most men didn't and never would (and thus he attracted a lot of women), was still disrespectful to them in some respects. Though I haven't been as guilty (or abusive) as some of my brothas out there, I have been guilty none the less. However, I'm no different than anyone else out there. Of all the people in creation, I have to believe that the percentage of us that have misused sex at one point or another in our lives is pretty high. The only difference between you and me right now is that I'm writing about mine and, through my writing, you're reminiscing on yours.

Just as we have with so many other things God has given us, we've taken something that was meant to be beautiful and turned it into something very ugly. How many of us hear the word "sex" and think of something beautiful? Even the happily married will sometimes initially think of impurity. Just like the words "religion" and "spirituality" shouldn't cause controversy, we need to reclaim sex. We need to bring it back to where it's supposed to be in our lives. One way in which we express our love for one another, as opposed to one way in which our lust manifests itself.

As for the ladies, what more can I say? I've been laying it out for you guys for a few chapters now. The solution is simple no matter where you fit into what I've been writing. If you're on that side of the fence that's tired of being used and abused by unscrupulous men, then the answer is simple: Don't allow it. The only women that are forced to deal with the type of men that will use them for their bodies and then disappear are the ones that allow it to happen. As I've stated in earlier chapters, if you carry yourself in a certain way, you'll attract only certain men. If you carry yourself like a lady, then a man will be forced to either treat you as such or he'll go running for the hills. However, if you carry yourself like a whore, then you'll only attract johns. And don't you be fooled either. A whore's price tag doesn't only consist of a monetary value.

There are many different ways in which a "john" is willing to pay you based on your particular weakness. If it's money for sex, then he'll provide it and use you accordingly. If it's material things for sex, he can do that as well. However, if it's attention you want, he'll say whatever you need to hear, all the way to the bedroom. But your body must be worth more to you than just mere words. If he can't show and prove to you that the words he speaks are real, then neither is he.

Though sex can be an *expression* of love, it's not always an *indication* of love. If you put a male dog in a room with 10 female dogs in heat, he'll have sex with all of them. It doesn't mean that he loves them, they were just available. Just because a man made you feel good doesn't mean that he cares anything about you. How he really feels about you will always be shown outside of the bedroom.

There's nothing wrong with wanting the love of a good man. There's nothing wrong with wanting a competent sex partner. Sex is a beautiful thing and in its proper place, it can add to the happiness in your life. But if you fail to search with your mind first, you're body will lead you astray. A lot of things that are no good for us come to us wrapped in beautiful packages. And since this sex without love thing is merely physical, I have to assume that it's all based on physical appearances. But take it from me, some of the most screwed up people in the world are also some of the most physically beautiful people in the world. I'll addressed my theories on that later is this book, but as it pertains to this particular subject, just because it looks good doesn't mean that it's good for you.

Women have often found themselves thinking that fine + money = happiness. So they're more willing to make a fool of themselves for guys that fit this description rather than for a guy that's proven that he's more about the person inside. They're more willing to give their bodies up for the pretty package in *hopes* that he's not like all the rest, rather than the average looking brotha that's already shown you what he's about by being a shoulder to cry on every time one of these guys has used you and dumped you by the side of the road. Women have to rise above the shallow thinking that has caused them to become parents sooner than they expected and caused them to contract STD's, some deadly, because some man was too cute to pass up and you slept with him without having the slightest clue about how many links there are in his chain.

Women need to take a step back and take a long, hard look at themselves. They need to take a look at what they're doing, where they're headed and where they want to be. I don't think that women really want to be disrespected by men, but at the rate they're going, they're leaving us no choice. If you're giving your body up to anyone who'll ask, if you ever meet the man of your dreams, unless you flat out lie to him, he'll be able to do the math. After a few discussions about sex, he'll soon find out that you've been around.

Now granted, people can change and we all make mistakes, but it will take a special man to overlook such things. Through God, all things are possible and that man may be out there, but why set yourself up for the struggle? Most men will just keep looking for something a little less challenging. Why not get control over that libido before it becomes a problem? On the flip side of this scenario, if you give yourself up to anyone who'll ask, that's a self-esteem problem that will be noticeable to most men, especially those that are looking for someone to exploit. And you also run the risk of getting a reputation, and how hard do you think that will be to live down?

I refuse to believe that in those hours when a woman is all alone that she's actually proud to be sharing her body with a man (or men) that she already knows doesn't care about her beyond her naked body. Somewhere inside, women still have the ability to carry themselves with dignity and respect. I have faith that there are still women out there that are ready to lead a different kind of revolution. One that begins with closed legs, an open mind and a clear vision. A vision of what they want from a man in the vertical sense, rather than the horizontal. Also more importantly, a vision of what a woman could and *should* be in terms of perception *and* reality.

There are women out there that have made some of the mistakes that I have talked about in this chapter, and have vowed not to make them again. There are women out there that will make us men treat them right *before* we reach the bedroom or they'll tell us to get lost. There are women out there that want to help lead other women back to purity. I believe that there are women that want to change so that they can be effective and positive role models for their sisters, nieces and daughters. At the same time, there are women that already possess these qualities. Whether you want to change or you're already there, I applaud you. You've got your work cut out for you, but don't give up the fight. I believe that women can change this climate. I hope I'm right. My son will be a man soon.

# 5

## *"Saying goodbye is never an easy thing…"*

*"…but you never said/That you'd stay forever".* Those are lyrics to a song by 80's pop star Taylor Dayne. Now wait, before you go burning my book, that was a good song. One of the finest moments of Ms. Dayne's career. It was a song called "Love Will Lead You Back". Those of you that remember that song know that it was the jam. C'mon, admit it. It was a song about someone that wanted to leave a relationship, while the other person couldn't quite understand why. The lyrics I've quoted here were the very first lyrics of the song. It was one of those break-up songs that gave the listener hope. It gave us hope that somehow things would all work out. Though the love of your life was walking out the door, some strong wind would come along and blow them back into your life. The chorus went like this:

*"Love will lead you back/Someday I just know that/Love will lead you back to my arms/Where you belong/I'm sure, sure as stars are shining/One day you will find me again/It won't be long/One of these days, oh/Love will lead you back."*[1]

Isn't that so sad? Taylor Dayne, ladies and gentlemen. So, so emotional. Oh, if only life were really like that. If only break-ups went that way. If only, when someone completely broke your heart, you could still have that hope that somehow it would all work out. For some of us, this is a dream that eventually comes true. However, for most of us, when that break-up comes, no matter how much hope we may have, no matter what Taylor Dayne says, the love of your life isn't coming back through that door to stay.

One of the most difficult things to go through in life is a break-up. As it has been with a lot of things that I've talked about throughout this project, I have some experience in this area. I've dumped, and I've been dumped. Personally, neither one was easy. Leaving someone that you love can be just as trying as being left. Obviously, it's usually more traumatizing to be left, but depending on how much you love a person, leaving them can be very difficult. Although when we're in love, being on either side of this equation can be very difficult, it's one of those things that life will put you through and you'll be forced to deal with the reality of it.

Sad to say, especially when you've been dumped, we're never really prepared to deal with it. All of a sudden, you wake up one morning, and the love of your life is no longer in your life anymore. All of a sudden, storm clouds are producing rain, with no sign of a rainbow in sight. All of a sudden, some of the simplest task to complete on a day to day basis, become the most difficult to get through without breaking down. It's like that dream that you have when you're falling. You just keep falling and falling and falling and falling, and all you wanna do is reach the bottom so that you can tend to your wounds, get up and try it again. Easier said than done.

There are many reasons we break up. I've spent a lot of time talking about all of the ways we can and should come together, so I guess it's now time to talk about what to do when it's over. First of all, there's a lot that can lead to a break-up. We dare not talk about breaking up without covering some of the things that we can do to ourselves and to each other to bring about an end to a relationship. Sometimes we're just careless with what we have, and sometimes a break-up is just necessary. It's just what has to happen. We'll talk about all of that in this chapter.

This chapter will be a different from the other chapters in more ways that just subject matter. As I mentioned in the intro to this book, I have a deep love and appreciation for music. You've noticed how often you catch me quoting from songs. It's just that, for me, music is one of the purest forms of expression that we have. How often have the words of a song best summed up how you were feeling, no matter what you were feeling? I know, it's happened all too often to me.

So in an interesting twist, this chapter will be surrounded by song. I'll use lyrics and phrases from some of the songs that best describe what I'm saying at any particular time throughout this chapter. For all intents and purposes, I'll "sing" this chapter to you. I'll periodically use the words of another to best sum up how I feel. (Some of these songs may be a bit over some of you guys' heads; check the end of the book to find out where you can find some of these songs that are playing in KJ's CD changer).

*"Ain't no stoppin' this, no lie/I promised to stay monogamous, I tried..."*[2]

Before we get to my personal experiences with the break-up, let's talk about the many reasons we finally reach the end of the road. We can start by going back to that old stand by, infidelity. This leads to most of the break-ups. There are many reasons that infidelity comes about. It could simply be a strong attraction that your partner has to another. It could be a situation where you and your partner have grown apart. It could be the lack of affection being given or received. Or it could be that you're just involved with someone that's plain ol' no good. Any one of these things could lead to infidelity and thus a break-up.

Rather than re-writing the first three chapters of this book that dealt with the incompatibility issues that can lead to this, we're gonna focus on what you should do when faced with a situation where the break-up should happen. We won't talk about every single thing that leads to it, but rather what to do when it happens to you, whether you're the doing the leaving or being left. We'll talk about what to do when love won't lead them back. What to do when you're done falling, how to tend to your wounds, get back up, and most importantly, try again.

Probably the most painful thing to find out in a relationship is that you have been cheated on. As I stated in previous chapters, it's a violation of trust that, more times than not, can't be repaired. When you've given your all to a person and have been faithful to them, to find out that they didn't return that same respect to you can be devastating. It feels like someone just walked up and punched you in the stomach. You feel sick. You feel betrayed. And worse than that, you feel inadequate. You start to think to yourself, "If I'm not enough to satisfy you on my own, then what's the use?"

All of these things are natural to feel, and sometimes valid. At the time that this is all being revealed to you, you're really not in the position to consider all the reasons a person may cheat on you. We naturally just assume that it's just a sexual thing. You'd be surprised to find that most times, it's deeper than that. Usually, there's something else missing from the relationship that leads to infidelity. The sex is just the way in which it all manifests itself. It's almost like a child lashing out through violence when there's actually a deeper issue at hand. The sex is just what usually comes of that deeper relationship problem.

Before anyone starts to think that I'm naive, read on. I'm not in any way suggesting that some people don't just cheat for the sake of cheating, but usually there is a deeper problem. Sometimes it can simply be that lack of communication showing its head, and therefore you missed the problem altogether. Or maybe you didn't read the first three chapters of this book and hooked up with the wrong person, thinking that you can change them. Yes, some men are dogs and some women too. If you found them that way, don't be surprised if they revert back to their old ways. If you got with someone that's likely to cheat on you just for the sake of cheating, they probably showed you that side of themselves early on. If you chose to ignore it, then you get what you pay for.

*"Baby, you can't have all of me/Cause I'm not totally free/I can't tell you everything that's going on, baby/There's a few things in my past/That should not be explained/ I'm asking you baby/Be with me, for a little while...*"[3]

Don't front like ya'll didn't know what Aaron Hall was singing about. You can ignore that line "I do love youuuuu". That song ain't have nothing to do with love. One of my favorites has always been the relationship that started through infidelity. You know the ones. When you guys started, one of you, or in some cases both of you, were already in a relationship, cheating on someone else. But somehow, when you came together, there would be faithfulness abound. Somehow, we'll shed our wicked ways and fly the straight and narrow. "I was a cheater before, but I'm gonna treat you right", they seem to say. I'm not saying that it isn't possible, but you have to be leery of those situations. They're either showing you their willingness to be unfaithful or their inability to work through their problems with their current partner without cheating.

At any rate, make them prove that they have the ability to be faithful before you leap. But I'm getting ahead of myself, while at the same time going back to the beginning of the book. For those of you that take greater care in choosing a partner and still find yourselves in the position of being cheated on, don't just assume it was sex that caused you partner to stray. Once it's revealed to you that there's someone else, then it's time for investigation, rather than jumping to conclusions.

After your investigation, you have to weigh your options. As I stated earlier, a lot of times when someone cheats, they're looking for attention or crying out that something's not right at home. It's not always to suggest that they want to leave. In fact, a lot of times when they're caught, they're rather remorseful and really don't want to lose what they have in a relationship. Believe it or not, a lot of times it *is* a mistake. Something that got out of hand. That's not to suggest that they shouldn't have to pay for their mistakes, it's just to say that there isn't always malicious intent. But after you've investigated this thing, no matter who's at fault or what the problem is, you then feel like you're sitting across the table from someone totally different than the person you thought you were in love with. And no matter who's at fault, something has to be done about it.

Whether it's a mistake or a deliberate act, infidelity cannot and should not be accepted in your relationship. If you're married, the first thing that you should try is counseling. There's a lot of emotion that goes on when this type of thing happens and if you're married, you have a lot more to lose than a girlfriend and boyfriend would have. You took a vow before God and you should work to save it rather than just throwing it away. However, this book is primarily aimed at single people such as myself. If you find yourself in this situation and you've talked it over, you still don't think anything's gonna change (meaning that the cheating will stop, no exceptions), and your trust has been violated beyond repair, then it's time for a change.

When someone cheats on you in your pre-marriage relationship, it's time to end the relationship. Some feel that that's a harsh view and that people should be given a second chance, but I don't completely agree with that. If someone cheats on you once, then it gets easier and easier to cheat on you if you let them stay. Why? Because if you allow them to stay, no matter what you may make them do to earn your forgiveness, in the end, they got away with it. If the consequence isn't losing you, then they'll never learn. The thing is, you don't ever want to go further into a relationship with someone that can't respect the fact that they're *in* a relationship. You don't want to fall deeper into the rabbit hole. The further you fall, the harder it is to let go, and you don't want to be head over heels in love with a cheater. It's easier to walk away when you're mad, and you should use that. Don't let that emotion go wasted.

Anger is an unfortunate emotion to feel and we do a lot of regrettable things when we're angry, however, that wouldn't be one. It's best to walk away while the pain is still fresh because it doesn't get any easier when you've reinvested yourself, your heart, your trust and your love through forgiveness, just to have them cheat on you again. If there's anything worse than having your heart broken, it's having it broken twice by the same person over the same thing when you could've done something about it the first time. The second time would be your own fault for believing that they would change, and that would really hurt.

*"While all the time that I was lovin' you/You was busy lovin' yourself/I would stop breathin' if you told me to/Now you're busy lovin' someone else..."*[4]

Now some of you are wondering how I can suggest that a matter of the heart can be so cut and dry. Why should a person that legitimately made a mistake be banished forever and never given a second chance? What if I'm kicking my soulmate out of the house? Well, here's the twist. I'm not suggesting that people don't deserve a second chance. If your partner cheats on you and are really remorseful, apologetic and is willing to work their way back into your life, then a second chance can be given. However, here's the other twist. All of that should be done without you in their lives. Sometimes people need time to grow up and be responsible.

It's disrespectful and irresponsible to cheat on someone that you've committed to. Like I said before, if the consequence isn't losing you, then they'll never change. And if they don't lose you in the process, then they got away with it. They took a gamble and won. You may have been mad for a little while and they may have had to show a little more love and affection for a while, but eventually things will go back to normal. There has to be some separation between you and this person. And not just a week or two, you need to approach it as though it's a permanent break-up. Because it should be until something changes. The reality is they may not ever change and you don't want to be on a "temporary break-up", waiting for things to go back to normal, and they never do.

If your partner cheats on you, they should be made to walk that road to forgiveness alone. How ridiculous is it for you to walk it with them? There's probably no more lonely feeling in a relationship than the feeling you get when you've been cheated on. Why shouldn't someone that broke your heart be made to walk alone as well? Sometimes when we lose something that's dear to us due to our own stupidity, it actually makes us better people. It helps us to realize that some things are important to us and they shouldn't be taken for granted. But it's usually *losing* something that *really* drives that home to us, and not coming close to losing something.

It's almost like a student in school that maintains a C average due to lack of effort. They'll maintain that average and never do better because they're getting by. But it would take them failing a class to get their attention. But just as it is with that student, it still may not bring about improvement. That student may be destined to be a failure. They'll either see this as an awakening and resolve to do better or sink deeper into the abyss. The same can be said for a cheating lover. They may resolve to be faithful the next time around, or they may prove to be the cheater that they revealed themselves to be with you. You'd hate to find out that it's the latter after you've given them a second chance without reprimand.

Out of this tragedy, what you want to do is inspire that person to *become* a better person. Their reasoning for becoming a better and more respectful partner in a relationship shouldn't be simply to get you back. Their motivation should be to be a better person and partner, period. Whether they get you back or not, the motivation should be that the next time they get involved with someone, whether it's you or someone else, they'll do it right. Getting you back can be a goal, but it shouldn't be the only goal.

By breaking up with a cheater you can possibly do two things: You could make them a better person *and* you can teach them that a real man or woman doesn't stand for cheating. A clean break can do this. As I said earlier, this is not to suggest that eventually this person wouldn't deserve a second chance, but let some time pass. Let water go under that bridge. Go it alone and you never know. You may find someone that treats you better. You may also find that after a little time apart, that same person that you sent packing may actually grow up. After a few months on the outs, people can make some remarkable changes in their behavior.

Having said all of that, sometimes it can actually be partly your own fault that your partner cheated. This is where it has nothing to do with sex. If you're neglectful to your partner, it can lead to cheating. If you're emotionally unavailable to your partner, this can also lead to infidelity. If you're physically unavailable to your partner, guess what? That can also lead to infidelity. It can cause them to lash out in the way of a wandering libido. However, it's still no excuse. Sometimes the cheater will use this against you. They'll suggest that they cheated because of your shortcomings, and therefore, deserve a second chance. Only half of that can ever be true. No cheater *deserves* a second chance. A second chance can be earned, but it's never deserved when you've done someone wrong.

Even if your partner cheats on you due to your shortcomings in the relationship, that's no excuse for not trying to talk it out with you before they go running off into someone else's arms. If you're involved with someone that only knows how to solve a relationship inadequacy through sleeping with someone else rather than talking it out with you, then you don't need to be with that person. Even if *you're* lacking in the relationship department, rather than break your heart through cheating, your partner should walk away instead. Just because you're not giving them everything that they need, that's no reason for them to break your heart in this way. It may be a reason for *them* to leave *you*, but in a situation like this, it's important to be a man or a woman about it. If you feel the need to cheat and you can't resist the urge, then you should leave before someone really gets hurt.

*"One thing is sure/And that is change/When the water is rising, you can't remain/ Move to dry land, move to dry land/You gotta move on..."*[5]

I know that it seems that I've simplified all of this. That I've made it seem that it's all so easy to let go of someone that you love. Not so. Nothing could be further from the truth. Like I said before, sometimes it can be just as hard to leave as it is to be left. This is where we have to be strong. Though you may love someone, it's so important that we love ourselves more than we love anyone else. It's never easy to deal with infidelity. It's never easy to leave the one that you love. When they've hurt you, you feel weak. But somewhere inside, you must find the strength to do what's best for you.

For those concerned about letting go of your "soulmate" over a little infidelity, ask yourself this question: Did you envision your soulmate being a cheater? If the answer is no, then you know what you need to do. If that's really your "soulmate", then they'll find the strength to change their ways. They'll find the character to respect you and the relationship that the two of you once shared. They'll find the resolve to work their way back to you, no matter how long it takes. And given a couple of months on their own, they'll come back to you with a renewed spirit to make things work and do it right this time. But this is all if, and only *if*, they're really *deserving* of a second shot. It's about having pride in yourself. It's about not accepting any less effort than you're willing to give in a relationship. If you're giving all that you have to make it work and you're with someone that feels that it's okay to disrespect you in that fashion, then you have to have enough love for yourself to move on.

It takes a great deal of strength to do this. Simply put, you're not just leaving them alone, you'll be on your own as well. That can be a little scary sometimes, but it's not the end of the world. Being alone doesn't always have to mean lonely. It'll be rough at the start, but I promise that it's easier than being with someone that's cheated on you, and having the uneasiness of not knowing whether or not they'll do it again. Just remember that whatever will be, will be. If it's meant to happen, then it will. If you're meant to be together, God will always come through. And if you're not, you can't be afraid to move on without them. Learn from the experience whatever you're meant to learn, and move forward.

*"I'm so glad time and spaced was shared together/Songs were sung and laughter filled the air/But just as life is long/We must move on/And chart our own course to the rising sun...*"[6]

Speaking of moving forward, what do you do when you've grown apart from someone? This form of breaking up is quite difficult to figure out. The reason being, it's so hard to actually tell when it should happen. You don't quite know when to give it one more shot or if you've already given it all that you have. You don't want to make the mistake of leaving too soon, but it can be more painful leaving too late.

As hard as it is to walk away from love, you don't wanna make a mistake by leaving, when just a little more work and being a little more focused could've made it work. It's not as clear-cut as infidelity. We know my views on that now. If you did it, you gotta go. It's just that simple. But whether or not a couple has grown apart or not depends on whose point of view it's being seen from. To one, it may seem that you've grown apart, but to another it could be just a case where things have become stagnant. Who's right and how do we know which way to go? I can share my experience with you while telling you how I think you can tell the difference between putting your back into it and quitting altogether.

The longest relationship I've ever had with a woman lasted about 5 ½ years. When we first became a couple, we were still pretty young. Like a lot of women that I've wound up dating, I met her on the job. Just like a lot of young couples, in the beginning, we were inseparable. We went everywhere together and did everything together. We learned a lot from each other, both good and bad. I can't speak for her as to what I may have taught her, but I feel confident that I taught her some things. But what I learned most from her was how a man should be treated if he's treating his woman right.

For example, for the longest time, I never understood why a woman should fix a man's plate. I mean, if he's got two legs, why shouldn't he get up and fix his own plate? Maybe it came from being raised by a single mother, but I always felt like a woman was almost being a servant if she did that for a man. However, this young lady was raised in a different environment. She was taught that if your man was a good man, taking care of you, putting food on the table and clothes on your back, the least a woman could do after her man's had a hard days work was fix his plate. In short, if he's deserving and pulling his weight, it's no problem. However if he's not…

Anyway, at the height of our love, there wasn't anything that we wouldn't do for one another if we could. I was her little handy man and I put together anything she'd buy for her house that she felt was necessary to have. Usually with some complaining because most of it was short notice, but nevertheless, I did the job. Meanwhile, she picked up dry cleaning at a moment's notice and played the role of stepmother to my son from a previous relationship. If I needed money and she had it, she was always there for me, and I did the same for her. In fact, I was even there with that when she didn't really need it.

After we broke up, we had a running joke about all of the things that I bought her without my knowing it. She once showed me a bracelet in church one Sunday. She hadn't worn it in a while, and I had never seen it. However, she couldn't believe that I didn't remember it. "How can you not remember this bracelet, Kelly? You bought it!" she said, furrowing her brow at me. After a little back and forth, she finally realized that I had no knowledge of "buying" the bracelet because she had taken money that I gave her and bought it without telling me. But that's kind of how we did things. If she needed it, I gave it without asking why, and she did the same for me.

We shared many bonds. Outside of our love for one another, our major bond was Prince and our love for his music. We shared that same love for a lot of other artists, but Prince was the favorite. I think we saw him 4 or 5 times in a two-year span. He kept coming back and so did we. Another bond we shared was basketball. The two of us, along with my mother, were Detroit Pistons season ticket holders. If she and I did bump heads about anything, it was her love for Michael Jordan.

It was then, and still is my opinion that no true blue Piston fan can have love for Michael Jordan. It's just not possible. There's just too much bad blood there. We respect his ability, and for the record, in my opinion, he's the greatest basketball player to ever walk the earth, but that's about it (as if that isn't enough). But I could never convince her that she couldn't really be loyal to both. That should've been a sign that things weren't going to work out between us. Just kidding, although she could've probably said the same thing.

For anyone that knew us, we were made for each other. We seemed to click on some other level. Truth be told, we clicked the way a husband and wife would. She could finish my thoughts, and I could finish hers. I could send her shopping for me, and without me even being there, she could tell what I would and wouldn't wear and buy me an outfit. We were a well-oiled machine. It seemed that marriage was just a formality. Though we both still had some personal goals that we wanted to accomplish before marriage, we both felt that once those things were accomplished, we'd go ahead and do it. All we had to do was reach those personal goals, and we were home free. However, we couldn't see some of the problems that were waiting for us just over the horizon. You just don't expect to grow apart from someone that you click so well with, but that's exactly what happened.

*"How do we ever lose communication?/How do we ever lose each other's sound?/Baby, if U wanna, we can fix the situation/Maybe we can stop the rain from coming down..."[7]*

Before we knew anything, we were both starting to do a lot more things separately. Things that we normally shared, we started doing alone. Movies that we usually took in together, we started seeing separately. We used to have a ritual of going bowling together, especially on Sundays. There was a bowling alley close to where I lived, and on Sundays they would have open bowling from 9pm 'til 2am. $8 a person, all you can bowl. If you bowl at all, you know that was a hell of a deal. We were usually inseparable on this one, as we loved to bowl. But soon, she wasn't coming out with me anymore. She would tell me that she had to get up too early for work the next day. Although I could respect that, there was a time when it wasn't a problem.

Outside of the fact that we were beginning to grow apart, there was the fact that we were getting older. I can guess that it started making less sense to her to stay out 'til 2am when you know you've got to get up and go to work the next day. You can throw in the fact that she had a much longer drive home from the bowling alley than I did, and the fact that I was in charge on my job, therefore, I could go to work the next day pretty much when I wanted to. I guess I had a little more leeway in that area than she did. But the fact remained that some of the things that we used to do together, we were now doing apart.

When things like that start happening, it's easy for other people to start coming into the mix. People that share your interests. When she eventually stopped bowling with me, I kept going. Sometimes with my mom, sometimes with my brother, and sometimes with other females. Once you start doing things separate from your partner, sometimes your interests will change as well. And, in some cases, you're allowed to explore some interests that you may have put on hold for the sake of the relationship. Inevitably, you meet someone else that shares some of those same interests. So, as harmless as it is in the beginning, you start to do things with other people. Not in the interest of cheating, but rather so you don't have to do things alone.

You tell yourself that it's all innocent and that you're just doing this so that you have to be alone. Besides, there's nothing wrong with having friends of the opposite sex when you're in a relationship, right? After all, it's not like you're married. As long as you keep it on a friendship basis, it's all good. And, if you can keep it on that basis, there is nothing wrong with it. But before you know it, they become contributors to your growing apart from your partner. They become a shoulder to cry on when there's trouble in your relationship. They become that spare tire when your partner can't or won't do something with you. Only problem with spare tires is that sometimes we leave them on too long, never actually repairing the tire we replaced in the first place.

However, this "spare tire" that I speak of is not always a member of the opposite sex. Sometimes, some of our friends of the same sex can be that "spare tire". Sometimes, once we start to drift away from our significant other, we'll drift back to our friends. Those friends we left behind long, long ago. And of course, they're more than willing welcome us back into the fold. "Welcome back, we missed you", they seem to say. They become who you hang out with now. They become who you do things with. They become who you spend some of your spare time with, instead of at home waiting to be with your "boo" like you used to.

Again, there's nothing wrong with that. Sometimes, these things just happen in a relationship. We just start to go in separate directions, and before we even know it, we're on different agendas. And that's what happened in my relationship. It started with her moving further away from me. What was once a 15-minute drive when we first started dating, turned into a 30-minute drive. Though she made the move out of necessity, it put an incredible strain on our relationship, damaging it beyond repair. Eventually we would live only 10 minutes apart, but the damage was already done. Throw in the fact that we both worked a lot of hours with staggered schedules and began to see each other only once week, and the end was nigh.

*"It's sad to think/We're not gonna make it/And it's gotten to the point/Where we just can't fake it/For some ungodly reason/We just won't let it die/I guess neither one of us/ Wants to be the first to say goodbye..."*[8]

That was when we should've made a concerted effort to spend more time together, but we didn't. It wasn't long before she and I began to argue constantly. Once again, we began to remind friends and family of a married couple. An unhappily married couple. It wasn't quite "The War of the Roses", but there were some pretty heated moments. And then there were those friends of the opposite sex that I spoke of that began to muddy the waters. Admittedly, I was always more guilty of this than she was, but she had her fair share that would come up from time to time. I believe some of it, from her perspective, was done out of loneliness and having to be without me sometimes. But sometimes it was done out of revenge for me having female friends that I refuse to give up at her request.

Sometimes, I think she befriended other men just to show me how it felt, and it worked. Once she accepted a gift from one of her friends because a female friend of mine had bought me a gift, which happened from time to time. I never accepted them in lieu of anything. I was just being polite. Now, I'm not stupid and I know what the gifts were for, but I felt that as long as I didn't act on it, it shouldn't have been a problem. There was nothing malicious on my part, just free stuff (sorry, I know that's selfish). However, when she accepted a gift from her friend, which came around Valentine's Day and included roses, she told me that she accepted it purposely to hurt me. I wish I was lying, but that's what she told me. I was shocked. I don't know if she meant it or not, but she's never taken it back, so I have to believe that she did.

That was the first time I could remember throwing someone out of my house, but that's what I did that day. I couldn't believe that someone that I loved would purposely try to hurt me, but that's what she did. She didn't succeed in that department, but she did succeed in the pissing me off department. Although that wouldn't be the last time someone I loved would purposely try to hurt me (the next time, it worked in a fantastic fashion), it was a stunning event that showed me that no matter how much love you have for a person, some things aren't meant to be.

This was the first time I really began to think that we weren't going to make it. In the beginning of our relationship, neither of us would have ever done anything like that. But that's what we had become. We began sniping at each other like we didn't even know or love each other. The truth is, we didn't know each other anymore. It was another 2 or 3 years of spinning our wheels before I would finally decide that we'd had enough of each other.

After a couple of years of said wheel spinning, I finally realized that we were never going to make it to the altar, and if we did, we'd have to spend some time apart first. I tried as hard as I could to make it work, and I feel that she did too. But it just wasn't going to happen. Our two-part harmony had disintegrated into off key caterwauling (thank you Mr. Burns). It seemed that every other day we were fighting, and usually about the same things over and over again. That said to me that we weren't making progress. Never really settling the arguments, but rather just dropping it.

Everything in my life was going well. I had just been promoted on my job, I finally had a good working relationship with my baby's mama, and my life in general was working. The only thing that wasn't working was my love life. On top of that, I fell prey some of the pitfalls of a man with a little bit of power.

Once I was promoted on my job, I gained quite a bit of responsibility. I even gained a little bit of power within the company that I worked for. Power that I wasn't even fully aware of. I worked in video production for a cable company, and once I was promoted, I was in charge of production in five cities. Though they were small suburban cities, it was still five cities. Don't take my joy from me. Anyway, that was a pretty big deal at the time, at least to some of the people I worked with. Especially some of the women I worked with. Hence the aforementioned pitfalls.

If you've ever met or been a man with any sort of power on your job, you know that it sometimes acts as an aphrodisiac. And with that, I began to attract all types of women at work. Although I feel that I'm a reasonably handsome man, that, mixed with a little power and a title just put me over the edge with some of the sistas at the office. Mix that ego stroke with the fact that my relationship is on the rocks, throw in a dash of one particular female that caught my eye and threatened to lead me astray, and the relationship was over.

My renewed popularity with the ladies gave me confidence. Confidence that even if I found myself single, I'd be able to manage. Sooner or later, I'd be back on my feet. I decided that with everything going in a positive way for me, I couldn't stand to be weighed down with an unsuccessful relationship anymore. I decided that it was time to move on. Now after all that I've written here, I know it seems like I was just itching to get out there and see the world. It seems like I was just ready to get out there and have as many women as I could. And that's what my girl thought when I eventually told her that I thought that we should go our separate ways.

However, I was actually pretty scared. It had been some 5 ½ years since I had been on my own. Knowing what I knew about women and how they had changed, I really had no desire to go out there again. At the same time, I had run as far as I could with my current situation. The constant arguing was a sign to me of how far apart we had grown. Besides, that kind of mental anguish isn't healthy and can wear on you over a period of time. Something had to be done, and I didn't think she'd ever agree to breaking up with me. We had tried it once before and it didn't work. She would always be so tough when we argued, but whenever I talked about leaving, she changed. She'd always say that she didn't want me to leave. So if this were to end, I'd have to do it alone. I'd have to be the bad guy. So I donned my black hat, got on my horse and rode out of town.

*"I guess I'll do what I gotta do/And break her heart/I don't wanna see her cry/But it's hard to live a lie/I gotta do what I gotta do/And break her heart/Though I love the girl, I know/That the best thing is for us to be apart..."*[9]

When I finally told her that I thought it was time for us to part, it was one of the hardest things I've ever had to do. It wasn't hard in the sense that I thought I was making a mistake. In fact, I felt quite confident that I was doing the best thing for both of us. The hard part was the fact that I never wanted to hurt her, but I knew that I couldn't leave without doing just that. At the time, I couldn't imagine having someone that I loved look me in the face and tell me that they didn't want to be with me anymore. I imagined it had to be one of the worst feelings in the world.

No matter what I would say, I could never say anything that would make her feel anything but rejected. No matter how I tried to explain that we weren't moving forward as a couple and that a clean break was what we *both* needed, she only saw me abandoning her. Having caught wind of some of the women that were pursuing me on my job, she accused me of leaving her to sleep with other women. We all know that you don't have to break up with someone to sleep with other people, so that accusation made no sense and I told her so. It was all about the fact that we had grown too far apart to come back together, in my opinion. It was simply what had to be done for both our sakes.

Once things started to go sour and we saw the distance growing between us, we both should have taken a break. It may have saved our relationship. Conversely, it may have made the break-up easier. Who knows which way it may have gone? But we loved each other and we thought that would be enough. It's always hard to accept the fact that you've grown so far apart from someone that you love so much. On the other hand, the longer you hold on, the harder it is to let go. I feel that once there was physical distance between us, then the emotional distance followed. We were both still growing, but in separate directions. By us not spending as much time together, we weren't growing *together*.

By the time we were physically closer to one another again, we had become strangers. It also didn't help that once we did become physically further apart, we both started doing things to the relationship and to each other that didn't make sense. I realize now that I should have shown a lot more respect towards her feelings about my friends of the opposite sex. That led to her retaliation and thus contributed to the decay of our relationship. At the same time, I feel that she could have shown me a little more often that it mattered to her whether I stayed or left, and not just when it appeared that I was walking out the door. At the risk of sounding like I'm defending myself (I've bravely stated a lot of my shortcomings as it pertains to the relationship), there were other issues that I had with her and the relationship. But rather than air them all, I'll just say that I think by the end, we were both better suited for other people.

All in all, I felt we made the mistake of staying together too long. Most times when you grow apart from someone, that's the way it goes. You tell yourself that love will find a way, somehow. The thing is, you can't start from the middle. When you realize that you've grown apart from someone, you have to start again from the beginning, because you're strangers now. It's hard to do that when you already know and love someone, but you have to re-learn each other. But if you find yourself in a relationship that's like the one I was in, where two people that once saw everything eye to eye are now fighting every chance they get, it's time to take a look at the door.

As I stated earlier, sometimes a relationship has simply grown stagnant. It just needs a little life breathed into it. But if it's clear to you that you and your partner have gone in separate directions, seemingly never to return, maybe it's time to shut it down. It may be temporary and it may be forever. For the record, you should approach it as forever. Just like I said when talking about infidelity, you don't wanna be holding out hope for that miracle return and nothing of the sort happens. Keep your options open, yes, but remain realistic.

We also made that classic mistake that most people make when they break up. We tried to remain friends without any down time. It's so important that you take that down time. Get away from each other. Give each other room to breathe. Whether you've been left, if you did the leaving or if it was mutual, there needs to be some space. The going out together, the spending time together, the continuing to have sex, it all needs to stop if you're not together. All it does is lead to more holding on to false hope.

The problem with breaking up and still acting like a couple is that if you don't get back together, someone's really gonna get hurt. The old folks used to call it "sweetheartin'". Doing all sorts of relationship type things, when there's no relationship. Sooner or later, somebody's gonna want more, and if it doesn't happen, somebody's gonna get hurt. If it's a break, make it a clean break, even if you're thinking in the back of your mind that, "love will lead you back". Truth is, you may be the only one thinking that way, which could also lead to some hurt feelings. When the break-up occurs, no matter how it went down, there's bound to be some hurt feeling and some bruised egos.

The problem is, you never know when any of these things will surface. You could've had the most amicable break-up in the history of relationships. Everybody left with their heads held high. You've foolishly agreed that you'll double date sometime in the future. Unlike the movie *The War of the Roses*, everyone's okay at the end. All the CD's were split up properly, there's no dispute over bills and there's no need to get Judge Judy involved. But you never know when someone's gonna realize how much they've loved, they've lost, is hurting over or is missing the other person. When that comes out, it can be both loud and ugly.

You need to allow time for these emotions to take their course. In the end, you just can't be afraid to pull the trigger if that's what needs to happen. It's better to be alone and happy than to be together and miserable. Leaving was a very difficult thing for me to have to do, but in the end, we were both better for it. It doesn't always work out that way because love isn't a perfect science and sometimes we leave without trying everything that we possibly can. But even she can agree now that it was the best thing for us. As of writing of this book, she's happily engaged and I'm sure she'll make a wonderful wife.

The first two forms of breaking up that I've covered have been based on relationships that were exclusive in nature. However, there is another way in which we can break up, and that is the non-exclusive break-up. The break-up that comes from a relationship in which the parties involved aren't exclusive with one another. That relationship where no one necessarily wants to commit, but they eventually expect the same treatment as someone that's in a committed relationship. All the benefits of commitment, with supposedly none of the hassles of commitment. Believe it or not, these break-ups can be, and a lot of times are, more painful than the break-up of an exclusive couple. The reason being, once you've given that much of yourself to something that you never really had, and then you still wind up losing it, it can hurt quite a bit.

It's like you've failed before really completing your mission. You've put in all of the work, but in the end, you have nothing to show for it. Sure, you have the same type of memories that an actual couple would have after a break-up, but there's always that nagging feeling that they were never really yours. Of course, that's also true sometimes with the couples that are *supposed* to be exclusive, but you get my drift.

The non-exclusive relationship is fool's gold. It seems like a good idea when you first start it. There's no commitment and no expectations, just a little fun. We can be so stupid sometimes. I don't know how it is that we always get into these things, fooling ourselves the whole time. Making ourselves believe that things will always be the same way and no one will ever catch feelings, and if we do, we'll both feel it at the same time and live happily ever after. Like I said, fool's gold.

This is not to suggest that all of these relationships are just two people with fear of commitment issues. If you go back to Chapter 1, you'll remember that I spoke about knowing your situation. If you're dating someone that's single and are letting it be known that they're dating others, then know your situation. Don't make yourself a partner until you're sure that the feeling is being reciprocated. You can't, and nor should you want to, force someone to commit to you. It'll never work out. Sometimes, people just hold on too tightly to someone that they want to be with so badly, even though they know that they're sharing.

Once that happens, they expect the other person to feel the same way, and when it doesn't go that way, it turns into a big mess. Here's a tip: Don't assume anything. If you haven't sat down, discussed it and come to an agreement with the person that you're dating, then chances are, you're not in a relationship. You're still single. In order to be in a relationship, everyone must be in on the joke. That's important. I can't stress that enough. If you're my girlfriend, that should be something that we both decide on, and not just you because you feel like you've found what you're looking for. If I don't feel like I've found what I'm looking for, then we have a problem.

Sometimes, this kind of thing just happens. You start out as friends and you don't wanna pressure anybody. You just wanna date and have a good time. Hey, every now and then, there might even be a little physical activity, but that's okay. You're just friends. But soon after that, as things tend to go once it gets physical, feelings start to come about. Still, don't wanna bring any pressure to the situation, but you're really starting to like one another. Not enough to give up that all important freedom, oh no, but that's still your boo. They're Number 1 on your list. You still like having the option of spending time with whomever you want, but you spend most of your time together. Whenever you go out, you're going with each other. You make each other's birthdays special, just like a couple would do. But you're not a couple. You're not a couple, but you're always together. But I must stress the fact that you're not a couple. Understand?

Obviously, I'm being facetious in my presentation of the scenario, but that's pretty much how it goes. That's the way we look at the non-relationship relationship. We fool ourselves into believing that we're free. But the same rules are subconsciously, and sometimes consciously, enforced. Although we tell ourselves that we're not attached, once those feelings come into play, we're subject to the same things that people in relationships are subject to. Those feelings of jealousy, neglect and all that.

We've told ourselves that these things wouldn't be a problem, considering the fact that we're not exclusive and everyone's free. What we foolishly always forget, or better yet ignore, is that once someone falls in love with you, whether you like it or not, somewhere in their minds, the two of you are in a relationship. We're stupid enough to believe that avoiding commitment is the best way to keep anyone from getting hurt. I'm laughing as I'm writing this. What's worse than that is, once that feeling of commitment *does* enter into one's mind, they expect things to go accordingly. Depending on how much is being given in the "relationship", I don't necessarily disagree.

If you're involved with someone and you're not exclusive with them, you may not believe it, but you have certain responsibilities. Especially when things start to change and feelings come into play. The responsible and adult thing to do when this happens *should* be to sit down and decide where the "relationship" is going. If it's going somewhere you don't want it to go, you should end it right then and there. I know a lot of you don't want to hear that because you'd like to have your cake and eat it too. However, to keep feelings from being trampled on, this is the most responsible thing to do.

If you have to be involved with someone without being attached to them, and you find yourself faced with someone that's falling in love and you don't feel the same way, then you need to let them go. Hell, it makes more sense to just start with someone new. If you're not in the position to reciprocate, then let them go. Don't be selfish and keep a person around that clearly loves you and wants to be with you, when you clearly don't share either of those feelings. Sometimes both parties can fall in love and simply have a fear of moving forward. That's something that can be worked through with just a little communication. However, it's never acceptable to play with someone's feelings, whether intentional or otherwise.

Now, I know a lot of you are asking yourself, "Shouldn't this have been covered in Chapter 1?" I felt that I couldn't properly tell you about the non-exclusive break-up without first telling you exactly how it comes about. All the reasons (excuses?) we give for getting involved in them in the first place. If I may be allowed to explain it again, simply put, none of us really wants to be alone, no matter what we may say. At the same time, a lot of us don't want to commit. So we've created a situation where we give ourselves the illusion of freedom. As long as we feel free, we feel comfortable. But know this, it's nothing but an illusion. No matter how many you may date, eventually one becomes more important than all the rest. One becomes a priority over all of the others. One becomes more deserving of your time than the others. Between you and me, it's a relationship, but I'll never tell. It'll be our secret.

How do I know all of these things, you ask? Well, after I had been in a relationship for 5 plus years, as I stated earlier, I was afraid to go out there (into the dating world) again. The climate had changed, and the way that women were at that time was certainly not what I was used to when I had someone. So, I often found myself in these non-relationship relationships. Part of me yearned to be free for a while after having been attached for so long, but at the same time, there weren't any suitable candidates for a relationship even if I wanted one. Thus, there were some people that I became involved with, without committing to.

A couple of them became very special to me, and I even fell in love with them. But because I couldn't get everything that I needed from a woman out of these women at the time, we could never go any further. Did I follow my own advice and let them go once I realized this? Well, yes and no. There were some that I let go of rather easily. Yet had I let them all go right away as I'm suggesting that you should, how would I be an authority on how things can get out of hand if you don't? If I don't screw it up, I have no opinion and you have no book. So hopefully, you'll benefit from my pain and mistakes.

Moving on, in the case of those that I did love, it was hard to let go. No matter the situation, it's hard to say goodbye to someone that you love. Although there are those that looked on from the outside and thought I was just being a dog (some in my own family), the women I were involved with knew better. They knew the things that they were doing to keep me from going completely exclusive with them. I haven't named names thus far in this book, and I won't start now, but I'll just reiterate that women are just as capable of a wandering libido as a man. And if you're a man that's even possibly looking for a mate and you're auditioning women and they began to show behavior that was usually only attributed to men, it'll make you cautious.

I wasn't just looking for any woman that would have me. I had a son to consider. The next woman I committed to could have very well wound up being my son's stepmother. I wasn't just going to hook up with anybody, behaving any way. As much as these women claimed to love me, sometimes their behavior suggested otherwise. Considering the fact that in some of these instances I was in love as well, even though I wasn't exclusive with them, it still hurt me and changed the relationship. No longer did I feel as though I was looking at potential stepmothers and potential mothers to my unborn daughter. Once they broke my heart by doing things that they promised me they wouldn't do without at the very least being as up front with me as I was with them, I couldn't trust them. Whether you're in a relationship or not, a liar is a liar. If you can't trust them before you commit, then how will you be able to afterwards?

Don't get me wrong, since I wasn't exclusive with these women, I did date others at the same time that I dated them, and they had every right to do the same. That's the rules of the game, and if you play, you may have to pay. It always seemed that I wasn't putting my heart on the line to them, but I did. They'd usually find that out after I had found out about their indiscretions and displayed to them how they had hurt me. Because I happen to be a mentally strong individual, women tended to mistake me for invincible. The truth is, no matter who you are or how strong you may be, when you're in love, you're vulnerable. The difference between these women and me was that I was always up front with them so that there were no surprises. But when they did things like date other men, they often lied and told me that there was no one else.

The act of dating other men wasn't unfair considering the fact that we're talking about single women here. It was the whole telling me that I was the only one they were seeing, causing me to feel guilty about what I was doing, that was unfair. I always felt as though I was using them, considering the fact that they had fully committed to me, while I still dated freely. However, they were no more committed than I was. I was simply Number 1. Somehow, that should have mattered to me, and to the average brotha, it would have. But I never have and never will be the average brotha.

Again, considering the fact that feelings became involved and there was already a misuse of trust, the relationships should have ended there. And for the record, I did try. But their unwillingness to let go, combined with my love for these people, kept these types of relationships going on in my life. Why? Just like I said, no one really wants to be alone, and that included me. Instead of starting over with someone new, I held on to them as well. On the surface, it seems that I got what I was looking for. After all, there was no commitment. That wasn't my issue, though. I understood that I took a risk getting involved with people in this manner, but I felt that since I was so honest and so open with them and never kept them in the dark, the least they could've done was return the favor. But sometimes, no matter what rules you may establish at the beginning of the game, things begin to go their own way, feelings get hurt, and lives are changed.

Which brings me to another responsibility that we have in these types of relationships. That responsibility is to make sure that you're not using someone. In fact, this should be our main responsibility. This happens all the time in these types of relationships. There's nothing like having someone in your life that loves you. Once that happens, even if we can't return that love, we're reluctant to let that person go. It just feels so good to be loved, and if someone truly loves you, it's usually on display. Once you start to receive that love, you get selfish. You don't wanna live without it. So you selfishly hold on to that person that you refuse to become exclusive with, because they love you and you enjoy receiving the benefits of that love. Simply put, you become a user.

As I said before, once that type of thing starts to happen, if you can't return that love, then the right thing to do is to let the other person go. But then, what would you do for love? How will you get through the day without hearing some-one say "I love you"? Who will do all of those "in love" things for you? That's exactly why we hold on, even though somewhere deep inside, we know we're wrong. Never thinking of that other person that we will eventually crush with our undying desire to remain "free".

Now, I know there are those of you out there reading all of this that are say-ing, "If I tell you from the beginning and you fall in love, then it's your fault if you get hurt. *You* remember Chapter 1, KJ. They should know their situation". Well, that's only a half-truth. I used to live by that credo as well. I've always said that if a woman got involved with me and fell in love after I told her what the deal was, then it was her fault if she didn't protect her feelings. Eventually, I learned how responsible I could be for another's heartbreak, even though we weren't exclusive.

Yes, any woman getting involved with me should have kept her wits about herself and attempted to protect herself the best way she could. But once I real-ized that she was falling in love and I didn't and never would feel the same, and didn't at least make an attempt to quell the situation, I became just as responsible for her broken heart, if not, more. Still don't believe you can be a user in this sit-uation? Then let me tell you what happened to me. It was one of the worst expe-riences I've ever had with a woman.

*"Take me back in time/Maybe I can forget/Turn a different corner/And we never would have met/Would you care?"[10]*

After bouncing around from non-relationship to non-relationship, I kind of became comfortable with being single. Although I still had the desire to find someone that I could call my own and eventually marry, it had proved to be increasingly difficult and I was becoming discouraged. I didn't want to end up single for the rest of my life, but I was starting to resign myself to the fact that it may be a reality that I would have to face. Throw in the fact that the "leading candidates" were not living up to their campaign promises, and I was on the hunt again.

Eventually, I met a young woman that would change my life. Ultimately, the change was positive, but she would take me through a lot of negative before I'd get to those positives. Again, this was someone that I met at work, which usually makes it easy for me to get to know someone. I'm not very aggressive when it comes to women, so I don't know what to say to them often times. However, when you meet them at work, you have the perfect excuse to strike up a conversation. That was how we met, and after a couple of weeks of being afraid to say anything, I finally got up the nerve to start speaking to her, outside of the usual "hello" and "have a good night".

At the time, she had a boyfriend, but according to her, things weren't going that well. Of course, just by her telling me that, she was sending me a signal. There were plenty of reasons for us not to date. Besides the fact that she was still involved with someone else (whether it was working out or not), she was much younger than I was. This always has and, after this relationship, still will be a concern of mine. It's not that people who are a few years apart can't have successful relationships, but if the maturity level isn't there with the younger individual, then it will be more trouble than paradise. That was mainly my concern. When telling a female acquaintance of mine about my attraction to someone much younger than me, she told me "Go ahead and give her a chance. You never know, she may be able to handle it." I responded by telling her that I knew that if I wasn't careful, this girl would hurt me. It scares me sometimes to think that I haven't learned to follow my first mind.

Soon after ignoring that loud voice in my head, we began eating lunch together at work and talking on the phone regularly. Her youth was such a breath of fresh air for me. Physically, she was just about perfect. She was one of the most beautiful young women I had ever come in contact with, much less dated. But that didn't attract me nearly as much as her spirit did. She just seemed so free (remember that). She seemed so willing to live for the moment (remember that, too), something that I felt that I had kind of forgotten to do. When I was with her, I felt alive. According to her, when she was with me, I made her feel like a woman.

As time went on, she eventually left her boyfriend because of his infidelity (remember that, Pt. 3), and we became inseparable. Mind you, we never committed to one another. After breaking up with her boyfriend, she expressed her desire to continue to see me, and yet remain free. With the fact that I enjoyed being free and still had reservations about entrusting my feelings to someone so young, this seemed to be the perfect scenario for all involved. We both felt as though we had the best of both worlds. I could have the experience of dating a young (ego stroke), vibrant woman, and she could have the experience of being involved with an older, more sophisticated man than she was used to.

As time went on, her feelings began to change about being in a committed relationship. As she began to develop feelings for me, she began to lose the tolerance she had for me dating other women. I could see that she was falling in love with me, though sometimes she was reluctant to admit it. I began to care for her as well and began to spend most of my time with her. However, she had a hard time breaking away from her ex-boyfriend. She was back and forth with it. One day she wanted him back, the next day, he made her sick again. Young people. Eventually, she decided to leave for good. And eventually, she wanted me all to herself. That indecisiveness alone made me skeptical. I refused the relationship, telling her constantly that she wasn't ready. Although we had become much closer, I still wasn't sure.

She was the closet thing that I had to a girlfriend at the time. In time, she would do everything with me from family functions to company Christmas parties. Though I was still protecting my heart from her, it was becoming increasingly difficult not to fall in love with her. Whenever she told me that she loved me, I could see in those dark brown eyes how sincere she was. There was something about the way she looked at me that just melted me inside. This is what scared me the most. I fought for so long, but I could see that when I finally did fall, I was gonna fall hard.

*"I don't understand it/For you, it's a breeze/Little by little/You brought me to my knees/Don't you care?"*[11]

Have you ever seen one of those nature specials where they're in the jungles and the predatory animals run down their prey and tear them limb from limb? Well, that's what happened to me when I fell in love with her. She was the predatory animal and I was the limb from limb. I knew that once I crossed that bridge that there was no turning back. But I couldn't continue to deny how I felt about her. I still suggested that there be no commitment because she still wasn't mature enough. There was still times where she would lie to me. This was something that was a problem from the beginning, but it wasn't that big of an issue because she wasn't my woman. For that reason, I didn't understand why she lied because she was still single, but she would do it anyway.

Just like the women that I spoke of before, I felt that it was a way to make herself appear pure, while I appeared to be the user. Like she was all about me and only me, while I was still out dating. Also like the women I mentioned before, that wasn't necessarily true. Although I still dated others, I told her that if she could show me that she really wanted to be with me and could be honest with me, I'd be willing to give the others up and give it a try. But, from my perspective, she had shown me an inability to be honest when she thought it would place her in a bad light. You can't begin a relationship with someone that's already dishonest with you. You have to wipe the slate clean and prove that you can be honest with someone before you can expect them to just trust you.

While I continued to resist the relationship for what I thought were valid reasons, we actually became closer still. By this point, there was nothing I wouldn't do for her. I loved her that much. If she needed help with something, I was there. Whether it was emotional, financial, or whatever, I was there. This was the closest that you could be to someone without necessarily calling them yours. However, the way we talked and the way we went about our business, for all intents and purposes, we were a couple. Though things weren't exactly like I wanted them to be, any other woman I still dated played a back seat to her and I was inching towards giving in to her requests.

In the beginning of this "relationship", I resisted because I didn't want to appear to be "schooling" her because of our age difference. I never wanted to talk down to her. I wanted to treat her like a woman, even though she was still immature in some ways. I wanted her to grow at her own pace. I never wanted to "mold" her, as some older men tend to try to do when they're dating younger women. Though there are some women that want that, and maybe even need that, you can alienate others that way. I never wanted to do that with her. I felt that if she stayed close to me, she could still learn from me without me trying to shove it down her throat. With her being so young, I didn't want her to rebel against me.

Though I was proud of myself for approaching this with such wisdom and control, I began to shift to stupid and unhinged rather quickly. Subconsciously, I began to think that if I just committed to her, I could begin to teach her how to do a relationship right. I thought that if I could just show her that she was becoming a woman and that some of the games that she were playing were okay if she were single, but not if she wanted to be in a relationship, then maybe it would work. I wanted to show her that it's not a part-time thing. You can't be in a relationship when it's convenient for you, and then shift to single when you're in a club and meet somebody cute. If it's being done right, when you commit to someone, you're committed until further notice.

I would often tell her that if she were willing to do this thing right, that I would see signs of it even *before* we made it official. However, she would always tell me that if she could get a commitment out of me, then she would act right. I never believed that with her or any woman. If I were a woman, I wouldn't believe any man that said it either. But as I stated in Chapter 2, sometimes love acts as ether. When you're under that ether, you don't quite know where you are or what you're doing. Needless to say, she soon put me under. I began to kid myself into thinking that if I gave in to her, she would straighten up and fly right. Much to my chagrin, she is no relation to Orville and Wilbur (the Wright Brothers).

There finally came a point in the relationship where I decided to jump into the cement with both feet. Little did I know, once my feet were firmly planted in that cement, she would dump me in the ocean like something out of a *Sopranos* episode. I decided that it was time for us to give this thing a serious try. I was deeply in love with her, and she seemed to be just as much in love with me. Shortly after my decision, she decided that it was time for her to move out of her mother's house. She eventually found herself an affordable apartment, something nice for a young woman just starting out. She didn't have much furniture to move, so I gave her money to pay some movers to take care of it for her. Once she got her own place, there were various things that needed to be put together, namely her bed, so that she wouldn't have to sleep on the floor her first night in the new place.

After getting off work, I drove the nearly 30 minutes to her apartment to put it together. I was tired after having worked all day, but she was my princess and I wasn't about to let her spend one night on the floor. Having spent all of the money that she saved on other minor moving expenses and a security deposit, she didn't have anything left. So before I left, I gave her more money so that she could go grocery shopping. I was trying to show her what commitment was about. I was trying to show her what I had shown many before her. Once you have my love, there's nothing I won't do to make sure that you're taken care of. With her being so young, I was trying to show her what a real man was about.

*"If you asked me to/I just might change my mind, and let you in my life forever/If you asked me to/I just might give my heart/And stay here in your arms forever/If you asked me to..."*[12]

Where is this going, you ask? You thought this was a break-up chapter, huh? Stay with me, we're getting to the "good" part. Two weeks after she moved into her new place, it was her birthday. I decided to try and make it a very special one for her. I told her that she could pick the restaurant where she wanted to eat, and I would take care of the rest. The only thing she had to do was pack an overnight bag. Her birthday fell on a Sunday that year, so the plan was to make the entire weekend special for her. She picked her restaurant and we had a wonderful dinner that Saturday night.

After that, we were off to the rest of her surprise. I rented her a room in one of the more expensive hotels in town. In the room, she could open the drapes and see the entire city. At night, this scene was especially beautiful. Once we reached the room, a dozen roses and two of the most adorable stuffed animals that you're ever going to see greeted her. I chose two puppies because once she moved from her mom's house to an apartment, she wasn't able to take her dog, which she absolutely adored. I figured that the stuffed puppies would maybe help to ease that pain. From there, we ordered room service for desert. Cheesecake. When she called down to place the order, she was surprised and seemingly genuinely pleased when guest services, making the assumption that I had come with my wife, referred to her as Mrs. Jackson over the phone. She actually seemed to blush with pride.

Although I had no actual plans for the next day, which was her birthday, we decided to see where the day would take us. Driving around downtown Detroit, out of the blue, I suggested that we take in a baseball game. The Tigers were terrible that season, so good seats weren't hard to come by. I bought us a couple of tickets down the 3$^{rd}$ base line. We were about 15 rows off the field. That was the closest either of us had ever been at a baseball game. It was beautiful day out, which made it all seem so perfect.

Through the two years we had been dating at that point, I don't think I had ever seen her smile that much in a weekend. She genuinely enjoyed everything we had done. At one point she looked over at me and told me what a wonderful birthday she'd had. And she told me that she loved me. I responded by telling her that we could be this happy everyday. I told her that this weekend was supposed to serve a dual purpose. It was to make sure that she had a wonderful birthday, but also to show her just what kind of man she could have on her arm. I felt that at this point, I had passed every test she could have possibly had for me. I wanted her to know that I was ready. I was just waiting for her.

There are some weekends that happen in relationships that change everything forever. They're turning points. You may realize that you love a person on that weekend. You may finally give in to a person on that weekend. You may finally connect with a person on that weekend. You may finally realize that it's all worth a try on that weekend. You may realize that you've found the person that you want to spend the rest of your life with on that weekend.

This was supposed to be our weekend. Whatever our particular turning point was going to be, it was supposed to happen on that weekend. As the old folks used to say, I had completely "showed out" that weekend. All she had to do was see the writing on the wall, and follow accordingly. This was supposed to be our moment of truth. And it was. I had no idea how right I was. This was the weekend that would represent our turning point. I just had no idea which way we would turn.

*"Your friends act sorry for me/They watch you pretend to adore me/But I'm no fool to this game/Now here comes your secret lover/(He'll) be unlike any other/Until your guilt goes up in flames/Did you know, when you go it's the perfect ending/To the bad day/I'd gotten used to spending/When you go, all I know is/You're my favorite mistake..."[13]*

After that weekend, I thought it was going to be smooth sailing from that point on. Sure, there were bound to be bumps in the road, but I thought most of the *major* difficulties that we would have were behind us. I had no idea what she had in store for me. There was one factor that I underestimated about this situation that a friend would eventually bring to my attention after it was all over. He told me that when you take a young person, send them out on their own for the first time, out from under the watchful eye of their parents, all hell can and most times will break loose. Whether they be moving out on their own or going off to college, it's just like they've been let out of jail.

If you've ever noticed, when some prisoners are let out of jail, a lot of them usually wind up back in at some point because they can't control themselves. They can't handle the *responsibility* of freedom, and they begin to do things that don't make sense in the name of freedom. Soon they come to realize that freedom *is* in fact a responsibility and should be handled accordingly. They usually realize that while doing their second stint in jail. If you're not responsible with your freedom, you can wind up screwing up your life. In relation to this story, I had forgotten about the fact that she had been "let out of jail". She had her freedom, but had no idea about being responsible with it. She could either be responsible about it, or abuse it. Guess what she chose?

Not three weeks after our "weekend", she began to change on me. She had always been the type to go out to the clubs every now and then, but that increased once she had moved out on her own and had no one to answer to as it pertained to what time she came into the house. If you remember Chapter 2 of this book, you'll remember how I feel about the clubs. It's not my type of crowd, but I'm especially leery of any woman that I'm dating spending too much time there. I would always have that fear that there were too many "elements" to lead her astray. But if you're dealing with a strong woman, she knows how to go and have a good time without putting anything that she has at home in jeopardy by doing something stupid. This young lady wasn't that strong.

Once she started going out more, we started having more problems. She always assumed that it was *just* because she was going out. That wasn't entirely true. It was the number of guys that I eventually found myself competing with that was the problem. They came to the forefront as a result of her going out much more. It wasn't like I couldn't handle a little competition. And after all, no matter what I was doing for her or how much love we shared, we still technically weren't a couple.

However, we *were* when she needed something done. She never called either of theses new suitors when an entertainment center or kitchen furniture needed to be put together or when she needed gas money. That was still what she called me for. But she wanted me to know that she was still free. Though this was hard to swallow at times, it was nonetheless true. Besides, she wasn't making me do the things that I did for her. The only thing she *was* making was a fool out of me. Nevertheless, I did what I did for her out of love, and God will bless me for that. And speaking of God, He was trying to tell me something. But I wasn't ready to listen.

*"I don't wanna push you baby/And I don't want you to be told/It's just that I can't breathe without you/Feel like I'm gonna lose control/I've got a pocket full of money/ And a pocket full of keys that have no bounds/But when it comes to lovin'/I just can't get you off of my mind..."[14]*

Soon after all of these things started happening, I got this strange feeling that the relationship had changed forever. There was a spirit about the whole thing that wasn't right. It was as if God began speaking to me about what I was involved in. I have this sense about myself that God tells me when things aren't right in my life. It's just up to me to hear His voice and follow His command. He placed it on my heart that she was seeing other men rather heavily and being dishonest whenever I asked her about it.

I've always been the inquisitive type when it came to my relationships, and I always asked if there was someone else. Whether we were exclusive or not, I felt that I had the right to know. I had always been honest with the women that I had dated, but I always suspected, based on past experiences, that they would never be as forthcoming with me, and she was no different. By this point in the relationship, I had pretty much stopped seeing anyone else but her. Not because she had asked me to, but because it was what my heart was leading me to do. I didn't feel comfortable being with someone else, when deep down inside, I wanted to be with her. It made no sense to me. So if I wanted to see her and she wasn't available, I never used a "substitute". I would just rather be alone.

For about a month, I had began to ask her if she was seeing someone else, and for about a month she told me that though she had friends, there was nothing going on. There was no one else in her life but me. I completely had her heart.

For about a month, I had the feeling she was lying to me. For about a month, she was. Finally, one night when were together, I just asked her over and over again, until she finally confessed. Not only was there someone else, the relationship had gotten physical at one point. I don't know what made me angrier. The fact that it had gotten physical, the fact that I had been so straight with her while she continuously lied to me or the fact that God was trying to warn me and I uncharacteristically didn't listen. Granted, all of those things made me angry, but at the time, none more than her continuous lies.

I couldn't understand how she could claim to love me so much and look me in the face over a month and lie to me every time I asked her if there was something that she needed to tell me. At this point, I lost all trust in her. I still wasn't missing the fact that we had no commitment, but I thought we had something stronger than that: love. She didn't have to remain "faithful", but she could've at least remained honest. Our love should have guaranteed me that much.

Her reasoning for not telling me was because she didn't want to lose me. I didn't know what she thought would happen when I found out about her lies. But, as I stated earlier in this book, some people that lie never actually believe they will be caught. With any trust that I had for her lying completely obliterated at my feet, I could hear God's voice loud and clear in my ears. I'm ashamed to admit this, but I still didn't listen.

I'd be a liar if I said that on top of all of the anger and betrayal that I felt, that I wasn't hurt. It hurt me to know that while I was putting in all of this time and effort, it was all for someone that couldn't care less when it came down to doing what she wanted to do. Again, it wasn't about her being "faithful" to me. It was more about the fact that after all that we had shared together, all that I had given to her in the way of time, companionship and love that it wasn't enough.

It wasn't enough to make her see that though she wasn't committed to me, she still stood to lose something by casually screwing around with someone. She didn't understand that it didn't matter that we didn't have a formal commitment. She still had a responsibility to me. Once you've committed yourself to love someone and they've returned that same commitment, you have to be careful of your actions. It doesn't mean that she couldn't see whomever she wanted, it just means that she should have been honest with me about it.

Foolishly, I simply chalked it up to her *just* being young and immature in the ways of love. Though that was true, her lesson learned should have been me walking away from her. When we're young, we do stupid things and we have to learn from them. That usually entails losing something of value to us before we actually do learn. Though she acted irresponsibly with my heart, I knew that she still loved me. However, that shouldn't have been enough to make me stay.

I should have left to show her that she shouldn't be so careless with something that she loves. And just as I stated earlier in this book, if over time she proved herself worthy of another chance, then, and only then, should I have given her another chance. And if she didn't, then it just wasn't meant to be. At the time, she begged me not to leave. I should've ignored her request, but I felt sorry for her. She seemed so sincere as she apologized to me through tears. Like a sucker, I agreed to stay. Wrong, wrong, wrong.

Once I agreed to stay, she promised that things would be different. Another promise that went unfulfilled. It seems to me that when she promised to do things differently, that meant that she'd try a little harder next time to keep me from finding out. This proved to be difficult for her. The fact of the matter was that now that these things had come to the forefront, no matter what she told me, if I didn't *know* it to be true, I assumed she was lying. We had reached the point of no return.

There came a point where she finally realized that I was going to be a hindrance to her "freedom". She wanted me to allow her to continue seeing me, while she "dated" whomever she wanted. At this point, after all that I had done and continued to do for her, I felt that it would be a waste of time to do so. I never changed my approach to the "relationship" considering everything that I had found out. I was still there for her in every way that you could be for someone that you loved, even though she didn't deserve it.

I felt that we had come too far to go backwards. If she couldn't see herself being with me and only me by now, there was no point in going forward at all. It was as if I was seeing the relationship that I'd had with my ex-girlfriend all over again. If we're going to start spinning our wheels, let's not pretend about it. If you don't see a future after all that I've done, then it's time for both of us to move on. The truth of the matter was that through her "dating", she had met someone at work that she *really* liked, and I was holding up progress with my presence.

Once all of this came out, I began to ask questions about this "wonderful" man. Things like, "Where is he when you need something done? Why doesn't he step up? Why doesn't he ever take you anywhere like I do?" Her response was that they didn't really know each other like that, but she felt that he would do those things. Now, understand me. The only thing he had ever done for her up to this point was ask her over to his house, but never out on a date. And whenever she would suggest that they go out, he came up with an excuse as to why he couldn't take her out.

Also, let me interject that this isn't an assumption on my part. I'm not guessing about what happened, or rather didn't, between the two of them. This is *her* account of things. This is what *she* told me about their relationship. Everything that I found out in terms of what he wasn't living up to came out of *her* mouth, and I'm not paraphrasing. Word for word, she told me that he never even came close to doing what I had done for her.

Now, to the intelligent readers out there, you know what this sounds like. But to her, she couldn't, or rather wouldn't see it. And when I would point out to her what was going on, you know what her response was to me? "Well, this is just something that I want to do!" I couldn't believe it. It was like someone had come along and completely brainwashed her. It was like she had no idea of how she was *supposed* to be treated. But, I'm getting ahead of myself. Let me break the camel's back real quick.

By the time "Mr. Right" came along, I had begun to wear down. It seemed that she was hurting me on a weekly basis and my blinders were *finally* starting to come off. She had planned a trip out of town with her best friend's family, when an unfortunate event took place. Due to some poor judgment on her part that I won't detail here, she lost her trip money. I won't divulge how much money it was, but it was a considerable amount.

She called me at work hysterical and in tears about what had happened to her. I immediately left work to be with her. When I pulled up and saw her sitting in her car with tears streaming down her face, it's a scene I'll never forget. I never saw her before or ever again cry like that. It was one of the hardest things that I've ever had to sit through. I just held her and consoled her. I felt so bad because she had been looking forward to this trip for a while.

Once I calmed her down, she left to go and meet her mother. She wasn't sure what she was going to do about her trip because she had essentially lost all of her money. So, out of compassion and stupidity, I followed her poor judgment with my own. When we left one another, I went to the bank and got her more money. Now, I didn't come close to replacing everything that she'd lost, but I gave her enough to be able to go on the trip and still have a good time.

There are a lot of stupid things that I've done as a youth, but not very many as an adult. I've always been pretty cautious as an adult, especially after my son was born out of wedlock. But that trip to the bank was without a doubt, the single most stupid thing I have ever done in my adult years as of the writing of this book. (For the record, she did offer to repay me after we fell out completely, but in an attempt to top my previous level of stupidity, I refused; love makes fools of us all) Read on…

That night, she came to my house. She was still pretty distraught over what had happened to her. Then, I surprised her with what I had done. It was like a cloud had been lifted from over her. Her eyes just completely lit up. Other than "the weekend", I had never seen her so surprised. Even at that time I questioned what I had done. Later on, I realized that subconsciously I was making one last effort to show her who she was dealing with. I was hoping that this gesture would finally wake her from her sleepwalk and show her what a man was about.

On top of all of this, Mr. Wonderful was nowhere to be found. I was not shy about bringing that to her attention. I reminded her that when she found herself in a tough spot, there was a reason that she called me first. Because she knew how I would respond. If she couldn't see what was in front of her by now, then there was really nothing more that I could do. From there, she went on her trip and had a wonderful time. She called me three times a day while she was there to tell me that she loved me, she missed me and how much she appreciated what I had done for her. But it must have been something in the air up there, because when she came back home, the honeymoon was over for good.

*"I wish I wasn't in love with you/So you couldn't hurt me/It just ain't fair how you treat me/No, you don't deserve me/Wasting my time thinkin' 'bout you/And you ain't never gonna change/I wish I wasn't in love with you/So I wouldn't feel this way…"*[15]

Soon after her trip, she expressed to me her desire to pursue a relationship with this other guy. Just to paint a picture for you, months had passed by this time and he still had yet to take her on a date. Again, that came from the horse's mouth. Whenever I would ask her about how interested he really was if he was never willing to take her anywhere in public, I was met with that same response: "This is just what I wanna do!" Never an explanation as to why, I assumed because she didn't have one.

At this point, I decided that it was time to finally let go. It was a very painful decision to make. To be honest, I had no idea, and therefore I was not prepared, for what lay ahead in the pain department. Strangely enough though, it wasn't so much letting go of someone that I loved that was the most painful. It was being replaced by someone that hadn't had to jump through nearly as many hoops as I had to in order to gain her affection. From her own lips, he literally did nothing for her, and she willingly gave up what we had for that. Shortly after that, they consummated they're "relationship". He promptly followed that up by not calling her for a week.

She cried on my shoulder about it, and once again, I consoled her when in fact she had gotten what she deserved because of how she treated me. Some said I was a fool for doing that, because most men in my position would've thrown it right back in her face, and she was reluctant to tell me for that very reason. But I'm a Christian. It's not up to me to punish her or turn her away. I couldn't in the name of revenge ignore the requested help of someone that I was still very much in love with. It's not in my nature, and some of those same people that told me to turn her away had at one point or another been in her position and benefited from that same nature. It was hypocritical of them to say that I should leave her where she lay.

As a Christian, I told her what she needed to hear. I actually consoled her about a man that she had *played me* for. I told her that a man will only do to you what you allow him to do. I told her that she never demanding anything out of him, so she wasn't going to get anything out him, short of what he gave her. He was only out for one thing, and she gave it up without a fight. She didn't respect herself, so she couldn't expect him to do it.

I reminded her that even though she and I didn't work out, I gave her a blueprint on how she was supposed to be treated. If any man comes behind me and doesn't live up to that, or at the very least tries to, she should send him packing. A man that won't even take you out does not fit that description. I told her to never forget how he made her feel the next time he actually did call, and to use that as motivation to move on from that situation.

Now, after you step on a good man for a loser, and then that loser plays you, then you go back to the good man for comfort, and instead of kicking you out the door (which he would've have certainly been justified for doing), he gives you comfort, you would think that even the most unenlightened person in the world could see where they should be. But not our hero.

She seemed to understand what I was saying and agreed that she deserved better. She even expressed an interest in trying once again to save what we had. However, at this point I was a little too skeptical, and a little too damaged. And I was right again. The next day, she *ran into him* at work (they worked in separate sections of the building). He offered some half-assed explanation as to why he hadn't called for a week after doing his business with her. When I asked her how she felt about that, she gave me a response that nearly floored me. She said that part of her wanted to believe him. That said to me that all of her did believe him.

*"How could an angel break my heart?/Why didn't (she) catch my falling star?/I wish I
didn't wish so hard/Maybe I wished our love apart/How could an angel break my
heart?"*[16]

At this point, my heart was completely broken. Contrary to belief or what you
may have read, it wasn't just that my ego was bruised because someone had pre-
ferred to be with another instead of me. It was bruised by the fact that she put me
down for someone that wasn't even half the man I was. We had our arguments
and disagreements, but I can't imagine that I've ever said or done anything that
bad that she was willing to take so much less in exchange for what I *thought* we
had. In fact, whenever we would have one of our marathon discussions where I
would pour out my heart to her, tell her how much she meant to me and suggest
to her that if she could just see the light, maybe there was still hope, before she
would tune me out in disgust, we would always come back to one recurring
theme: "This is just something that I want to do!"

Can you believe that? Neither can I. She would often say to me, "If it doesn't
work out between me and him, then, oh well. If I'm making a mistake by letting
you go, then I'll deal with it when the time comes". Ah, youth. If there's a downfall to that free spirit that she had, it was that feeling of invincibility. That feeling
that she'd be able to get up without a problem if she let the chance of a lifetime
slip away. Never fully understanding that what she had in me, some only see once
in a lifetime, and never see again. But, I guess she's got her life figured out in a
way that the rest of us don't.

In relationships, there's nothing like that feeling of rejection. I was understanding first hand what my ex-girlfriend was feeling when I left her. However,
she wasn't being left for someone that couldn't hold a candle to her. She wasn't
being left because I was lost and confused. She was left because we were no good
to each other anymore. She hadn't laid herself out for me in ways that I would've
never laid out myself for her. It was truly for the greater good.

My situation was a little different. This young lady wanted me to stay around
while she felt her way through. And if she turned out to be wrong, then she
wanted to have me to fall back on. She wanted to be able to have me over one
night and tell me how much she still loved me, and then have him over the very
next night, trying to mold him into me. This may sound a little arrogant, but he
could never be me on his best day. She should have known that for the simple
fact that he never even put that side of himself on display. For example, neither of
us ever visited the other's house before we went on our first date. I don't think I

should be sitting up in a woman's house, and vice versa, before I've even taken her out on a date.

*"Sunshine, blue skies/Please, go away/My girl has found another, and gone away/With her went my future/My life is filled with gloom/So day after day, I stay locked up in my room/I know to you, it might sound strange/But I wish it would rain...*"[17]

When you love someone as much as I loved in this "relationship", it's devastating when you get to the end and you have nothing to show for it. However, nothing can match the pain of having it go away simply because of something that someone "just wants to do". I was very depressed after it was over. Once I decided to walk away (she may dispute that, but I was the one that said that I couldn't do it anymore; she never asked me to leave), it was like my world had come crashing down around me.

She was so much a part of my life for 2 ½ years that I felt lost without her. The lift that she brought to my days, even when we weren't on the best of terms, was gone. I missed everything about her. It was like I had become a zombie. I got no sleep at night. I got no sleep in the day. I lost weight. I became nonchalant about everyday activities. I felt like I was dying. It was one of the hardest things I've ever had to get through, but when I wrote this chapter, it was the final dose of therapy that I needed. It wasn't just getting through the pain that got me, it was trying to understand how it could happen the way that it did. How could some one willingly go from the penthouse to the outhouse?

We had several conversations after the end about what had happened between us. There were days when I could hear in her voice that maybe she had realized that she'd made a mistake. But her pride wouldn't allow her to admit it to me. It seemed like she felt that she had to see it through to the end because she was either going to prove me wrong about the choice she made, or go down in a blaze of glory trying. I once told her that she would have to work much harder to keep that relationship together than she ever would to keep ours together. Simply put, she was the only one that cared, so she'd be the only one trying. Just like I was when she and I were together.

He never wanted a woman, and that's why he would disappear on her for days, and sometimes weeks at a time without her hearing from him. If he really wanted her, this type of thing would've never happened, no matter what excuses he gave her. However, it never stopped her from chasing him. She told herself that she didn't want a relationship from him and that it was "just what she wanted to do". It's a shame when you lie to others, but the greater shame is lying to yourself. If she weren't pursing a relationship, she would've never let it destroy what she had with me. But I guess now I'm lying to myself, because that's exactly what she did.

Whenever I tried to tell her how she was being used and that she should have more respect for herself, she responded with anger. She always told me that I was "tearing her down". Maybe it's just my way of thinking, but I don't think that you can tear someone down with the truth. By telling her to respect herself and to demand more from any man that she dates before she gives up her body, I felt that I was building her up. When you go to church and the preacher starts "steppin' on yo' toes", as we say, you don't stand up and yell "Stop tearing me down!" Don't kill the messenger.

If you don't like the fact that what's true about you isn't flattering, then change the message by changing the way that you're living. That's the way we should receive the message in the sanctuary, and that's the way she should've received my message. I wasn't tearing her down, I was showing her love. I had never treated her the way that he did, and the thing that hurt me more than seeing someone make a fool of her, was the fact that she didn't seem to mind. It changed the way that I viewed her from that point on.

*"Tears fall gently in my garden/As I wait in vain for my sweet baby to call/I guess what my own brother told me was true/He had been with my sweet baby/And she never really loved me at all..."*[18]

There were times where she tried to strike up a friendship with me shortly after things had died down, but that just proved too difficult for me. Every time I heard her voice or saw her face, it was hurt and anger all over again. I couldn't wrap my mind around the fact that someone that I thought could be so sweet could cause me so much pain.

Once she came to my house and apologized for what she had put me through. I asked her why all of a sudden she felt the need to apologize to me. She told me that God had placed it on her heart to apologize to me. I told her that I felt that God had told her all along that she was wrong. It wouldn't have taken the God that I know a month or two to tell her that she was wrong. He usually let's us know that type of thing right away. Sometimes, we just ignore Him.

She then continued that she wanted to make sure that every time that I thought of her, that I didn't have a bad thought. It was clear to me that nothing had changed. Her apology was simply a selfish gesture. She was more concerned with her "legacy" than anything else. She didn't apologize because she mistreated someone that had done so much for her. She just wanted to make sure that I only had happy thoughts of her. How could she think such a thing was possible? After all, this was one of the worst experiences I'd ever had with a woman. A few weeks later, we had one more conversation, in which I told her that it was best that we don't talk anymore because it was clear to me that she cared nothing about me or how I felt. It was 2½ months before she would ever attempt to call me again. I didn't answer the phone. (This story will be continued later in the book).

When things like this happen to you, you find out who your real friends are. You find out who really cares about you, and who's just talking. There we many nights where I couldn't sleep because of the hurt and anger that I felt about what had happened to me. There were some nights that I just needed to vent. There were two young women that were there for me.

They listened and listened and listened. At times, they got pretty angry as well. Because of the love and friendship that we shared, they were obviously very angry with this young lady for putting me through what she did. However, they marveled at the fact that I still found it in my heart to defend her and would forgive her, if she'd ever asked properly. Where they thought she was a little off (I'm cleaning it up here) for walking away from what she had in me, I cut her some slack. I told them that we all go through learning experiences in life and this is just one of hers, as well as mine.

What she will eventually learn in life are some of the same things that I've talked about in this book thus far. That true love is really hard to find. That there are very few men out there that really know how to treat a woman. That when you sit down and ask God to send you someone to treat you right, you'd better be ready to live up to it when He does. And if you're involved with someone that loves you in a way that you can't or aren't willing to return, then be woman enough to walk away. Don't continue to take from that person. Don't continue to reap the benefits of that love if you can't return that same love. Don't be selfish. If it's not what you want, then let it go so that someone else can reap those benefits.

If you don't, then what you run the risk of doing is ruining a good man. Someone that's willing to give to a woman from his heart. If you use and abuse him, he may begin to think that women aren't worth that kind of effort and become one of the very men that you're tired of running into on a regular basis. There are a lot of women that are having to deal with the wrong type of man because women like the one that I just finished talking about have abused their love and kindness, and turned them into misogynists.

*"Strange, baby/Don't you think I'm looking older?/Something good has happened to me/Change is a stranger you have yet to know/Well, you're out of time/I'm letting go/ You'll be fine/Or maybe you won't/You're out of time/I'm letting go/I'm not the man that you want..."*[19]

For any of you out there that have gone through something similar to what I've described here, I hope what I've learned can help you get through. What I've learned here is that some people aren't deserving of my love. I know it's a little different to hear a man say that, as it is usually us that are abusing our women's love. But if you're a good man, there are women walking this earth that aren't worthy of your love. Remember that. Do what you can to avoid that kind of woman. And if you get caught up with one, don't allow the experience to corrupt your thinking. There are still good women out there. It's just that, unfortunately, they're becoming just as scarce as good men.

Just like women shouldn't give up on the idea of a good man, we men shouldn't give up on the idea of a good woman that will appreciate what a good man can do for her. We have to learn to recognize the same signs that women have to recognize about us. When this young lady that I was with left her boyfriend due to his infidelity, I should've known that she was no different than he was. Why? Because she pursued a relationship with me before that one had ended. Isn't that the pot calling a kettle a kettle (relax, I know how that goes)? If she were that disgusted by his behavior, she should have left him before she even met me. On top of that, the first time that she "strayed" from me, I should have gone running for the hills.

Infidelity isn't something that you can just tell about a person when they're in a relationship. If you're involved with someone that's single, you can tell a lot about what they'll be like in a relationship. For example, single people may date more than one person, because that's what being single is. There's nothing wrong with that. However, if they bounce from bed to bed, all in the name of being single and free, then you know what type of person that you have on your hands. If they have no restraint about themselves just because they're single and have the *right* to sleep with anyone they want, then they'll have no restraint in a relationship. Even single people should use restraint when choosing whether or not to sleep with someone.

At the risk of rehashing the early part of this book, being single isn't a license to go crazy. You should still respect yourself and limit the amount and the type of contact that you have with others. If you're involved with someone and the two of you aren't exclusive and you find that they're a little bit *too* free with themselves, you have to walk away. It'll only get worse before it gets any better.

I feel that I was treated the way that I was because I was with someone that doesn't understand the gravity of life. She didn't take our love seriously. Again, she may dispute that, but how else can you explain how this thing ended? She didn't understand that you have to weigh things out before you do them. We have to learn that even though life should be fun and lived to the limit, we should always take it seriously. There are serious consequences to not being a little more analytical with what were doing in our lives. We tend to believe that as long as we protect ourselves from the physical dangers that exist in the world of dating, then we're okay. But there are emotional dangers out there as well.

This young lady was not ready for what God had placed in front of her. Her youth led to a lot of the mistakes that she made with me. However, it can't all be blamed on youth. Some of these things she should have know better no matter how old she was. There were times when she would tell me that she was grown and could do whatever she wanted. That was the naive in her. Being grown doesn't mean that you just do whatever you want. Being grown means understanding that you *shouldn't* do whatever you want to, because everything that we want to do isn't necessarily good for us. Being grown is about that type of wisdom. To know the difference between what we should and shouldn't do, for our own sakes. By the end, it seemed as if she didn't even love herself. That's the only way that I can explain letting go of someone that loves you and that you love, in exchange for someone that doesn't even care about you beyond the physical.

*"I'm learning to live without you now/But I miss you sometimes/The more I know, the less I understand/All the things I thought I knew, I'm learning again/ I've been trying to get down/To the heart of the matter/But my will gets weak/And my thoughts seem to scatter/But I think it's about/Forgiveness/Forgiveness/ Even if/Even if you don't love me anymore...* "[20]

I also had to bring myself to forgive her, whether she deserved it or not. This was very hard to do, considering the fact that she never really asked me for forgiveness for what I felt were the right reasons. She never seemed to think she had lost anything from where I was sitting. Whenever I talked to her, she always seemed to have this tone of voice that suggested that *she* felt sorry for *me*. At times, it was even condescending. After everything I had done for her, you could imagine how that made me feel. But no matter how angry and hurt I may have been, I still had to forgive her. It was just the right thing to do.

It was also the necessary thing to do. The hard part about forgiving someone that's broken your heart is that you never really want to do it unless they beg for it. You never really want to do it unless you think that they're coming back to you. If they come to you from a position of strength and ask for your forgiveness, you actually feel worse. You almost feel like they're rubbing something in your face. You have to rise above that. You have to make sure that you're not selfish. You have to forgive them whether you get that satisfaction of feeling that they're really sorry or not.

More importantly, you have to forgive them so that you can get on with your life. It's all a part of letting go. Holding a grudge is just another way of holding on. That's not good, especially if you're holding on to someone that doesn't want you anymore. You have to forgive for your own piece of mind. If you don't, to quote the band U2, you'll be "stuck in a moment and you can't get out of it".

In the end, the most important lesson that I learned was to obey the voice of God. As I stated, He gave me numerous signs that I was going down the wrong road. He gave me numerous signs that I wasn't supposed to be treated this way. He gave me numerous sings that she would never appreciate what He had done by sending me her way. Because I didn't heed His voice, I paid for it. All the heartache and pain that I experienced was due to my own disobedience. Had I listened like I was supposed to, she could've never hurt me to the degree that she did.

God did not send us here to suffer. That's not His intent, even though it's a part of life. Our suffering could be kept at a minimum if we would just learn to listen and obey His voice. How do you know when God is speaking in your life? That's like salvation, it's a personal thing. The Bible says that we have to know God's voice for ourselves. So you have to determine when God is speaking to you, and act accordingly. Here's a hint: That little voice inside you telling you to do right when you're about to wrong isn't your conscience; it's GOD!

Lastly, when I was beaten down about this whole thing, there were a lot of thoughts running through my head. They were the same thoughts that would run through anyone's head that's been mistreated by someone that they love. How am I gonna go on? How am I gonna make it without her (or him, if that's your situation)? I wish I could turn back the clock. Why can't she see that I'm the one she needs? Why can't she see that no one could ever lover her like I do? Will I ever be able to love again? WHAT AM I GONNA DO? After having all of these thoughts, I was reminded of something that my uncle said one day.

My uncle, who is my Pastor, was eulogizing my brother, Paul, who died in '89. He stood over the pulpit, and as he spoke to the family, he talked about how it's okay to grieve for a while when you've lost someone that you loved so much. However, one statement he made will stay with me forever: "All of our hope was not bound up in Paul".

What he was saying was that even though my brother had gone home, we still had to live. As much as we loved my brother, our reason for living wasn't going into the ground with him. We had to carry on, though it may be hard. Now, losing the love of this young lady was in no way comparable to me losing my brother. Let's not get that twisted. However, the message that my Pastor gave me was still applicable in this situation. All of my hope was not bound up in this relationship. I had to carry on, though it may be hard.

*"The verses of my life/Are moving past/And so now the chorus I must hear/I've got to define my life and times/Before I can give you more than tears/Cause sometimes, it's alright for a season/But then it's time to go..."[21]*

What I eventually noticed during my days without her was that nothing stopped. People still got up and went to work everyday. Buses kept running. Trains kept moving. Mail was delivered. Birds kept flying. The sun rose everyday. When nature saw fit, it still rained and snowed. On a more personal note, the people that loved me before I met her still loved me. My son was still just as special to me. My mom was still my heart, soul and backbone. I was still gainfully employed. In essence, God was still in charge, no matter how she treated me. I had forgotten what was really important in life. And just like everyone else, I had to go through some pain to be reminded of that.

I had been a hypocrite. I had told her not to be involved with someone that mistreated her, and yet I stayed with her. But that day was over. There were plenty more fish in the sea that would be more than willing to have the love of a good man, and I was still fishing with pretty good bait. And though I had become more cautious and aware about who I shared my love with, I was still the same loving individual that I was before she attempted to corrupt my way of thinking about the opposite sex.

I began to love life again. I learned that no matter how life may try to knock you down, you have to get back up every time and keep fighting. I came to understand that what she lost would be on her mind soon enough. I remembered that God doesn't put anything on us that we can't handle. I also learned that just like God gave me to her and she squandered that opportunity, He'll send someone along that's willing to love me the right way. Life's too short to waste wallowing in self-pity. It's okay to grieve for a while, but I have to carry on, though it may be hard. All of my hope is bound up in God.

*"When I was down, You came and lifted me/When I was bound, yes, You set me free/ The things that You do makes it clear to see/It's all a master plan/Oh, no greater love that I've come to know/And when I refuse, You still love me so/With open arms, You came and rescued me/And erased all the pain, yes all the pain... "22*

# PART II
## Reclaiming our children

# 6

# *"Teach them well and let them lead the way..."*

Looking back on everything that I've written so far in this book, it would almost seem that in some cases, we have no hope. However, there is always hope, we just have to start at the beginning. A lot of the relationship problems that I've talked about so far in this book can be traced back to the breakdown of the traditional family. Because we have so many single parent homes and babies raising babies these days, there isn't a lot of home training going on. Now, I'm not a psychologist or Dr. Phil or anything like that, but there are some things that you don't have to be a licensed therapist to notice.

The traditional family, especially in the black community, has changed dramatically over the years. This has lead to our children not being raised properly, and thus growing into unproductive adults. And when we are productive, it's usually in the wrong way. We make babies, but we don't properly nurture and care for them emotionally and psychologically. Our young mothers aren't quite mature enough for what they've taken on sometimes, and by the time they are and are ready to impart some wisdom onto their children, it's sometimes too late as the streets have already claimed them. Our young fathers are in a position no better than the young mothers. Most of them, having grown up without any real guidance or role models themselves, aren't adequately prepared to be role models that offer any real guidance to their seeds.

When you think of some of the things that we've discussed so far in this book as it pertains to sex, women's lack of self respect, men's mistreatment of women and the problems that men and women have together in their respective relationships, a lot of these things started in the home. A lot of the morals and values that we once had, seems to have all faded away. There was a time when families stayed together, and now we seem to get married for a couple of years, have a couple of kids and then go our separate ways. What's often lost in the shuffle is what this kind of thing does to our children.

There are many reasons why these things tend to happen, a lot of them already covered in the first chapters of this book. By not making sure from the beginning that we're compatible with the potential parents to our children and our potential husbands and wives, we often make mistakes that not only damage us, but more importantly, damage our children. By becoming involved with people that either won't be around or don't particularly share our morals and values, we place the proper raising of our children immediately in jeopardy.

This is something that I referenced throughout the first five chapters of this book. It seems to me that the younger the parents got, the worse the children became. Once teen pregnancies moved from epidemic to all out explosion, you had less and less parenting being applied. Some of the things that a lot of us were raised on have now gone absent from our homes. Unfortunately, those things that we're no longer teaching are the very things that kept us from completely losing our way before. We have forgotten to train up our children in the way that they should go, so that when they become old, they won't depart from it. That doesn't mean that they won't stray, but we haven't given them the tools to find their way back. The only way to keep our children from growing into some of the adults that I've described in the early part of this book is to start from the beginning. It's time to reclaim our children.

There were a lot of reasons that I took on this project. There were a lot of things that I wanted to say about a lot of different things. The majority of this project focused on male/female relationships. It would seem that I was only concerned with the love, or lack thereof, that men and women have between one another. However, there was another motivating factor. In fact, it was the main motivating factor. It was the youth of today. I wanted to deliver a message to them. I wanted to explain a few things about life to them. I have one son now and I hope that I can teach him something through being a good father that's always there for him. But I also wanted to give him a blueprint in writing that he could reference throughout his life.

I hope to have a daughter one day and I'm hopeful that these words, along with a mother and father that will love and nurture her, will help to mold and shape her into a woman devoid of some of the self-esteem issues that so many of the types of women that I've referenced in this book seem to have. I have nieces and nephews that will hopefully be inspired by something they've read in these pages. I feel that if we're going to turn it around here on earth, as with a lot of things, it has to start with our children. Though the song sounds clichéd, I do believe the children are our future. It's time again for us to teach them well and let them lead the way.

Our children face so many challenges today that are extremely different from the ones that we faced growing up. I'm a 36 year old man and I can't imagine what Steffen, my 14 year old son, goes through on a day to day basis. It was a big deal for us to have a drug dealer in our high school, yet my son may have had one in his class in Jr. High for all I know.

As I mentioned in the intro to this book, the first time I saw a man get shot was outside my high school. My son has to face the possibility of one of his class-mates bringing a gun to school because he's been teased once too often. If there was a loose girl in our high school or neighborhood, she stood out because she was rare. What my son is facing are young girls that think that they're women and wear shorter skirts than I've ever seen because someone at home thought it was cute (I'll get to that later). It's situations and distractions like these that can keep our children from reaching their full potential in life.

Television, movies and music are much racier than they were when I was a young pup. We didn't have *Sex and the City*, we had *Dynasty* and *Dallas*. Our music was a lot tamer. The only thing our parents had to worry about was Prince, because he was the only one at the time that would go on records and say the unthinkable. The hip hop that we listened to (music that our parents considered noise) would be music to their ears today if they were to do a lyric comparison. Some parents today would trade in every song from today's hip hop stars that degrades our women and glorifies the street life for the songs about hard times and Jam Master Jay (R.I.P) that Run-DMC recorded.

At the same time, as a fan of hip hop, I still must defend the music. Just like my son, the new generation in hip hop faced different circumstances than some of the pioneers of rap faced growing up and it's reflected in their music. That's also a discussion that I'll have later in the book. Also, the temptation to abuse drugs and to have sex prematurely is facing our young people. We as a society have glorified these things seemingly to the point of no return. But there's nothing going on with our children that parenting and prayer can't handle.

## *THE RESPONSIBILITY OF RESPONSIBILITY*

*"No child is bad from the beginning/They only imitate their atmosphere"*
*—Taken from "Sexuality" by Prince, from the album Controversy*

I know that throughout this book, I've quoted many songs, movies and other entertainment sources. But, what can I say? I'm a child of the '80's. We were raised in that pop culture-type society. Our movies and music (especially with the explosion of the music video and the invention of the VCR) were just as important to us as previous generations' movies and music were to them. As I got older, I began to understand why old songs by The Temptations, Smokey Robinson, Marvin Gaye and Earth, Wind and Fire or the movie *Sparkle* evoked so many memories for my oldest brother and sister.

In that same way, a Sam Cooke song or a Bill Cosby movie seemed to take my mother back. There's usually some fond memory attached to those songs or movies that brings a smile to your face. In addition to that fond memory, sometimes it reminded them of a simpler time in their lives. A time when things were different. But as time rolls on, things change. As we get older, we realize that we have to become more responsible. As we start families and have children, we start to realize what being an adult is really all about. Those songs and movies sometimes remind us of the innocence of youth. At the same time, they remind us that things ain't the way they used to be. We think back to a time when we didn't have a care in the world. But once that song fades out, it's back to reality. The reality of adulthood, the reality of parenthood, and more importantly, the reality of responsibility.

There are two different reasons that I quoted that song at the beginning of this section. Number one: There's truth in what Prince said there. Number two: I wanted to show my mother that, believe it or not, there were actually some positives to my listening to Prince all the time that even she could appreciate. Although he was a bad boy, he did give us something to think about from time to time in between his extracurriculars. It's strange that a message like that could be found in a song with that title. If you're prudish, you would never listen to a song with that title and thus you'd never hear that line.

However, it's just one of the many dynamics of Prince. He used to hide the most positive messages in the strangest places. But, I digress. There is a misconception about children that has always been there from the beginning. It is the misconception that they don't understand and pick up on the things that we say and do. We not only think that they don't understand when they're babies, this continues on until they're walking, talking, riding their bikes and so on and so on.

We've always underestimated the understanding and the perceptiveness of our children. Therefore, we're irresponsible with our behavior both with them and around them. We allow them to hear and witness things that they shouldn't, under the assumption that they don't understand. However, when they begin to act out what they've seen, we pretend to be alarmed. "Where did you learn that word?!" we've been known to ask angrily, as if we've never heard or said it before. "Who taught you how to dance like that young lady?!" we ask with uneasiness, knowing full well that we were doing that same dance just last week at that back-yard barbeque that we had, assuming that our children were too young to pick up on what we're doing. Again, that's where the wisdom of Prince's words ring so true. Our anger towards our children is wrong. They're only imitating their atmosphere.

My mother has a degree in sociology, which is in essence the study of people. Before she achieved that, she was a full time mother. So she knows a thing or two about parenting *and* people. She always told me that a mother can start to train her child from the womb. By eating properly and going to bed at sensible hours, you could teach your child early on to do those same things once they arrive. Once they do arrive, she taught me that it was never too early to begin to shape their behavior. Teaching them right and wrong, establishing boundaries and teaching them the importance of sharing with others at an early age can help to prepare them for the rest of their lives.

It's never too early to instill some values in your children. As I stated earlier, without even trying, we can teach our children things through our own actions. Imagine what we could do if we actually tried to teach them something of value. However, there's a down side to our children being like sponges. If we're display-ing some less than positive behavior, they'll soak that up as well. What we teach them when they're young, whether right or wrong, will shape them for the rest of their lives. While we once understood this and taught our children things that would eventually turn them into responsible adults, we eventually began to teach them some things that would serve more as a hindrance to them.

With our parents becoming younger and younger, we have more and more ill-prepared people raising our children. If you put two young people together that are too immature to realize not only the importance of safe sex, but the responsi-bility of taking care of another human being as well, they're going to "raise" a child that doesn't have the necessary skills to become any more responsible than their "parents" are.

When our young people have these babies, they're more like big brothers and big sisters rather than the mothers and fathers that they should be. Now, we all know how annoying little brothers and sisters can be. They always wanna be with you. They always wanna tag along whenever you go somewhere. They wanna dress, walk, talk and act like you. Our children can be that way as well. The only difference between a little brother or sister and your child is that word called "responsibility". Though we're partly responsible for helping our parents to mold our younger siblings into model citizens, we're completely responsible for teaching our own children. But how can you really teach when you don't know any better yourself?

When our children are young, they have a lot of wild ideas about what life is gonna be about. They think that once they're grown and on their own, they'll be on easy street. They figure they'll be able to stretch dollars in ways that we as parents couldn't quite figure out. They'll have the best house, with the best car. They'll wear the best clothes and they'll eat fast food every night. And they'll do it all making $9 an hour. Lights, gas and phones aren't necessary utilities to them, they're luxuries (and don't forget that our children are growing up in the cell phone and can't live without cable/satellite era). Those bills will all work themselves out. I can't understand why it is that we couldn't budget the way that our kids plan to. I mean, if we could, we'd all be a little better off.

If you have any children, you know what I'm talking about here. In fact, if you've ever been young (because some of us like to pretend that we were never young and foolish), you know what I'm talking about. We all thought that once we were on our own, we'd show our parents something. However, as I've told so many young mothers that wanted their flowers from their kids while they can still smell them, your kids will never know what kind of a job you did in taking care of them until they have to take care of themselves. It's just a matter of finance and knowing how money works.

Our children may know how to count money, but that doesn't mean that they have a complete concept of money and how it works. Once they understand that, they'll understand what it takes financially to run a household and take care of children. Then, and only then, will they realize what mama and daddy did to take care of them and any siblings they may have had.

The fact of the matter is that some of us aren't really grown and on our own until we're in our mid to late 20's. Obviously, at 16, 17 and 18, we aren't fully prepared to adequately take care of ourselves. Even if you've got good parents that have taught you well, you still have some life experiences to learn from and some maturity to gain on your own. If we completely understood these facts at those ages, one would hope that we would take more precaution when engaging in sexual activity. Either better protection or abstinence all together. Because if we fully understood at those ages that we couldn't adequately take care of ourselves and that we weren't as mature as we were going to need to be to make it in life, we'd understand that having another mouth to feed and another mind to mold is something that we're just not prepared for. Having never really embraced adulthood completely, how can our young people expect to become adequate parents?

The answer is they can't. When you've got someone that's young and still naive about the world, they can't provide proper guidance to a child. They simply don't have the tools. Most young people think that you change a diaper or two, feed the baby and you're all set. Sure, they expect to have to buy some baby clothes here and there, but most of what they need they expect to get from the baby shower. You see, when you're young, you foolishly feel invincible. You think that you'll never grow old the way your parents did. Everything will stay the same from the age of 18 and on.

Young people simply don't think too far ahead like most responsible adults do. They don't understand when they're laying down to have sex with no condom that when you have these children, they grow just like flowers. However, you don't have to clothe a flower. A flower won't grow to one day ask you for a $100 pair of gym shoes. A flower won't grow to one day ask you to buy them a $300 video game system. A flower won't need clothing at the beginning of every school year, and sometimes during the school year, because what they had last year is not only out of style now, it's too small. Flowers won't eat you out of house and home. Flowers simply need water and sunlight just to grow. Our children shouldn't just grow, they need to be raised, and it takes the help of God, some wisdom, love, courage and a whole lot of finances to do that.

These young parents don't really understand the fact that these children are forever, just like they were forever to their parents when they were born. They have no idea about staying up all night with a child that's sick or simply won't go to sleep. I'm sure that they feel that it won't be a problem since they're used to staying up all night after a few hours of clubbin'. The only problem is that babies have the worst sense of timing. The only time they choose to get sick or want to stay up all night smiling that smile at you as you look at them with weary eyes, wondering aloud why tonight of all nights this child has chosen not to rest, is on nights when you're really tired and could use a full night's sleep.

They seem to need shoes right around the time that the light bill is due, and if you're not checking on a regular basis, they won't tell you until you're broke and can do nothing about it. They sometimes need motivation when you're at your wits end and feel like giving up yourself. And sometimes, when they most need a positive role model, we're into some of our most negative behavior and need to straighten up because they're watching. And after all of that, I still haven't scratched the surface of real parenting.

One of the most important elements to parenting is patience. It is patience that keeps us parents from killing our children sometimes when they make the same mistakes that we made when we were coming up. That patience tells us to calm down and talk to the child before we wind up doing time over them. It is patience that keeps parents from unnecessarily spanking their children when they don't quite know what they've done wrong. It is patience that allows us to suffer through some of those periods of indecisiveness when our children don't quite know what they want to do with their lives. It is patience that allows us to wait and see and give our children a chance, even when it seems that they aren't turning out like we wanted them to.

That patience is necessary because sometimes it takes our children a long, long, long time to finally see the light and understand the wisdom of what we tell them and the fact that we're not trying to rain on their parade when we discipline them. You will discipline that which you love. Outside of love, patience may be the most important tool in parenting, simply because our children in one form or another will try that patience. That needed patience is something that young people simply do not have.

Usually, when some of our young people become parents, there's usually a parent somewhere still exercising patience with them, hoping to God that this is a one time only mistake and that things will eventually still work out. How many of you that are reading this, know of any young people that truly have patience? Even though there are exceptions to everything, there aren't very many out there. So if you don't have that patience, how are you going to raise a child? How can you turn a boy into a man when his immaturity in some ways still makes sense to you because you haven't fully developed yourself? How can you turn a little girl into a woman, when in some ways, you're just as naive as she is? More times than not, it's not gonna happen. Most of us that have actually matured into responsible adults when our children are born are still gonna make some mistakes from time to time while raising them. After all, raising children is not a perfect science, and our children truly are like snowflakes. They're all different.

It's not that there isn't any on the job training that goes on there. Making some mistakes with your children happens with all parents. However, our young parents are already behind the curve on that one, considering the fact that they're still maturing. They still have to learn that life isn't what *they* thought it would be about. They still have to come to the conclusion that mom and dad were right about a lot of things and that there's more to being a parent than spoiling your kids. They still have to come to grips with the fact that some of the better parents actually do say "no" to their children because everything our kids want isn't necessarily good for them.

They have to understand that without patience, without good monetary sense and an understanding of how money works, and more importantly, without the complete understanding of the word "sacrifice" and knowing that once that child is born, your needs become secondary and that's final, they will not be adequate parents to these children. In short, they need to grow up before they can properly aide their seeds in doing the same. However, sometimes it takes our young people a little while before they actually grow into their own. By then, if they've been teaching their children the wrong way, it may be too late to turn back. At that point, we have inadequately raised children, and that leads me to my next point.

## *"IT TAKES A VILLAGE…"*

There was a time when that saying still applied. For those of you that aren't familiar with it, the saying goes, "It takes a village to raise a child". Don't get me wrong, the saying is still true. It's just no longer being applied the way it was intended. As I'm going through this chapter, I'm attempting to connect the dots of our changing society. Since I started this book by talking about how some of the adults nowadays are making poor decisions in relationships, with their bodies, and in life in general, it stands to reason that some of these adults were probably raised improperly. They weren't taught any morals or values as children, so they couldn't apply them in their adult lives. Usually, in cases like those, these people were raised by inadequate parents. So it stands to reason that they wouldn't be well adjusted adults.

The bottom line is these messed up people came from somewhere, and it was usually a messed up home. There are many reasons that some of those homes were messed up, but nevertheless, they were messed up. It wasn't all due to young parents that weren't mature enough to raise children, but that's where a lot of it came from. But not only have parents failed when it comes to raising more responsible children, our communities have failed as well. In fact, those same communities failed the very same young parents that I've been speaking to for the last few pages. With that, we had to face the results of improperly raised children. Children that more times than not, grow into irresponsible adults.

As I stated earlier in this chapter, my mother taught me that it's never too early to start teaching your children right and wrong. It's never too early to start teaching them morals and values. She also taught me that once your children reach the age of five, they're starting to develop their personalities. By then, they're on their way to becoming whatever their going to be in terms of personality, demeanor and mentality. So it is imperative that we instill something positive in them as soon as possible. When that teaching isn't applied early on, the results can sometimes be disheartening. It can not only be reflected in a child's behavior, it can be reflected in their grades and even their relationship with their parents. They can become disrespectful to all that oppose them, lazy, unproductive and extremely disobedient.

While some of this behavior is evident when our children are very young, some parents dismiss it as a part of growing up, some parents assume that they have plenty of time to correct this behavior, and strangely enough, some parents see some of this behavior as no big deal and assume that at one point or another, their kids will grow out of some of these things. There's something very wrong with some of these theories.

Considering the fact that I only have one child, I don't claim to be an expert on child rearing. In fact, most of what I've been writing on the subject I learned either from listening to my mother, watching what she did in terms of raising all of her children or witnessing the influence that she had over so many other children. I have to believe that she did a solid job considering how we all turned out. So my feeling is that most of what I'm regurgitating here does work.

There inevitably comes a point in the parent/child relationship where the child challenges their parent. They may challenge your authority or they may challenge the rules of your household, but nevertheless, at some point most children will challenge their parents. This is a turning point for both the parent and the child. If you as the parent hold firm to your position, then your child will have to respect that and they'll understand who's the boss if you are unwavering in your position. However, if you as the parent aren't up to the challenge, things could change forever in your child's favor. What's happening more and more these days is the children are winning the war, the prisoners have overtaken the wardens and the lunatics are running the asylum.

As I stated earlier in this chapter, with the age gap between parent and child becoming smaller, the relationship has become more along the lines of siblings rather than parent and child. In some cases, some parents have sacrificed the parent/child relationship in favor of forming a "friendship" with their children. Though there's nothing wrong with sharing a level of friendship with your children, it's almost like being your friend's boss on the job. It's okay to remain friends, but there still must be some sort of separation between supervisor and subordinate if we're to do our jobs properly.

That same mentality must be applied if you're a young parent. You'll obviously have a lot in common with your child, as a 17 or 18 year age gap ain't what it used to be. However, there still must be some separation between parent and child. When the kids start to head down the wrong path, we can't view them as a little brother or sister that's screwing up. That's your child and the responsibility of raising them is squarely on your shoulders. But when you're that young, some of that wrong behavior doesn't seem like that big of a deal to you. You haven't even completely come to understand how right your parents were about *your* need to grow up and change *your* ways.

What's worse than our inability or refusal to correct our children when they go astray is our willingness sometimes to join in on the confusion. Instead of us monitoring and correcting the way that our young ladies dress and carry themselves, we've begun to enable and aide them in their attempt to grow up too fast. Rather than making them wear skirts with some length to them, as opposed to those handkerchiefs masquerading as skirts, and flat or reasonable shoes until they're old enough to do otherwise, we've decided that we'll go shopping *with* them. You get a skirt shorter than theirs and matching pumps with the six inch heels. Then mother and daughter leave the mall and you can't tell whether they're going to the "track" or the strip club, but either way, they look like working girls. (For those unaware, the track is where prostitutes "work", and a "working girl" is a form of slang for a prostitute).

I used to tell my mother whenever I saw a young lady with a skirt on that was too short that it wasn't a skirt, it was a sk, because the skirt was too short for the rest of the word to be applied. As for the fathers, rather than tell our young men to pull their pants up above their waists or explaining to them exactly what the belts were meant for, we've decided to let our pants hang down to the floor as well because we're under the impression that everyone wants to see our underwear. All in the name of being cool and trying to win approval from our *children*, we've sacrificed our parental roles. Instead of going out and making some friends in our own age group and allowing our kids to do the same, we've decided to befriend people that don't need us as friends. They need our guidance. They need our leadership. They need us as parents.

If there's anything sadder than this type of thing happening with the young parents of today, it's when it happens with the older parents of today. Rather than accept the fact that our time has come and gone, we've decided that we won't teach our children something that we should know at a later stage in our lives: There was nothing in the streets when we were coming up, and there's nothing in the streets now.

In attempt to hold on to our youth, we've resorted to running the streets *with* our children. That's no longer your daughter, that's "my girl". That's no longer your son, that's "my homie". We try to mask this behavior by suggesting that it's just a closeness that we're sharing with our children. We try to suggest that we're trying to spend more time with our children. However, just as I've explained with male/female relationships in this book, there's spending time and there's spending quality time.

For example, my mother and I get season tickets to the Detroit Pistons' games every year. When we go to the games together, that's quality time spent together. However, if I were off to a night club and she told me to wait until she got dressed so that she could come along, well, that's just spending time together. See, we think that just because it's time together that we'll never forget, that there's quality in it. I don't know about you, but I've spent time doing a lot of things in my life that I remember like it was yesterday, but I still wish I hadn't done them. Whatever kind of time we spend with our children will never be forgotten by either the parent or the child. It just seems to me that if I want my son to remember anything, it should be how I influenced his life in a positive way, and not how we went to the club and got drunk *together*.

This kind of thing starts when our children are young. When our little girls wear miniskirts and put on little heels, we think it's cute. I don't want to seem extreme here, but things are different now. There was a time when our little girls played dress-up and put on mommy's clothes and make-up. That was cute way back then. The problem isn't our little girls playing dress-up. The problem is that mommy's wardrobe has changed.

Where little girls once dressed up like mommy and looked like they were going to church, they now put on mommy's clothes and look like they're getting ready to hit the streets looking for a man. Again, rather than putting a halt to this kind of thing, we laugh it off, thinking it's cute. But what our little girls are saying when they play dress-up is "I wanna grow up and be like mommy". So mommy needs to ask herself, what am I putting out there for my daughter to aspire to?

Instead of asking that question, we laugh it off and before we know it, she's 13 dressing like she's 23. Then we wonder why some sexual predator snatches her up on the way to school and rapes her. Before the uproar gets started, understand what I'm saying. I'm in no way defending a rapist for doing what he does to our young women. It's a vile and disgusting act. What I am suggesting is that we not allow our young ladies to dress in a way that invites such attention. Why do we give these losers extra incentive to choose our children?

The rapist is no different in his crime than a home burglar or a car thief. He's going to attack that which gives him the least amount of resistance to do his crime. In essence, if he's looking for a victim, do you think he'll choose the girl who's got on jeans and a regular shirt or the girl with the low cut blouse and the skirt that's almost up to her butt if they both walk the same blocks to school? Young ladies must be made to understand that a woman dresses like that to entice and draw attention from the opposite sex. They also must be taught to be careful what you wish for, because you just might get it.

Considering the fact that our young ladies develop physically much faster than they did in years past, we have to be more mindful of the things we allow them to wear. And have you seen the way that some of them walk? It's like they're trying to dislocate a hip or something. We have to be more mindful of what types of lessons we're teaching them. We have to put something more substantial in their heads besides what shoes go with what skirt and what type of man we want them to marry. If you give them a solid foundation in their lives, more times than not, whether or not they marry the right man will take care of itself.

Our children will no doubt be influenced by what they see in the streets and by their friends. We have to counter that with those morals and values that I keep going back to. If we don't teach them our way at home, they'll learn someone else's way in the streets. And as we all know from our own experiences growing up, everyone wasn't raised like us. If we don't coral our young men and women before they get out of hand and stop them from behaving as if they were grown men and grown women, they'll eventually begin to do grown man and grown woman things. That's not good when you ain't grown.

In the end, whether the parents are young or old, if they haven't completely taken themselves out of the street life and the immaturity of youth to become parents instead of friends to their children, the children's chances of becoming responsible adults are greatly reduced. To quote that saying again, "It takes a village to raise a child". That means that not only do our parents have to do a better job of raising their own children, we as a community need to do a better job of helping to raise these children. I'm sure that some of you that are older and are reading this book can remember a time when you did something wrong, and just about anybody on the block could either give you a whippin', or at the very least, tell your parents what happened and let them take care of it.

My mother told me that when she was coming up, if any adult in the neighborhood caught you doing wrong, not only would they whip you, but once word got back home about what you did, your parents were waiting there to give you another one. That was a way to make the children understand that not only was improper behavior not going to be tolerated at home, it wouldn't be tolerated anywhere that an adult could see you. There was a responsibility that was felt amongst all of the parents to make sure that all of their collective children turned out okay. They wanted to instill in those children that someone was always watching. That was the village raising the child. Things are different now.

These days, you can hardly say anything to another person's child. Parents have caught a case of the "not my child's". If you tell some of these parents anything negative about their children, the first words out of their mouths is "Not my child!" Some of these parents are willing to fight you if you say something negative about their children. What's worse than that is that sometimes the parents actually know that what you're saying is true about their kids, but they resent anyone else telling them that their child is doing something wrong.

They see it as an attack on their parenting as opposed to someone just telling them that once their "baby" was out of their sight, they did something wrong. As if it's not possible, and as if we didn't get out of hand ourselves growing up when we were out of our parent's sight. What this leads to is our children feeling that they don't have to respect anyone outside of their front door. Not the elders in their neighborhood, not the elders of the church, not the teachers in school, not anybody. Some parents feel that that's exactly the way that they want it. They don't realize the harm that they're doing when they create an environment where their children only have to respect them. It's a disaster waiting to happen.

With all of the negative influences that are available for our children to latch on to, we should welcome anyone willing to assist us in monitoring our children's behavior. Our neighborhoods are full of malcontents that wish to lead our children astray. There were always pimps and drug pushers in the 'hood, but now they're running a little more rampant and their looking to claim our children into their army to do their dirty work while they sit back in their luxurious houses and drive their expensive cars, all gained from product that our children risk their own lives to sell, while aspiring to live out the dream (or rather nightmare) that these people have laid out for them.

These are the types of people that get a hold of our young men and teach them the irresponsible side of manhood. They teach them how to make babies and walk away from the responsibility of it, because as long as you're out here in the street selling drugs, child support isn't an issue. They teach them how selling drugs is a victimless crime because the fiends are gonna get high whether you sell it to them or somebody else does, so you may as well get paid.

They teach them that a regular 9 to 5 is for suckers and it don't make sense to put all of your time and effort into a job like that just so that you can put money into some white man's pocket. They never enlighten our children to the fact that there's a very short list of things that you can do for a living in this country that won't put money into some white man's pocket, and drug dealing isn't on that list. You see, the village is still raising our children. The problem that we have now is that the village is corrupt.

## *PRETTY IS AS PRETTY DOES*

Just as we were when we were children, kids are always in a hurry to grow up. We have to be ready to slow them down. We have to remind our children that they have a long life ahead of them. They should enjoy the time that they have as children, because once you move into adulthood, ready or not, there's no turning back. This is especially paramount with our little girls.

Those of you from the country probably remember your grandma or some older relative talking about those "fast tail gals". They were usually talking about one of those little girls that thought she was grown when she was 15 or 16. Always wearing make-up and tight clothes. Always trying to put a little extra in her switch when she walks. You know the ones I'm talking about. 'Lil so-and-so from up the street that everybody in the neighborhood is trying to talk to.

She's always got her hair done up in a style that's too old for her years, and considering that she's one of those over developed young ladies that I spoke about a minute ago, if you catch her on the wrong day, she looks like a grown woman. She can recognize 20 inch rims on a SUV from 50 yards away, but when the time comes, she'll be too dumb to realize that she's 20 credits short of graduation. She can't tell you the capital of the state she's living in, but she can tell you what club will let you in without checking ID.

She can't tell you what she's gonna do after high school, but she can tell you what she's gonna do and how she's gonna do it if that boy from up the block calls her tonight. And to top it all off, she dresses this way, acts this way and wears her hair this way because her mother thinks it's cute. In fact, mama is always telling her how fine her baby is and that she should carry herself this way. What mama don't realize is that she's doing more harm than good.

We have to be careful of the ways in which we praise our children. Sometimes, in the name of building self esteem, we give our children the wrong types of praise. It's okay to make sure that our children feel that they're special just like anyone else. It's okay to boost our children's self esteem by telling them that they're beautiful. It's also okay to instill certain things in them because chances are someone will come along one day and try to bring them down. Our children have to be strong in the face of these things because other children can be cruel sometimes. However, it's a whole other story when we teach our children that they're better than others. We sometimes do that directly and indirectly.

Now, for the sake of this experiment, let's take off our parental glasses. Those of you that have children, pretend for a brief moment that you don't. Let's look at the children just as we do the adults. I'll preface all of this by saying that beauty is truly in the eye of the beholder, so you can all figure out for yourselves where you fit into what I'm about to say.

In this world, there are beautiful people, there are average people and there are ugly people. It doesn't make one better than the other, it's just the truth, but stay with me for a minute. Now, if that's true with the adults, then it's true with the children. If it's not, then where do these people come from? Moving on, there are also beautiful children, there are average children and there are ugly children. Now, stop with that look of horror on your face. Don't act like you haven't noticed some of these children with less than stellar looks. And for those of you that have some of these children, remember what I said: For the sake of this experiment, pretend that you don't have any children with a face that only a mother could love.

For those of us fortunate enough to have some of those beautiful children, I'd like to speak to you for a moment. We all know when we have children that are pretty, handsome or whatever you want to call it. If we don't know it, others will make us aware of it. While we're all so proud of ourselves for coming through for the team and creating such beautiful people to help beautify the landscape of the world, what seems to be a blessing in physical gifts could also be a curse to both the child and the parent.

How can beauty be a curse, you ask? Here's how. It starts in the home with the parents telling our beautiful children that they're beautiful on a regular basis. Again, there's nothing wrong with a little self esteem building, as long as it's done with some sort of wisdom. Simply put, it's okay to tell those pretty girls and handsome boys that they are such, just don't forget to add this phrase: "...but that doesn't make you any better than anyone else".

I know some may think that it takes away from our message of praise, but it's so important that our children understand this. As beautiful as some of our children are, we must instill something else inside of them besides the importance of looking good. If you don't teach them anything besides that, they begin to develop a mentality that suggests that they're better than others because of their physical features. As they get older, this mentality will come back to haunt them.

We as a society have placed too much emphasis on physical beauty, and this affects our children as they grow up. They began to strive more for a beautiful face rather than a beautiful mind. I have a theory about some of the beautiful people in the world today. First, I'll ask you a question: How many of you have either met or been involved with someone that was physically out of this world, and then found out that they were mentally *from* another world? You know, lights on, nobody home. A couple of sandwiches short of a picnic. Dumb as a box of rocks. You know the ones I'm talking about. I have a theory on how some of these people come to be the way that they are.

Now, some of these people are just dumb, plain and simple. That's true with some beautiful and some not so beautiful people. My theory is that some of the most beautiful people in the world are some of the dumbest because they're given more than us "regular folk". I see you frowning, but hear me out. All of us have been guilty of going the extra mile for someone that we thought was attractive.

We've done it on our jobs, for a stranger in the street, almost anywhere. We're usually a little nicer to people that are more attractive. They get out of traffic tickets, they get promotions on the job when they're undeserving, they've received better grades when they weren't deserving of them, they get free oil changes, and it goes on and on. I mean, you name it, and if you're attractive, it's happened in your favor at one point or another. Whether we've done it consciously or subconsciously, we've all catered to the beautiful people before. And the beautiful people know this.

The good looking people of the world don't play by the same rules that the rest of us play by. They consider themselves privileged because they're "beautiful". This is what some of us want for our children, so we build them up as soon as they show signs of having that winning smile. Where it hurts our children and turns them into one of those not-so-bright beautiful people that I've spoken about is in their ability and willingness to work and earn what they get in life, rather than having it handed to them. Whether it's through beauty, privilege or just spoiling a child, if you fail to make your children understand that they're no better than anyone else and you fail to make them work and earn whatever they get out of life, they'll become lazy and sometimes not too bright.

If we teach our young men that they can charm their way through life, and if we teach our young women that they can smile and wiggle their hips and shake their breasts to get what they want out of life, they'll never develop their minds, only their physical attributes. They'll be so busy developing their styling techniques, that they won't have time to develop their brains.

By teaching our children the importance of working for what they want out of life and using their brains instead of their bodies to succeed, rather than expecting someone to give them what they want based on their looks, you can help nurture and develop that side within all of us that feels a sense of pride when we earn something.

What I'm saying here I'm sure a lot of you disagree with, and that's okay. It's just that it's been my experience that most of the attractive people that I've come in contact with were usually a little short in the brain department sometimes. I've often found myself wondering how people so beautiful could be so spacey (see Ch. 5). It goes back to one of those things that we all do subconsciously. We assume that just because someone is beautiful, they're otherwise okay. As if they're not subject to the same shortcomings that the rest of us are. Because everyone bends over backwards for these people and treats them as though they were God's gift (and this is true with men and women), whether it's something major or minor in their lives, they never have to work hard for what they get. They feel a sense of entitlement and we're all guilty of making them feel that way.

When they screw up, we let 'em slide because they're beautiful. Some of us would rather be miserable with someone that looks good on our arm, than happy with someone that's average, but knows how to treat us. Of course there are exceptions to all of this, but those exceptions are usually people that came from homes where someone made these people understand that though they're beautiful, they should still earn what they get in life. However, because some of them use their physical attributes more than their brains, they fall into an unhealthy mindset of conceit.

While some of us "regular folk" aren't as blessed as some of these people are, we're "forced" to think our way through life, and thus we're a little more grounded. But it's all about what we teach these children when they're young. This situation is no different than a spoiled rich kid that gets everything he wants. If his parents never teach him the value of hard work and what it took to get rich, there's a good chance that he won't amount to anything.

To wrap this explanation up, we have to give our children a foundation that's rooted in something more than superficiality. We can't allow them to fall prey to the trappings of money or beauty. One of the ways that we can do that is if we as parents have avoided those same trappings. For those of you that are older and have fallen into some of these things, it may be too late for you to come back, so you may not be able to lead your children out of it. And for the younger parents out there, you may also be mired into thinking that your beauty will never fade and that having a brain is for people that never get dates. But if you don't get something in *your* head as well as put something in your child's head, it's those very same dateless brainiacs that you'll be working *for*, as opposed to working *with* one day.

If we don't arm our children with more than beauty and material goods, we're setting them up for failure. As the saying goes, beauty is skin deep, but ugly is to the bone. If you've got children that are looking down their noses at others, they're just pretty faces with ugly demeanors. And it will come back around one day.

## *LISTEN WITHOUT PREJUDICE*

I'm hoping that parents realize that there are a number of things that we can do to improve the situation between parents and children. There's also any number of things that we can do to improve the village that I spoke about. A lot of the changes have to start in each of our homes. In order to improve the village, each home within the village has to make some significant changes in terms of how it conducts itself.

As I stated earlier in this chapter and in this book, a lot of the adults that we're turning out are screwed up because the homes that they came from are the same way. Somewhere along the way, we changed the philosophy of the traditional family. Where we thought we were improving, we only made things worse. What's needed is a redefining of the roles. Mothers, fathers and children have forgotten what they're roles are supposed to be in the family. If we want to get back to a point where everyone is a little more stable in their lives and morals isn't just some old-fashioned word that we throw around, it's going to have to start at home.

As parents, we have to first re-establish ourselves as an authority figure in the homes. There was a time when we weren't communicating properly with our children. We weren't talking to them like we were supposed to, and our children felt as though the parents were just ordering them around, rather than really being there for them. There was a lot going on in their lives that we weren't aware of. We either weren't as diligent as we needed to be or, sadly enough, some of us just didn't care like we should have. In some cases, it wasn't that our children weren't willing to talk to us, they just didn't know how to approach us with their problems. After all, they're children.

Add in the fact that some of the issues that they had were things like peer pressure about sex, drinking and drugs, issues that you just don't feel comfortable going to your parents about in the first place, and you have a situation where both parent and child aren't talking to each other when they really need to. Sometimes, even we as the parents aren't as comfortable talking to our children about certain things as well. You throw all of this in the pot and mix it up, and you've got some trouble headed your way.

What happened as a result of this is that our children started to get into things that they shouldn't have. The drinking, the drugs and the premature sex that I spoke of began to take its hold on our youth. And don't kid yourself, sex acts as a drug once our children begin to have it. Just like drugs, once it gets into their system and their bodies get a taste of it, they began to crave it just as a junkie does his next hit. And just as the junkie does, they have no idea how devastating what they've taken on can potentially be. Instead of coming to their parents for guidance, our kids began to go to one another for some sort of direction. Imagine that, our children going to other misguided souls for advice on things of this nature. With that, the choices that our children began making became increasingly poor.

As parents, there came a point where you had to deal with some of those poor choices that were made. Sometimes it was a stint in rehab, sometimes it was a teen AA meeting and sometimes it was an unplanned pregnancy. Once the children became lost, there was an outcry from both parents and children alike. We had to get more involved with one another.

Parents had to care more about what was going on in their children's lives beyond the obvious grades in school. Children had to be more forthcoming with their parents. Rather than crying out for help through some form of self abuse, they had to just open up and talk to their parents. We wanted to break down the adversarial wall between the parent and the child. Let's talk more. Let's do more together. Let's not just be parent and child, let's be friends. Just as it has been with so much that I've talked about so far in this book, we took something that was a good idea, started it out right, and then took it too far.

As parents, it's extremely important that we know what's going on in our children's lives. It's also important to make them feel comfortable enough to come and talk to us about anything that may or may not be going on in their lives. In some instances, it may be important for us to have a sort of friendship with our children. However, that friendship can never override the parent/child relationship. There may be a point in your lives when your child reaches the status of adult where something like that may be more appropriate, but not when they're coming up.

In fact, in the name of respect, there should always be some separation in that department even if you've reached the level of adulthood. Mama should always be mama, no matter what the situation and the same respect should be given no matter how grown you are. In the name of being friends with our children, we've gone so far to the other side that we've forgotten where the friendship ends and the parenting begins. In an effort to be closer to our children, we've forgotten that we are, and should always be an authority figure and not a buddy. It's alright to connect with your children on a level other than a disciplinary one, but both the parent and the child must remember, understand and remain in their perspective roles.

With our parents being a lot younger these days, part of this "bonding" has taken on a different meaning. I touched on this earlier when I referenced the dress code that's taken place among the parents and their children. Not only is that a problem, we as parents have begun to "hang out" with our children. Not in the sense of me and my son chillin' out and watching some TV together, but rather going to the same "grown up" places and doing some of the same "grown up" things.

Nowadays, when you catch a young woman in the club, you may very well catch her mother ridin' shotgun for the evening. And just like I stated earlier, they'll never be introduced as mother and daughter. Instead, you'll probably hear something like "This is my girl". Even after our children have reached adulthood, there are still some places that we as parents don't belong with our children. To use the nightclub example, I'm not suggesting that after you have your children that your life is over, but shouldn't your clubbin' days be behind you? Maybe it's just me, but I don't think that my son and I should run the streets *together*. Even if I'm still running the streets, it shouldn't be in the same circles as my son.

When you have a true friendship with another person, you really care about them and their well being. If you're a true friend, you want nothing but the best for them. So when your friend is making some choices that aren't good for them, you're going to say something about it, all in the name of being a good friend.

Now, we all know that sometimes our friends can be a little sensitive when receiving that advice, but as I said, if you're a true friend, you only want the best for your friend.

However, the fact that you don't want to offend or hurt someone's feelings may hinder you in this scenario. You want to get your message across, but you don't want to offend or maybe even lose your friend over your point of view in this situation. So sometimes we're forced to tread lightly. We have to be as delicate as possible with what we're going to say because the friendship is so important to us and we don't want to lose that. Ultimately, your friend has to live their own life and though you may care a great deal how that life turns out, you're not responsible for it. When we become more friends than parents to our children, we set ourselves up for this type of scenario. When we allow the friendship with our child to override the parent/child relationship, we sacrifice our position of authority. Read on...

When we maintain our position of parental authority over our children, the words that we speak to them carry a certain kind of weight. How many of you that came from good homes with strong parents would take the advice of a friend over your parents? Not very many of you, I'm sure. Simply put, we don't see our friends as an authority figure most times, so whether or not we listen to and take their advice is arbitrary. It's a matter of choice. If it makes sense and is in line with what we want to do, we may take it. But if it's not, then we may choose to ignore it.

If you maintain your position of authority with your young children, it shouldn't be a question of whether or not they'll listen to you, but rather what the consequences will be if they don't. Our children should be made to listen to and respect what we tell them, regardless of how they feel about it, or else. Now, your "or else" and my "or else" may be two different things. Sometimes my mother used words, sometimes she used the belt. It depended on what the situation called for. Your mother may have used "time out". I have my own theories, but whatever works for you is what you should use.

Don't get me wrong about how we should respond to how our children feel about it. I'm not in any way suggesting that our children don't have rights and that we shouldn't hear them out and respect their opinions. But, as I stated earlier in this chapter, just like the financial aspects of raising kids, they won't fully understand the disciplinary aspects of what we're doing until they're older. Simply put, if you tell them that they can't do something and you told them for their own good, it'd be nice if they understood why, but their understanding isn't a prerequisite or requirement for compliance.

You can't let them do what they want anyway simply because they don't understand why you've taken whatever stand it is that you've taken. Sometimes they won't understand and that just doesn't matter as much as them respecting what you've told them and their following it accordingly. I know this may sound harsh to some, but there are times when the parent/child relationship is not a democracy, it's a dictatorship.

We as parents have to regain control of the relationship that we have with our children. Another way in which we can do this is to understand that this is not a popularity contest. Part of our overwhelming desire to be friends with our children is the need we feel to be seen in a favorable light with them. As I stated earlier, it's almost as if *we're* seeking *their* approval, when it should be the other way around. Though it would be nice if we always got along with our children, we have to understand that it's not necessary in order for us to do our jobs. Can't you remember when you were a child? Your mom and dad weren't popular. They were the equivalent of the police. If they came into your room and you were doing wrong, you scrambled just like crackheads do when the cops roll up.

They weren't popular with their children because they were the authority figures. We're bending over backwards to gain acceptance from children that we have to tell 5 or 6 times to take out the garbage and clean their rooms. We have to get back to the point where we realize that it's okay to be hard on them. It's okay to have expectations as far as our children are concerned. We can't be afraid to punish them when they're wrong. We're holding back on a lot of things because we don't wanna make our children angry. There's definitely something wrong with this picture.

I'll reiterate the fact that our children will be adults before they fully understand the wisdom of what we've done for them. That's why we can't be afraid to discipline them. That's why we can't be afraid to tell them "no". That's why we can't do things based on whether or not they'll understand it. If it's in the best interest of our families, then we have to do what's best. If we do all of these things, it'll be for the greater good.

Whether they realize it or not, these children need our guidance in order to grow into responsible adults. If you're going to let the children lead you, then you'll both be in trouble. Unlike us, the children aren't supposed to know any better about certain things. There are some things in life that they're just not supposed to be wise about. We must know the difference between having a good relationship with our kids and bending over backwards to have some sort of friendship with them. Trust me, you remaining in the parental role that you're supposed to be in is what's best for all involved.

## *LIVING VICARIOUSLY*

There are also times in which we overcompensate for some things that we feel are lacking in our children's lives. There are a lot of reasons that this happens, and sometimes it's to a fault. Sometimes it's in the interest of being friends with them, and we've already belabored that point. Another way in which we overcompensate is due to the fact that some of us feel as if *we* missed out on some things in our own childhood.

There's a certain amount of spoiling that will go on most times when we have children, simply because we love them. However, sometimes we spoil them because we feel that we didn't get what we should have when we were growing up. Sometimes that feeling is justified, and sometimes it isn't. This happens a lot with the younger parents out there. The ones that I spoke of earlier that think simply giving your children all of the things that you didn't have as a child, is parenting. Because they haven't come to fully understand the wisdom in telling your children "no" sometimes, in an effort to give their children all the things that they feel they missed out on, they give them too much.

I've known plenty of young mothers that came from families where they simply didn't get enough love growing up. Because of some of the dysfunction in families today, they didn't have enough people in their lives pushing them in positive directions. For that reason, some of them *became* young mothers and made other poor decisions in their lives because it seemed that no one cared what they did or whether or not they succeeded in life. That feeling of neglect lingers for a long time within some of our young women.

So in that search for love and acceptance, they fall for any man that *pretends* to understand what they're going through, and in order to hold on to that man, they'll share their body with him, thinking that they've found true love. They don't understand that the love that they've missed in their lives, whether it be from a mother, a father or family in general, can't be replaced by a man. There's a certain kind of love that a man can give you, but it can't replace what you feel you've missed from a parent. My mother taught me a long time ago that you can't replace a mother's love, and when you meet someone that's looking for that love, if they can't get it from their mother, they'll be searching a long time.

For a lot of these women that recognize that they've missed out on that love, they decide that when they have children, they'll never be so neglectful towards them. They swear to themselves that things will be different when they raise their children. Knowing the pain that comes with not being loved like you should've, they tell themselves that their children will never miss out on that love. It's a noble thought considering the fact they could easily go the other way and raise their children the same way they were raised, as so many of us, whether raised right or wrong, tend to do.

Yet in their quest to provide their children with a love that went missing in their lives, sometimes they overcompensate. Anything that they can do extra for their kids, they do it. They attempt to make their children's lives easier in every possible way. They want their children to have no stress, no worries and no troubles. They attempt to create a kind of paradise for their children, one that they never had themselves growing up. But sometimes, in the midst of all of this, they spoil their children, when all they wanted to do was create a better life for their children than they had themselves growing up.

Like a lot of us, they want to spare their children the same pain and struggles that they had when growing up. That's fine in the context of trying to keep our children from making some of the same mistakes that we've made in our lives, but where this can be a problem is when we give our children too much, trying to fill holes that aren't even there. It's a problem when we try to satisfy their every whim, just so that they can know that they're loved. It's a problem when we try to spend every waking moment with them so that they can know that we care, never allowing them to go out and grow and experience some things without us. I've seen this happen with parents that have small children, as well as older children. Where they're trying to be protective, they don't realize that by spending too much time with your children, you hinder their growth.

You have to allow them some space, and at the same time understand that you need space and time alone too. That's especially true with the single parent as it can be stressful doing it all on your own. It's also important as a lot of this behavior can be attributed to single mothers trying to overcompensate for an absent father. It's okay to be selfish sometimes and take a break from the children. This is similar to what I said about space in the male/female relationship. Parents have to understand that allowing their children to experience one or two things without them, doesn't mean that they love them any less. It's just a part of them growing up. By smothering your children in "love", you can make them too dependent on you, and sometimes you can cause them to pull away from you, seeking freedom.

This isn't to say that parents shouldn't be as involved as possible in their children's lives. It's rather to suggest that we understand the difference between being involved and shadowing. Go to school plays, functions and little league games because your presence is important, but don't go to class with your preschooler every day or hang out at the day care center. If they see you there everyday, they may begin to expect it and start to cling to you even more than they already do when they're younger.

As our children get older, there are certain stages of letting go that both the parents and the children have to go through. Those stages keep coming until the day one of us dies. It starts with the first days of kindergarten. Then it happens when they become teenagers in Jr. High and you have to start dropping them off at the corner because it doesn't look good to their friends (some of them would say it's "embarrassing") when mom and dad are there all the time. Then it goes on to high school when you have to let them date here and there, go to a party or two and (gulp) drive (I'm already afraid of that with my son being 14). And as they get older, they go off to college, move out on their own, they get married and so on and so on. It never stops, so the sooner you get started on some of this letting go, the more practice you'll have as you approach these stages (I didn't say it'll be easier, because I don't imagine that these stages are ever really easy).

These types of parents must also understand the importance of discipline. As I stated, when some are trying to give their children the love that they didn't get when they were growing up, or trying to fill the gap left by an absent parent, they tend to try and alleviate any and all difficulty their children may have in their lives, not fully remembering that difficulty is a part of life. They don't want their children to have an unhappy childhood if they've had one themselves.

So when it comes to discipline, they sometimes go a little light. Even when discipline is necessary to us parents that came from homes of discipline, we're sometimes reluctant to give it. Once a lot of us became parents, we actually came to understand that sometimes our parents disciplining us actually did hurt them more than it hurt us. Most parents don't enjoy having to spank or punish their children, but sometimes it's necessary.

Parents that were neglected as children must understand that discipline is done out of love and not hate. Even though we're angry most times when we're dishing out the punishments, it doesn't change the fact that we're doing it because we love these children. Had some of these parents that I'm speaking of been disciplined by someone when they we're growing up, once they became adults they would've understood the love that goes into it. Had someone cared enough to correct them in some of their behavior, there would've surely been some mistakes avoided. What they thought was growing up easy, without any discipline, was actually growing up without love. Some see growing up with rules and boundaries as difficult. Some see the rules mom and dad had as unfair, which leads me to that other group of parents that overcompensate for their children.

There are some parents out there that overcompensate for their children because they think that their parents we too hard on them. They act as if being hard on your children is some sort of crime. Now understand that I'm not talking about those parents that ran their houses like drill sergeants or parents that abused their children. I'm talking about those parents that dared to set rules in their houses and expected their children to follow them. Some of these young parents of today couldn't wait to get out of their parent's houses, and out from under their parent's rules. As children, there was nothing short of allowing them to run completely wild and do whatever they wanted to do that their parents could've done to satisfy them.

I've seen this one up close and personal. These are the ones that while growing up, swore that things would be so different when they go out on their own. They were going to run their house, their way, and it would be 10 times smoother than mom and dad's house could ever be. These are the ones that raise their children in this screwed up image that they've foolishly imagined will work. These are the ones that haven't realized that life will be nowhere like they think it will be once they really grow up. These are the ones that don't realize these things until their kids are 7 or 8 and all that time they've been raising them the wrong way. These are the ones that are turning out messed up kids.

There are some rules that some of our parents had while we were growing up that though they may not have been completely unfair, we don't necessarily agree with them and we don't plan to use with our own children. There's nothing wrong with that because it happens with every generation. We take what mom and dad taught us, put our own spin on it and move forward. The problem that we have is that some of our parents are so young when they have their babies, that they haven't fully grown to understand the wisdom in their parent's discipline, so they can't effectively pass it on to their children. If you're 18 or 19, you're still waiting for the day that you can do things your way.

Your parents already know that your way won't work because they were once where you are in their own minds and they try to advise you accordingly in hopes that through some miracle of God, you may actually listen. But in the back of their minds, they already know that the only way that you'll learn these lessons is to go ahead and put your plan into effect and fall on your face. That's how all of us learned that life isn't what we thought it would be. As I like to say, young people have a lot of bright ideas about what life is like because the weight of the world hasn't crushed their spirit yet.

Once that happens, they become a little more humble and a little bit wiser. The only problem is, now you have to convert your children from the old way, to the new. And at that moment, that's when you realize what a job it is to raise a disobedient child. At that moment, you feel your parent's pain. In the interim, the young people raise their kids in their own image. If they're wild and loose, then they allow their kids to be. If they swear, they do it in front of their kids, which in turn teaches the kids to swear. If they drink and smoke, they do it front of their kids. If they listen to music and watch movies with all types of profanity and sex in it, then their children are bound to partake in that as well.

It's not that some of the better parents out there haven't had a party or two that they couldn't allow the kids to be a part of because of the tone of the event. It's not that some of the better parents out there haven't listened to music or seen movies that their children had no business listening to or viewing. I myself listen to and watch things that I don't want my son to see or hear. But now, the kids that were sent to bed and shielded from some of these songs, movies and other adult activities, are becoming parents themselves.

When a lot of us were children, whenever we got sent to bed when the party was going on, we always felt like we were missing something. Even though we were right, it was something that we were supposed to miss. So what's happening with some of these young parents is that they're living vicariously through their children. I bet you thought that only happened in sports and music, huh? I bet you thought that parents could only do that if their children had some sort of talent or ability that we envied, huh? Not so. There are many different ways in which we can live vicariously through our children, and raising them improperly is one of them.

Allowing our children to do some things that our parents didn't allow us to do is another way in which we attempt to live vicariously through them. A lot of us have known people that have allowed their children to do certain things simply because their parents never allowed them to do it, never really exploring the reasons why their parents may have disallowed what they did.

A lot of us have known people that will buy their children just about anything they want, whether they deserve it or not, simply because their parents didn't do it for them when they thought that they deserved it. That's okay with some things, but some things our parents were correct in keeping from us. There are some things that are enjoyed by adults that our young people shouldn't be exposed to. Whether it's music, movies or whatever, there are some things that the young mind isn't able process properly, and thus it may have a negative effect on them.

There are some things that our parents didn't buy us sometimes because we didn't deserve it, and sometimes because they couldn't afford it. Again, without young people having that concept of money and how it works, they'll be older before they realize how they came up and what they're parents could and couldn't afford. I never knew how little we had growing up until I understood all of those things. My mother still laughs at the fact that my older brothers and sisters had me thinking that she had more money than she actually did. My son has often told me that "someone" told him that I had all of the money because he never wants for anything. I often told him that money didn't grow on trees and if it did, I wouldn't be talking to his broke behind, I'd be out in the yard.

Some of these parents don't figure some of these things out until it's too late. They don't realize the importance of watching their language around their children until some of those same four letter words come flying back at them from the mouths of their children. Then, and only then, is it time for discipline. When they cuss at us, we don't play that. We don't have that much of a problem with them cursing out the teacher at school or the old lady down the street, but they better not bring that home. Instead of us giving them something positive to mimic, we give them foul language and bad habits.

They don't see the importance of monitoring what their children watch on TV until they catch their daughter mimicking a booty video in their living room (sadly enough, even when some of these parents see that, they don't see a problem with it; we'll get to that in the next chapter). But once you allow your kids to live without the rules and structure that some of our stronger parents made us live by, you'll start to see some of those negative results. Even before the times that we live in now, there were always negatives facing our children. There were always things in the world that threatened their ability to grow up and become respectful, responsible adults. As parents, it's your job to protect your children from these things instead of allowing them to take on things that they aren't capable of handling.

If you raise your children without rules and discipline, it won't be long before they begin to disrespect you. Following the rules is a form of respect shown to the parent. If there are no rules, there's no respect. Though they don't quite know how to put it into words, a lot of our children actually crave discipline. When they get a little older, they actually seem to understand on some level that it is being done out of love, even if they do occasionally rebel and disobey.

Being hard on your kids, having expectations of them that go beyond good grades and setting life goals with your children is a way of helping to ensure their success in life. There's no guarantee that your kids will never stray if you raise them in a home of discipline, but it's almost guaranteed that they will if you allow them to do as they please. What these two types of overcompensating parents that I've spoken of are sometimes looking for in the way that they treat their children is love.

By giving their children what they want in the way of freedom, overbearing love, material things or whatever, they're actually looking for love themselves. Somehow, by making their children feel what they didn't as children, they're hoping to somehow experience that feeling of being loved through their children. Living vicariously.

There's a void in their own lives that they're looking to fill. Whatever it is you feel you may have missed in your childhood, whether you're right or wrong in this scenario, you can't reclaim it through your children. It doesn't matter if you feel that your parents raised you right or not, you have to raise your children the right way. Whatever is past is past. You have to move forward. You have to look to the future. You have to grow up so that you might help someone else grow up.

## *IT'S OUR TIME TO SHINE*

For every generation of children that comes along, there waits a new set of challenges. As I've stated before, the next generation will always face some different and sometimes tougher challenges than we did. Even though a lot of our children have it much easier than we did in so many ways (technology, more opportunities, quality of life), they still have their own set of worries. Their lives are technologically advanced, but so are the dangers they face. I mean, our parents didn't have to worry about us meeting a child molester over the internet in a chat room, and having us go out and meet him, potentially never to see us again.

Being a young person these days ain't no picnic, but neither is parenting one of these children. It's hard work, sure, but if you love your children, it's worth it. What parents seem to have forgotten these days is that natural instinct to protect our children the way a mother bear would protect her cubs. There seems to be a mentality that suggests that we should expose our children to more than we were exposed to in order to enlighten them. As I've stated so many times, we must be careful of that because our children aren't necessarily ready for the world we're so willing to expose them to. When we push our children out into the world too fast, we increase the chances of them becoming lost.

This whole chapter has been about parents reclaiming their roles, and more importantly, younger parents *learning* their roles. Starting with the younger parents, you have to understand that these are not baby dolls that you have, they're living, breathing human beings. Just like a job or your life as a whole, you only get out of it what you put into it. If you're not going to teach your sons anything more than smoking bud and drinking, then chances are that's all he'll grow to be. If you're going to teach him that a man never stays around to raise his son the right way, he may grow to treat his children the same way.

If you've instilled in him some sort of pride in walking around with his pants halfway to China, not really explaining to him where that originated because you don't know (or maybe you do), then how do you expect him to ever hold down a real job, other than rapper? By the way, since I brought it up, "saggin'" originated in jail. It was a way for the homosexuals in jail to let everyone know who they are. It wasn't something that made you hard, it was something that made other inmates that way when they saw you. I know that sounds vulgar, but that's the truth. So it's bad enough that we're not teaching our young men to become men, we're actually teaching them homosexual dress codes. I don't understand this.

Meanwhile, back in the village, I want to again touch on the importance of teaching our children to respect all forms of authority and not just ours. So many times, we lead our children to believe that they only have to respect our rules and they only need to heed our voices. This is a dangerous message to teach our kids, especially our young men. If we don't teach them to respect authority in all its forms, it's just a matter of time before they began to wonder why they even need to respect us as an authority. It's important that our children be taught to follow rules. Following rules can keep our children out of jail and alive. We're raising children that'll talk back to teachers, members of the clergy, other adults in the community, other adults in our families and it goes on and on.

We've even allowed our children to take disrespectful tones of voice when they speak to us. We have to be careful of this as well. You can't be afraid to tell that son of yours to take that bass out of his voice when he's talking to you. It may seem like a small and insignificant thing when that little girl of yours smacks her lips and does that whole chicken neck thing when she's talking to you, but our children's body language and tone of voice can be just as disrespectful as the words they use.

In fact, that body language is a pre-cursor to the other forms of disrespect that are sure to follow if you don't correct them. A lot of us just figure that's it's okay when they speak to us any kind of way as long as they do what we ask them to do, but their attitude needs to be correct when we tell them to do something. If it's not, then you must correct it.

We've become so unnecessarily protective of our children, that we don't want anyone else to say anything to our children. Although there are some out there that don't necessarily like children or know how to handle or speak to them, that's not true with every adult out there and that doesn't mean that our children shouldn't still be taught to show some respect to all adults. These are the same children that grow up and shoot at policemen.

Though we have our fair share of corrupt policemen in this country, we can't go around firing weapons at those who are legally allowed to fire back. These are trained killers we're talking about. The results can be, and most times are, deadly. We must not only demand that our children respect us, but we must demand that they respect authority. If we allow them to challenge all other forms of authority, then they'll soon challenge us.

*Withhold not correction from the child: for if thou beatest him with the rod, he shall not die. Thou shalt beat him with the rod, and shall deliver his soul from hell.*
*—Proverbs 23:13-14*

Even our government has taken sides as it pertains to the disciplining our children. A few years ago we decided that spanking our children was a crime. Parents are afraid to put their hands on children that they feed and clothe on a regular basis. Now, I'm not talking about child abuse here. I'm talking about the fact that sometimes, whether we like it or not, our children need a little physical contact to make them respond.

Somewhere along the way, we decided that spanking children teaches them violence. Child abuse teaches them violence. The streets teach them violence. Spousal abuse teaches them violence. Spanking your children when they need it does not teach them violence. It helps to keep them in check so that the law won't have to. When the cops correct our children, they do it with correctional facilities or bullets. I don't really want that for my son. A lot of people that are reading this will disagree, and that's fine. You have every right to raise your children the way that you see fit. However, if I feed and clothe it, I'll spank it when it's necessary. That's how my mother raised me and my siblings and that's how I'll raise my kids.

I'm not a violent person and neither are my brothers and sisters. We are no worse for our mother physically disciplining us when it was necessary, we are better. Like it or not America, she did it out of love. Now, my brothers and sisters will tell you that I got it a lot less from my mom than they did, and that's the truth. Although I had my moments growing up, my mother always told me that I got it less because I gave her less trouble than my predecessors. Again, my brothers and sisters will disagree and tell you that it was because I was the baby. I will tell you that I watched what my brothers and sisters did to set my mother off, and though I didn't avoid all of the mistakes that befell my older siblings, I did avoid most of them, and thus I got less whippings.

There was a time long ago that black parents whipped their children too much, mostly because that's how they came up. But it wasn't something that we just came up with on our own. It was taught to us by white slave masters long ago. It was how they "disciplined" us, and just like they forced their ways, their last names and their religion on us, they taught us their way of "discipline". Also, we as blacks weren't educated enough to understand that sometimes we could talk to our children and they will respond. Over the years, once we became more educated as a people, we learned to express ourselves more effectively and we leaned to discipline the children without physical contact.

Now, I must repeat myself again. Just like so many things in life, we took a good idea and took it too far. Once we got to the point where we wanted to talk things out with our children and respect their feelings and their space, we saw that it does work from time to time. However, there are always times, especially if you have boys, where our children will test us. There are times when they'll just about force you to resort to physical discipline. As parents, we have to be up to that challenge.

Too many parents are afraid of their children these days. They won't get physical with them because they're afraid of what the *child* may do to *them*. My mother had four boys. She kept a baseball bat in the house for such occasions. If any of us ever felt the need to get physical with my mother, it would not be an easy fight. My mother had a saying when I was growing up: "I'm willing to do time for you". If that didn't say it all to me and my brothers, nothing would. She was not afraid to do great physical harm to any of us if we were to ever decide that we wanted to put our hands on her in any way other than to show our affection.

Again, it's not that my mother was a child abuser or anything like that. She was just trying to make it clear to us that even though she was a woman and we were men, she was not about to allow us to walk all over her and do whatever we wanted while we were in her house. She wanted us to understand at all times that she was the parent and we were the children. There was no compromising that.

Another way in which we've become afraid is in terms of the law and its current views of physical contact between parent and child. We had a rash of parents (a lot of them young) that were abusing their children. We had a parent on videotape beating her child in the back of an SUV in a mall parking lot a few years ago in Indiana. Here in Detroit, we had a case of a very stupid woman leaving her two infants in a car with the windows rolled up, in 90 plus degree weather, to die while she was in a hair salon for 2 to 3 hours getting her hair done. Because of instances like these, we have become extremely protective of our children. There's nothing wrong with that.

(Here's that word again) However, we have taken this all too far. Those are issues of abuse in those cases and the law getting involved was what was necessary. But parents shouldn't have to be afraid of going to jail because they've disciplined their children. A couple of swats on the backside can go a long way in keeping a child in line. It's gotten so bad now that every little instance of a child being spanked is reported to protective services. Not only is it overkill, but some of our children have become aware of it, and used it against us. Some of these kids will tell you to your face that if you lay a hand on them, they'll call the police. As parents, we can't be afraid of these threats.

I've told anyone that will listen that I'm not afraid to discipline my son, even in this day and age of calling the cops on mom and dad. I've been known to tell my friends that every number that he needs will be on the refrigerator. If he wants to call the cops on me for spanking him for something that he did wrong, then he's more than welcome. Like I said before, if I feed it and clothe it, I'll discipline it.

In fact, I'll tell you a story that my mom told me about one of my uncles and one of my cousins. It seems that one day one of my cousins decided that he was going to run away from home because my uncle was going to whip him for something that he did. He eventually wound up at the police station, where they promptly called my uncle. When my uncle finally showed up at the police station, the officer told my uncle, "Now, Mr. Flowers, you can't put your hands on this boy when you get home". My uncle told them, "Then you keep him. Because what I do to him, I do out of love to keep him in line. When he gets out in the streets and do wrong, you guys will be shootin' to kill". With that, the cops told my cousin, "Son, you better go home and do what your father says". But they never told my uncle that he was wrong about what he said.

The reality is that if these kids are willing to call the cops on you for disciplining them and are willing to wind up in foster care with people that don't love or care about them beyond the check that they get for keeping them, it's simply because they don't know any better. Once they wind up in the system because they're being smart and trying to get back at their parents for checking them, then they'll know what real love is. Foster care is for kids that don't have any choice, not for kids that are angry with their parents. And once they get in that system, they'll run into a lot of kids that will make them aware of the fact that foster care is no picnic and those kids would trade places with anyone with a stable home.

Now, I'm not saying that all foster parents are just money hungry people working the system. My mom is a foster parent and she does that because she loves helping children. But let's be real. There are a ton of people out there that are just working the system. We can't be afraid to parent these kids in every way. A lot of us wonder why our society is in such decay and our children are running wild. I don't know about you, but along with a general lack of discipline, once we decided that physical punishment was no longer necessary, things started to change. A lot of parents have become afraid of these children now, and just like wild animals, these children can sometimes smell fear in us and they act accordingly. I can't stress enough that if our children don't have to respect us, then they'll respect no one.

When I was a child, I was afraid to get in trouble and it never had anything to do with any cop. They could've taken me and locked me up in any jail that they chose to, but whatever you do, don't call my mother. If she was willing to do time for me, I was willing to do time rather than face her. I know the PC (Politically Correct) cops will disagree with me, but the fear that I had of my mother was a necessary fear. Children don't have that fear of mom and dad anymore. We've all confused that fear with actually being afraid. God wants us to fear Him, but it's more out of respect than actually being afraid. I would've rather faced a cop than my mom not only because of the whipping I would get, but also for the disappointment that I would've given her.

You have to be at least willing to put you hands on your children in the name of love, because if you don't, others will do it in a much more hostile sense. I once knew a woman that wouldn't spank her kids because she remembered thinking that she hated her mom ever time she got a spanking. That's one of the silliest excuses I've ever heard for not spanking your kids. I mean, which one of us has never out of anger, at some point or another, said that we hated our parents? Kids say that all the time when something doesn't go their way, and unless you have some deeper issues there, they never really mean it. This woman admitted that she never really hated her mother, but she never even wanted her kids to have that feeling about her. She was naive enough to believe that children only think that way when we spank them. Not so.

They think that way whenever we tell them "no" to something that they really want. It's just kids being kids. It's not that serious, they're just pissed off, but not nearly as pissed as a parent is when they have to spank a child. Again, it actually does hurt you sometimes more than it hurts them. I'm not against talking it out if that works. All children don't need to be spanked. As of the writing of this book, I haven't spanked my son in nearly 9 years. I can't say the same for his mother, but simply put, he responds when I talk. He's a good kid, so there hasn't been a need for spanking. But he knows that I'm more than willing. If your kids get out of line, you have to put them back in, by any means necessary. If you don't, the streets or the police will one day.

We also must remember the importance of instilling some knowledge in our children. They'll never go anywhere without their brains, so we may as well make sure that there is something in them. I spoke about giving our children more than a pretty face. As I stated then, some of you I'm sure will disagree with what I wrote, but I'm sure that we all know a beautiful fool or two. People that some-how make it into adulthood, but can't do anything for themselves because they're so used to people doing things for them.

These are the types of women that marry for money because they could never make that kind of money with their own brains. These are the types of men that go from woman to woman, looking for someone to take care of him because he's too sorry to work for himself and too "fine" to get his nails dirty. That's not a real man. Our young ladies must learn to be thinking, individual women. So many times I see some of the most beautiful women in the world with some of the emptiest heads in the world. I referenced these women way back in the first chap-ter. They're the type that men crave, assuming all along that because she's beauti-ful, she's otherwise okay. At the same time, they have some of the same issues that anyone else is capable of having.

We must instill in our young ladies a mentality for success. We have a lot of young ladies out there that won't do a thing for themselves because they're wait-ing for some man to do it. Between them, they think that it's the man that's stu-pid. Between them, they feel that they're playing the man. The time and the energy that they put into playing the man could be put into bettering themselves and their situation so that they're not dependant on some man to take care of them, but they don't see it that way. Our mothers must teach our young women that this is the road to loneliness and despair. They must also be taught that prostitutes are treated the same way.

They must teach our young women that even if they have a man foolish enough to take care of a woman he's not married to, he'll do it because of her beauty and that will fade one day. Sooner or later, someone younger will come along, and God help you if she actually has a brain. If he ever meets someone that's beautiful *and* going somewhere, you'll lose quickly as she'll show him a world that he never thought existed. You can't hold him hostage forever with your beauty. Sooner or later you'll need substance or he'll trade you in for a newer model. Remember, unequally yoked won't work. Even if it takes a long time, it'll all soon fall down.

There's no doubt we as parents have our work cut out for us. I mean, it's to the point that we have to go through their CD collection nowadays just to make sure we're the strongest influence in their lives (I'll cover that next chapter). And the truth of the matter is that some of us parents still need a little raising and some rules and regulations ourselves. But we must remain strong in this struggle, and it is a struggle.

We have to understand that our children need us. Whether they can put it into words or not, they're counting on us to show them the way. We can't allow this task to fall into the hands of others that wish to do our children harm. We must fight the urges to be irresponsible and do right by our children. We should make sure that they're properly educated in school, in the ways of the world and in the ways of The Lord.

No matter what's happened in our pasts, we must raise our children for their futures. We must resist the urges to relive our youth out in the streets with our children. Understand that once these children are born, the role of parent is upon you and you must carry yourself accordingly. No more living vicariously through your child. As I said, the village is now corrupt, but it still wants to raise our children. We can't let that happen.

Remember to listen to these children when they speak. Nothing burns me up more than to hear a parent say that they had no idea what was going on in their child's life. These children tell us what's going on in their lives all the time. The question is, are you listening? Are you paying attention? To all the parents out there, it's time to make a change. We must reclaim our children. No matter what the song says, whether we believe it or not, the children are our future. Always has been, always will be. We have to teach them well and let them lead the way. They're counting on us.

# 7

## *"Music of my mind…"*

The music and movies that I referenced in the last chapter are a great point of concern these days as it relates to our children. As a lover of music and film, I've watched the way that movies and music have changed over the years. As I stated at the beginning of the last chapter, when I was growing up, Prince was the focal point of our parent's concerns. The only thing that our parents had to worry about was the man that would eventually drive Tipper Gore crazy and become the father of the warning labels that you see on CD's these days.

Prince was the only artist out there that would literally tell a woman everything, and I do mean everything, that he wanted to do to her. Hip hop was a few years away from really taking off in that direction. Even though I am one of Prince's biggest fans, that didn't always sit well with my mother. Though she never demanded that I didn't listen to him, there were obviously certain songs that I couldn't play around a good Christian woman like my mom. Out of respect for her, I had to edit my playlist.

Though I was being influenced by Prince's music in a lot of ways, my mother wasn't facing the same challenges that she, along with many other parents, are facing today (my mother is still a parent in the traditional sense, having adopted my two of my nieces). As of the writing of this book, music has even gotten to be too much for Prince these days as he has gone the other way now, completely removing all profanity from his albums and live shows. But for as much profanity and sexual content as he did put into his music in the past, our parents' concerns about what we heard from him seems rather minimal and trivial compared to what's on the radio today. After all, Prince never suggested that we kill anyone in his records. Comparing what he did to what's going on today, he appears to have basically just had a potty mouth and was some sort of sex addict. In comparison to what's on record these days, if a parent caught their child listening to an old Prince record, it'd be a relief.

# "CAN IT BE THAT IT WAS ALL SO SIMPLE THEN..."

For all of you parents out there that aren't very familiar with hip hop music, this chapter may be a little tough to follow. Some of the songs, artists and terminology may be a little foreign to you. In some ways that's understandable, but in some ways it's not so good. Your children are listening to this music and it's something you should be a little more aware of. Hopefully, this chapter will help you in that regard. Hopefully, I can shed some light on this thing of ours (and by the way, for some of you that don't know, it is our music). The general thought is that it's not good for our children. In some ways that's true and in some ways it's not. Hip hop is a very complicated thing to explain. Although I will not attempt to explain hip hop from beginning to end, I will try to explain it well enough so that we all can see how it relates to and affects our children. Try to stay with me, and if you can't, grab a young person and ask them to explain to what a "Jay-Z" is.

I still remember when hip hop really blew up. Not when Kurtis Blow, the Sugar Hill Gang or Grand Master Flash and the Furious Five first had hit records. With all due respect to those pioneers, I'm talking about when this thing really got big. When Run-DMC and LL Cool J became household names and the movie *Krush Groove* became a part of cinematic history. Hip hop was mainly about the music. It had a party atmosphere to it. There weren't a lot of the elements that are present today. There were a lot more songs with positive messages and images to them. It was a way for some of our young brothas and a few of the sistas to express themselves. It wasn't that there wasn't any crime in the streets, drugs being sold or gratuitous sex being had. It just wasn't making it onto wax in the way that it is now.

Run, DMC, LL and any other rapper out there probably saw it or knew someone that was close to some of this activity, and though it wasn't always being reflected in their music, that doesn't mean that it wasn't in their 'hoods. Songs like Run-DMC's "Hard Times" or "It's Like That" talked about the struggles that blacks were facing on a day to day basis. Through those songs, they put things in a perspective that pretty much everyone could understand, even if you couldn't necessarily relate. However, soon after that, the next generation of hip hop would come along and paint a grittier, more vivid picture of what was going on in the 'hood.

*Straight Outta Compton*. In my opinion, the second most pivotal album in hip hop history (the most pivotal being Run-DMC's *Raising Hell*, which took hip hop mainstream and made it platinum). This was the album that said it all. Literally. When N.W.A. (Niggaz Wit Attitude) dropped that album, the landscape of the music was changed forever. Before that, you had a few rappers here and there that would curse on a record. You had a few singles like "La Di Da Di" by Doug E. Fresh and Slick Rick and a few Luke songs that were out there with language in them, but N.W.A. took it to new heights.

You see, when those singles I just mentioned were out, hip hop didn't exist the way that it did once *Raising Hell* came out. *Raising Hell* meant that if you wanted to succeed in rap, you'd better start thinking album instead of single. So where N.W.A.'s impact may have been minimal in the era of the hip hop single, it was massive in the era of the hip hop album. Where they may have had a minor impact on the music if they'd had only 3 ½ to 4 minutes to share their views, they had a major impact on the music because they had a whole album to express what was going on in their 'hood. They took their own advice given on one of the albums songs, "Express Yourself". And express themselves they did.

Hip hop historians will say that Ice-T begat N.W.A., and that's true, just like so many came before Run-DMC. Hip hop didn't originate with Run-DMC, but they are still considered forefathers because they blew it up and put it on the map. At the same time, though Ice-T was one of the originators of West Coast rap, it was N.W.A.'s *Straight Outta Compton* that made it national and changed hip hop forever. Because of the brutal honesty of this record, the graphic and detailed nature of what they talked about and the reality of what they talked about from their South Central, L.A. neighborhoods, they touched a nerve in a lot of people, no matter what you may have felt about what these young black men were saying. Out of N.W.A. were born a whole slew of young men that wanted to get on the mic and tell of their struggles, in their neighborhoods. They wanted to tell of the things that they've gone through on their blocks. And they wanted to tell it with the same honesty that N.W.A. told it.

Over the years, hip hop would begin to express itself this way on a continuous basis. Soon it went from guys that talked about what they saw in their neighborhoods on a day to day basis to the theater of the absurd. Instead of the reality of an N.W.A., a Snoop Dogg, a 2pac, a Notorious B.I.G. or a Jay-Z, you had a lot of copycats coming along just trying to cash in. Where we once had a few poets telling stories, though rather grim, you now had a bunch of people making up stories just to sell some records because that's what was hot at the time. What started out as a few guys telling you what life was like in their neighborhoods quickly turned into a bunch of guys telling variations of stories that they'd heard from someone else for profit. Hip hop soon became big business. And just like a lot of things in this country that becomes big business, it became something that began to be marketed to our children.

I bet you guys were wondering where all of this was going. I know you were thinking to yourself that I had either gotten way off track or you had somehow started reading a totally different book on the history of hip hop and rap music. Nope, that's not it. As I stated at the beginning of this section, I just wanted to give those of you that didn't have a background in the music a little history. However, this is where I tie it all into parenting. There's a lot of music out there that is marketed directly to our children these days and we have to be careful what we turn a deaf ear to.

I referenced Tipper Gore a short while ago. Back in 1985, the wife of former Vice President Al Gore formed The Parent's Music Resource Center. This was in reaction to, among other things, Prince's song "Darling Nikki". Tipper caught her daughter listening to this song one day and got a hold of the lyrics. Once she found out what kind of girl Nikki was, she knew exactly what kind of man Prince was. She was outraged and as stiff as I think Tipper is, I must admit that I may have felt the same way had I come across my teenaged daughter listening to that song, knowing what I know about it. But where Tipper was trying to do some good when she created the PMRC, she created a double edged sword.

I have a question: If there's a house on fire on your block, what will you do? Chances are most of us will go outside to see the fire. Where I thought Tipper was actually being a good parent by being aware of what her child was listening to and, considering the platform she had, attempting to do something about it, all she did in essence was yell "fire" at the top of her lungs. Even though I'm an advocate of free speech and freedom of expression, I was in favor of warning labels, even in '85 when I was only 16 years old. I felt then and still feel now that parents should be informed when their children are listening to music with adult content in it.

What Tipper failed to consider was the fact that when that label hit those albums and cassettes (that's what those of us over 30 remember), she didn't drive the children away from the fire, she only brought them closer. The only thing that label did was increase the likelihood of kids buying the album. I won't lie to you, if I saw a warning label, I wanted that album. I wanted to hear what I wasn't supposed to hear. I wanted to know what Tipper was trying to keep me from. I wanted no secrets between Tipper and me.

## *"REALITY" TV…*

As our young men continued to grow and the conditions for young black men in this country worsened, it was reflected in rap music. Though we had the fakers in the industry (artist that simply regurgitated what they heard from other people and in other music), a lot of what was written and performed in hip hop music was very real in our society. Chuck D of the rap group Public Enemy once called rap music the CNN of the ghetto. He said that if anyone wanted to know what was going on in the black community, all they had to do was tune in to hip hop. A lot of those fatherless boys that we had in our society were now rappers with recording contracts. You could hear firsthand how the streets had taught them their version of what being a man was, as opposed to a father teaching his son the right way. And you remember how corrupt I told you the village is now.

You could hear firsthand the pain in their voices as they talked about pops not being there. You could hear how they sold drugs to support themselves and, in some cases, the illegitimate children that they had through irresponsible sex. You could hear how all of these things aided them in losing their identity. You could hear how they committed genocide on one another, killing their own in the name of street cred, territory, and all for the love of drug money. If there was ever a crystal ball to show you what affect an absent father and no real guidance or structure could have on our young men, hip hop music is that crystal ball.

In addition to the drugs, the killing and the glorification of money that went on in hip hop music, eventually another negative tone began to surface in the music. Our young men began to objectify women. As opposed to women, sisters, girlfriends and mothers to our children, women were now being referred to as "bitches", "hoes" and any other derogatory term you can think of, and being viewed as nothing more than objects that provide sexual gratification. Now women weren't completely blameless in the way that they were being portrayed in this music, but we've already covered women's roles in the way that men treat and view them these days.

A lot of this music was being created by men that never saw women any other way. Some of these guys came from homes with strong mothers in them that did their best to raise them right, but when you allow your children to get out into the streets and be influenced by what's going on out there, your chances of them being a little more respectable to women is considerably lessened. But when there's no father in the home and mom has to work to support the family, who else is gonna raise these young men besides the streets? If they're being raised by the pimps and the hustlers of the world, then respect for women is something that's way down on the list.

For example, I remember watching the documentary *American Pimp*. There was one pimp in the documentary that said that in order for a pimp to be "successful", he had to be willing to pimp his own mother if that's what the situation called for. Now, I don't know what "situation" would ever call for that, but just from that statement you can see the types of people that will raise our sons if we allow the streets to get a hold of them.

Once big business became involved in hip hop, they exploited it just like they did jazz, the blues and rock n' roll. And in order for big business to get bigger, they had to point this thing in the direction of our young people. Remember the Parent's Music Resource Center that I referenced before? Like I said, Tipper had a good idea, but it backfired. Where she wanted to make parents aware of what their children were listening to through a warning sticker, she only gave record companies a marketing tool. And also, like I said before, when I saw that label as a teenager, it made me want to buy that album as opposed to putting it back on the shelf. And it wasn't like they were carding us, so buying it was no big deal.

We were the same way with R-rated movies. All that did was make us want to sneak in. That label has the same effect on our children today. The more we label, the more they buy. Factor all of that in, and every album that has explicit content on it will go platinum. Factor in that platinum sales status and the record companies want more of that too. So the songs are then directed towards our children. They have many tools to reach our children as well. There are magazines, the ever popular word of mouth, and something that may be more destructive than the songs themselves: The music video.

If the music wasn't enough, eventually the videos came to the forefront. As if our women weren't being portrayed poorly enough in the music, we soon got visual aides. With rap music being funded more heavily by the music industry that pimped the so-called pimps and, quite honestly, by drug money, we were allowed to get on MTV and BET and show America how we viewed our women. Now these images were being played out each day in front of our children's eyes. This is another way in which all of the marketing and strategies of a corrupt industry began to target our children. With our children having more disposable income these days, they were targeted to spend some of that income on things that good parents would rather keep from their children until they were old enough for it.

They'd play these videos during hours that they knew our children would be watching. If that wasn't enough, they began to tie it in to call-in shows with nothing but teens in the audiences. Kids identify with other kids and when they see someone on TV that looks like them, dresses like them and are dancing and singing along to some of these songs, they wanna be down too. From there, the poisoning of our children continued. What started in the 'hood with drugs, alcohol and a "you'll never amount to anything" attitude was now being played out on record and in videos. Even though things were better for some of our children than they were for us when we grew up, it seemed that someone wanted to keep us down and keep us thinking that we were nothing more than what was portrayed on these records and in these videos.

Through the music video, we began to show our young people that life was all about how many possessions you can amass before you die. The cars, the jewelry and the big houses are what hip hop became all about. Considering the fact that this is the music of the youth now, they attempted to identify with artists that they had nothing in common with beyond skin color. All of these material possessions were things that young black people could only hope to gain in their lifetimes. Though there's nothing wrong with our children aspiring to have some of the finer things in life, sometimes we should present them with a realistic vision of how they may have to go about achieving them.

Since all of us don't have the ability to put words together the way that some of today's best rappers can, there's only a few other things outside of a regular 9 to 5 that one could do to achieve all of these things that they see in the video. Match that with some of the messages and themes that exist in the songs that the videos are set to, and if rapping ain't our children's profession, they'll soon be on the streets living out that other fantasy. Who's responsible? We'll get to that in a minute.

What videos have also shown our children is that women exist only to satisfy men sexually and to parade around half nude. They have shown our young ladies that it doesn't matter what's in their heads, as long as they look good in a bathing suit, can do any of the latest dances and are willing to wear as close to nothing as you can get, then they too can go to video shoots, rub elbows with celebrities, allow them to pour liquor all over their bodies and simulate sex with them. All on screen, all over the world, so that all of your family and friends can see. How proud you must be, mom and dad.

Yet, if you've ever heard any of these women talk, they talk as if they're actually in control of what's going on. They all want you to believe that they're not just some dumb girls that are being exploited by the video industry. They all want you to know how "smart" they are. They all want you know they're treated with the utmost respect on the set. They don't have to do anything that they're not comfortable with. I guess what's alarming to me is the fact that what makes it to the screen is what they actually *are* comfortable with.

When you hear these young ladies speak, they usually want to convince you of how different they are from the "other girls" that show their stuff on the video screen. But if you listen long enough, you'll find out where they feel the difference comes in between them and the "other girls". It's money. Somehow, our women have come to the conclusion that if they make enough money on the "project", then they're not being exploited. They feel that if they make $1,000 a day as opposed to making $300 a day, then they're not being exploited. That's just like an escort trying to convince you that she's not a prostitute because she's paid better and does her deed in a better hotel. A prostitute is a prostitute.

I'm sorry if I'm offending anyone, but if these girls were so smart, they'd make that money with their clothes on. This is the danger I spoke about in the last chapter when discussing the importance of educating our children, as opposed to them trying to get through life on their looks. Physical beauty will fade, and if your daughter is one of these "video hoes" (that's what they call them; that title is just dripping with respect), if she doesn't have a brain in her head, it won't matter how much money she makes in a day. Sooner or later she'll either blow it on clothes, on some man or up her nose. But make no mistake about it, a fool and his (or her) money is soon parted. That applies to all of us, no matter how pretty we are.

## *THE MUSIC MADE ME DO IT*

There was a time in my life when I felt that the music that children listened to had very little effect on what type of adults they would eventually become. I felt that way for two reasons. The first was I saw the way that I turned out. I listened to some pretty rough stuff as a teenager, both on the rap side and the rock side of music, and I turned out okay. I felt that since I saw it all as just music and entertainment and never let it affect my judgment, there was no reason that others couldn't do the same thing.

The second was the fact that I felt that with a little more parenting, we could keep our children in line, no matter what kind of music they listened to. I felt that parents that blamed their children's behavior on the music that they listened to were copping out. I felt that if they had tried as hard as my mother did, then their kids would be okay. It's amazing how your views will change once you have your own children. Needless to say, I feel differently now. Not completely, but there are many amendments to my thought process. Now that I'm raising a son in this environment, I've become more aware of what's being played out in his ears and on the television screen.

Where I was wrong as it pertains to the music affecting our children was in the fact that I underestimated a few things. I underestimated the power of the words these people speak to our children. I underestimated the job that my mother did raising me. I also underestimated my own mental strength, given to me by my mother. As much as I loved and studied music inside and out, I still underestimated its power. There were also a few things that I didn't take into consideration. I'll start with that.

As I stated earlier, when N.W.A. dropped *Straight Outta Compton*, it changed the music by adding more profanity and more straight forward sexual content and violence to it. That was 1988. I was 19 years old. I was pretty much the man I was going to be as far as the majority of my thought processes were concerned. Most times, something like that wouldn't affect a 19 year old the same way that it would a 12 or 13 year old.

Because I was almost a grown man when that album came out, I could process that information in a way that a younger person couldn't necessarily. But at the same time, I was heavily influenced by Prince growing up and he affected the way that I viewed a lot of things in life. However, as I stated before, Prince never killed anyone on his records, so his affect on me would be considerably different that some hardcore rapper's would be on a young man with a weaker mind and no moral foundation.

I had to come to understand that though I grew up on hip hop, I didn't grow up on *today's* hip hop. What we heard growing up wouldn't have had the same negative effect on our children as what they are growing up on today. Where we had Run-DMC, which were hardcore, yet clean 90% of the time, they had an N.W.A., which was hardcore, raw and explicit pretty much all of the time. Where we had LL Cool J making love songs for the ladies (although L could get raw sometimes), our children have a Jay-Z doing "Big Pimpin'". The difference between what we grew up on and what the kids of today are growing up on is night and day.

Where we had Jazzy Jeff and the Fresh Prince talking about "Parents Just Don't Understand", our children have some chick on a Nelly track singing *"I am getting so hot/I wanna take my clothes off"*. The first time I heard those lyrics, they were coming out of my niece's mouth. I wanted to kill her, no lie. She was all of 13 years old and had no idea how trashy that sounds. But, as the saying goes, one man's trash is another man's treasure. And maybe I'm getting older, but what used to be a treasure to me (hip hop), is becoming trash. I know the young people will disagree with me because this is their music now, but as I've stated so many times before in this book, maybe they'll understand when they have children.

Whether we like it or not, this music does belong to our children now. Even in all its hedonistic forms. However, the reason that its quality has taken such a slide is because we have too many young, underdeveloped minds in the industry. Because of the short sightedness of our youth, favoring money, women and drugs over true artistic expression, not only has the music suffered, we've allowed people that don't care about us or the music that we make to take it over and further corrupt what we've tried to build for ourselves. We've allowed this the same way we allowed them to ruin the blues and jazz.

Also, because so many of our young people make their money in the streets these days, it's not hard for some of them to put out records on their own. Although you admire their entrepreneurial spirit, you wish that they'd had that same drive to make their money honestly in the first place, and you wish that they'd invest in some measure of quality control. Outside of the vulgarity of today's music, some of it is just plain bad whether they swear or not.

When we were growing up, rap music was our rock n' roll. It was to us what rock n' roll was to our parents. It was our rebellion music. It was our "noise" to our parents. It was our method of expression. In the beginning, it was about our freedom and our outlet for creativity. But just like rock n' roll before it, rap music eventually became less and less about that freedom and expression. It became more about shock value and money and less about real music. Just like rock n' roll before it, once rap music became a "business", it was less about fun, and more about marketing. Once again, our children became "involved" and the music began to corrupt them.

# *BUT, WHAT ABOUT THE KIDS?*

So, the only remaining questions as it relates to this music and how it's affecting our children are who's responsible for what affect it has on our children, and how can we as parents effectively monitor our children and what they listen to, in order to shield them from some things that their young minds just aren't ready for? The answers are simple, but the explanations are not. All of us are responsible for what happens to the youth. Both the artists that create this music and the parents have a role in all of this.

Again, we have to all realize that we're all in the same village here. The responsibility of raising these children the right way belongs to all of us. There are things that these artists can do on their records that can aide in this process, and there are things that parents can do to help themselves. As parents, we are the first line of defense, but the artist has a responsibility to his customers as well. I'll attempt to explain.

I'm going to start with the hip hop artist. For the last few pages, I know that it seems that I've picked on hip hop music and all of its imagery, but I want to qualify a lot of my opinions and points of view by telling you about my current relationship with hip hop. I've already talked about the fact that I grew up on hip hop and I have great love and appreciation for the music. However, that doesn't mean that I'm just some old school guy that never left the '80's as far as rap was concerned. I feel privileged to have watched a form of music grow from its infancy to become a global force in music. It's literally the single most popular form of music out today.

Though the music has changed and gotten a lot harder over the years, I've still been right there with it. I still remember when that N.W.A. album dropped and what a rush it was. There was the rush of listening to something that you know you probably had no business listening to, but there was also the rush of listening to people so bold as to say literally whatever was on their minds at the time.

However, that was nothing like the rush that I felt when Ice Cube left the group and made his debut *Amerikkka's Most Wanted* and did the same thing that N.W.A. did, but with an intelligent message behind it. I still remember when Snoop Dogg dropped *Doggystyle* and how the world went crazy over this young genius. I still remember the first time I heard Biggie. It was like nothing that I'd ever heard before and he literally saved East Coast rap. I still miss him so much sometimes that I can't even listen to his music.

I remember when 'Pac started to blow up. I still remember how the girls went crazy over him, but because of their own superficiality and only seeing him as a handsome man, they never really understood the full scope of 2pac. I still remember when Eminem came on the scene. Here in Detroit, if you loved hip hop, you were so proud that someone with that kind of skill and lyrical brilliance could hail from this city. Though his content was out of this world, who could really deny that flow? And from a white boy, no less.

Last, but certainly not least, I still remember the first time I heard Jay-Z. It was actually around '90 or '91, but even with his first album, *Reasonable Doubt* in '96, I knew that I was hearing something special. By the time I heard *The Blueprint*, I knew that I was listening to the best rapper alive. By the time I heard *The Black Album*, I knew that I was listening to the most complete rapper I had ever heard. No one has ever possessed that much skill, flow, lyrical content and commercial appeal all at such a high and *consistent* level, all in one career, all in such a short period of time the way that Jay did. There are plenty that will disagree with that, but that's what makes hip hop so great. We all have our favorites and we all think they're the best.

The point I'm making is that I love this music that our people have created. I've listened to it, I've supported it and a lot of these people have my money. But just because I love it, doesn't alleviate it from its responsibility to our youth. Some of the hip hop artists of today have come to the conclusion that they don't have to take any responsibility for what they say to our children these days. Though I respect their freedom of speech and their right to feel that they don't have any responsibility outside of their own children, I think that they're wrong. Anytime you put out some of the things that these guys put out, there's a certain responsibility that goes with it. It's bad enough that sometimes their lives imitate their art, but when you create something that will reverberate within our children's minds over and over again, you don't necessarily have to change what you say, but you have to at the very least be willing to own up to some of its ramifications.

Too often they hide behind the guise of "keeping it real' and "just telling what's going on in the hood", but the problem is that they never balance any of this stuff out with any positives or with any real consequences to living the life that they glorify in their records and videos. Understanding that more times than not, they don't see a lot of positive images in their neighborhoods, they still have the positive of their own lives. They're on TV and they have multi-platinum albums outs. If no one made it out of the 'hood, they did. At some point while they're living in their multi-million dollar houses, they need to stop pimpin "the struggle" to our kids, and tell them that it's possible to make millions without getting shot at.

A lot of these rappers actually have children, which is scary in itself. I can't imagine saying what they say on record and allowing my children to hear what's coming out of my mouth. But here's the part where I defend the hip hop artists. Though some of their material isn't fit for children, if you were raised in the environment that they were raised in and around those things that they speak about in their records, how else do you know to express yourself? With what this country does to inner city youth in terms of living conditions and education, the only thing embracing them *is* the streets. The streets are the only thing that has love for them. The streets are the only thing that hugs back when these guys are growing up.

If you listen to these records, these guys will tell you, for most of them it's selling drugs, going to jail or hip hop. Biggie said it the best when he said you either sling (crack) rocks or you got a wicked jump shot. How's that for options? That's all that they have to look forward to growing up. Even though some of their content isn't appropriate for our children, I'd rather they do the music than drugs or jail (I've got no issues with the jumper either). Thank God for small victories. Much to the chagrin of Will Smith, I'd rather have these foul mouthed brothas making records about selling drugs and killing, rather than actually carrying out those acts on our people. We're all a lot safer if some of these guys are in the studio as opposed to on the street corner. We have to repair our situation, but one step at a time.

## *HOLLYWOOD OR HOLIER (THAN THOU) WOOD?*

Speaking of Mr. Smith, our rappers get more of a bad rap than Hollywood does for perpetuating the same things. The violence that's shown to our children on the silver screen is just as bad. How can we justify to our children Arnold Schwarzenegger's killing of hundreds of people in some of his movies, but never facing any jail time? Don't be fooled, our younger children can't tell the difference when Arnold's killing one day, and the next day he's the Governor.

I took issue with Will Smith for something he did a few years ago at the MTV Video Awards. Will won an award in the rap field that year, and in his acceptance speech, he brought up the fact that he didn't have to swear on his records to get his award. Considering the fact that it's an MTV award, from a channel that *used* to be about music until it was turned over to the likes of Ozzy Osborne and Jessica Simpson, I don't know how proud Will should be.

I didn't take issue with what Will actually said. In fact, I agreed with his philosophy. He had previously recorded a song called "Freakin' It" in which he challenged all rappers to say just one verse without a curse word. He was right. I don't know if very many could have at the time, or even now. He was stating something that I've already stated at the beginning of this chapter. There were too many rappers out that were cursing just for the sake of cursing and it was having a negative effect on our children. Where I disagreed with Will was on his timing.

While I had no problem with him putting it on record (because that's how it's done in hip hop) and challenging the hip hop community to clean up its act a little, I disagreed with him putting hip hop on front street on national TV, and in my opinion, trying to appease a white audience. From my point of view, he was tearing down the very thing that made him who he was. He may have made it someday anyway, but the reality is that nobody knows who Will Smith is if he never starts rapping. He never gets *The Fresh Prince of Bel-Air* television show, which served as a springboard to an impressive acting career, if it weren't for his rhyme skills.

Will Smith came from middle class Philly. 90% of the rappers in the industry can't say that they came from middle class anywhere. It didn't make any sense for Will to curse all over his records because the only trouble he ever had in his life was his parents lack of understanding about his Home Alone/McCaulay Culkin-like mishaps as a child. These other guys came from a different place, a place that neither I nor Will can completely identify with, although I may have been a little closer to it than Will.

They come from the ghettos. They come from the projects. These aren't exactly beacons for proper etiquette and grammar. It's the 'hood and that's how they talk. It's not right, but it's reality. It wasn't the right time or place for a hip hop veteran (and even if you don't like Will, that's what he is, and he was good) to take the music to task. A lot of the people that he was talking about were at the ceremony. Be a man and tell them face to face how you feel. Or, better yet, they have hip hop summits every year now. Take a flight from your L.A. mansion, go there and tell these guys how you feel about what they say on record. But make sure you wear a vest. Some of these guys are rappers pretending to be criminals, but some are the other way around.

Although most would never say anything publicly (except for Eminem, of course), I think he pissed off a lot of people in hip hop with that speech. Maybe that was his goal, I don't know, but I didn't think it was right. We as black people need to handle *some* of our disputes in private, away from the public eye. This is our music and we shouldn't use the white media to snipe at one another. If there's a problem with what belongs to us, we need to come together and fix it. Again, that's what the hip hop summit is for. I would've had more respect for what he had to say if he had said it at The Soul Train Awards, or even at The BET Awards. Those are our shows and may have been a more proper and appropriate forum to address this onstage if that's what he wanted to do.

People like Jay-Z and Snoop Dogg were at the MTV awards, sure. However, people like N'Sync, Brittney Spears and Christina Aguilera were also there. Not exactly the most threatening atmosphere. Nothing's jumpin' off at the MTV Awards. Security is tight. Every rapper, whether large or miniscule, attends the Soul Train Awards. In fact, there has been a riot or two that's broken out there, although that's not something our people should be proud of. I would've liked to see him say that there, where *all* of us were present, and then go backstage. Does he even go there anymore? Okay, that wasn't fair. But think about it anyway.

What Will did was a calculated move. He said something to appeal to a mass audience, which is good for a movie career that was still on its way up at the time, while at the same time addressing a legitimate concern in rap music. He tried to play both sides of the fence, but I still feel like he sold us out a little. What I felt that Will perpetuated was an attitude in Hollywood that rap music is not art. Now that he makes $20 million a movie, he can't identify with his rap brethren anymore. However, Ice Cube probably makes the same money because he writes, produces and directs as well, but I've never heard him disrespecting where he came from just to appease Hollywood. It's wrong for rappers to swear in their music because of the message that it sends our children, but it's okay for Will and Martin Lawrence to run around on screen for two hours in *Bad Boys* and *Bad Boys II* shooting people up and cursing like, well, rappers? Oh, but I forgot. They were cops in those movies, those were criminals they were shooting and cinema is art. Shame on me for not remembering. My bad, Will.

Of course, I'm being facetious. In my opinion, there's no difference between Jay-Z cursing throughout his album and Will Smith cursing throughout his movies. It's the same message being sent to our children. In fact, you can almost make an argument that Will is reaching more children than Jay at some points. With his brand of non-threatening music, parents are more likely to buy his albums for their children, thus causing them to identify with him and want to see his movies.

What's that Will? You say some of your movies are Rated R and children are forbidden? Well, that's where parents should come in. Just like they should when they're children are listening to some rap album with a warning sticker on it. You see Will, there really is no difference between you and DMX (for all of you parents that may be reading this, but aren't really up on your hip hop artists, he's another hardcore rapper). In fact, Will's wife, Jada Pinkett-Smith, went to school with 2pac and was one of his biggest fans. How does Will reconcile that? There are contradictions abound here.

In the end, I think that Will and I are feeling the same way about this. It's one thing for rappers to curse because that's how they were brought up and it's all they know. It's another thing when they're cursing just to sell records. It's also another thing when these guys are talking about "street life" when they're millionaires. You may still hang with the same people, but no matter how down you may still wanna be, you no longer share the same struggles as the other brothas. You don't have rent concerns because you own property in two states now. Ice Cube was once asked if he had lost his edge and why he wasn't as angry as he was earlier in his career. He responded by reminding the interviewer how much money he makes doing films in addition to his music now. "What do I have to be angry about?" he responded.

Although Will and I may disagree on his choice of forum to deliver his message, I see him working. I think he was trying to suggest that there be more positive images shown to our children through this medium of rap music. Though I brought up the fact that some of Will's movies have a lot of language and violence in them and he really has no room to chastise anyone, all of his movies aren't that way. For all of his *Bad Boys* movies, which I do enjoy, he's also made excellent movies like *Ali* and *Enemy of the State*, where he more than held his own on screen with an accomplished actor like Gene Hackman.

The point here is that Hollywood is just as culpable as hip hop and R & B music are for contributing to the corruption of the young minds of today. We can't just let them off the hook for what they put on screen for our children to see. They usually use that argument that what they do is art and rap music is just some form of garbage, but I don't see the difference. Depending on your point of view, they're either both garbage or they're both art, and I tend to believe the latter. It's all theater because these rappers are just telling stories, just like Hollywood does.

Hollywood has also used the argument that while children may see what they put on screen for 90 to 120 minutes, rap music is played over and over to our children. There was a time when that argument was true when you factor in the amount of radio time songs get. However, things are different now. With the DVD craze the way it is nowadays, those of us that have children know that our kids can, and sometimes will watch the same movie over and over and over again, day after day after day. So that argument is flawed as well.

Hollywood is filled with the same violence and sex that populates rap and R & B music. At the same time, a lot of the rappers today are now starring in movies. Most of them take the same themes from their music and put them on screen. With the exception of a few (LL Cool J, Ice Cube, Will Smith, 2pac, Queen Latifah), these movies usually resemble nothing more than a 90 minute music video. The same sex, the same violence, the same glorification of money, and that's right up Hollywood's alley. And now that hip hop and the dream factory have gotten into bed with one another, we as parents have to step up our game.

So what are a parent's responsibilities where all of this is concerned? I mean, you can't be with your children 24/7. That being said, there are things that a parent can do to keep these things from completely taking over their children. The first thing that we must do as parents is be part of the solution and not the problem. This goes back to what I spoke about in the last chapter when discussing our willingness to be more of a friend than a parent to our children. When we become aware of what our children are listening to or watching, we shouldn't be so quick to just join in with it.

Like I said, I'm a big fan of hip hop. I also love movies. Some of my favorite series include all of the *Beverly Hills Cops* movies, all of the *Lethal Weapon* movies, all of the *Matrix* movies and any movie with Robert De Niro in it, so you know there's bound to be some language and violence there. However, when my son was 5 or 6, he wasn't going to be sitting right next to me while I watched all of this language and violence being played out on the screen.

There are some that would suggest that allowing him to see and experience these things is better for him. There are some that would say that by shielding him, I'm making him vulnerable to the ways of the world. While you can't completely shut your children off from these things and you might want to allow them some leeway, it should always be when they're a little bit older and lot more able to discern fiction from reality. In short, they should be able to handle and understand what they're seeing and it should be given to them in moderation.

Now that Hollywood and hip hop have formed this marriage, they've taken what was imagination as far as lyrics and content in the music, and made it visually real for our children to see. As I said before, it's nothing but a long music video now. I would like to see Hollywood be a little more responsible about the stuff that they put out, but since that probably won't happen, it's up to us as parents to monitor our children's entertainment intake. Now, I'll give rapper DMX a free pass because the movies that he makes, though violent, are nothing more than action flicks that actors like Wesley Snipes or Bruce Willis make all the time. Though not as good, they're along the lines of the *Lethal Weapon* movies that I've watched. But when we have movies like *Baby Boy*, that stars R & B artist Tyrese, I wonder what we're trying to prove or say to our children.

Now, maybe I didn't get this movie because I don't come from South Central, L.A. like the movie's director John Singleton does, but I felt that he took a good idea and a good message and completely screwed it up. Unlike his masterpieces *Boyz N The Hood* and *Higher Learning*, the emphasis on sex added nothing to the social commentary and message that it seemed he was trying to get across. It seems that Tyrese's character "Jody" saw the solutions to all of his problems in his penis. Every time he had a problem, the solution seemingly was to go and have sex with his girl or his other baby's mama. If there was a message in that, I completely missed it.

In fact, even his mother had that problem as she was willing to put everything in her life on hold for a man that had been in and out of jail, almost got her sent up by growing weed in her backyard (and she instantly forgave him), but was obviously good in bed (or in the hallway; if you saw that movie, you know what scene I'm talking about). I guess that's where Jody got it from.

Well, maybe I did understand that movie. Maybe not. I don't know, but the point is, I've known parents that will allow their children to sit up and watch this movie. A movie where you have sex, or references to it, in just about half of the scenes. A movie where there's all sorts of gun violence (and of course it's black on black crime). A movie where you have Snoop Dogg's character cursing out a small child and just about raping the boy's mother right in front of him. A movie where you have a nude Ving Rhames cooking breakfast, for God's sake. That alone is something that our young children don't need to see.

The bottom line is, whether I understand what Singleton was trying to get across or not, this isn't a child's movie. It's an adult's movie. Even though it's based in reality, and I respect that, it's a bit much for our young children to handle without possibly being influenced the wrong way. I know that in the end, Jody survived and everything was okay, but he also played a role in taking another young black man's life, and it doesn't matter if he saw himself as right or wrong in the equation. Who's to say where a child watching this movie sees himself?

If a child sees himself as Jody in this movie and he takes the life of Snoop's character (basically in self defense), I guess we see it as all good. But what if he sees himself as Snoop's character? There are a lot of corrupt young men out here that don't see themselves as wrong in how they're living. Maybe I missed it, but I don't know that the line was properly defined in the movie. It's like we just told a story about some stuff that happens in the 'hood from day to day, but we never actually focused on a moral of any kind. It was a story of survival. Again, maybe I did get this movie. I guess I just didn't agree with the lack of a defined message. I didn't need to see *Boyz N The Hood II*, but there should've been something other than the struggle. If we're not struggling to gain something, then what are we struggling for?

There are some of our young men that will watch that movie and see Snoop's character as a hero, and Jody as soft. Throw in the fact that Snoop Dogg is a favorite among young people that listen to rap (Hollywood's marketing to the young people), and they may identify and sympathize with him and miss the point all together. Even though I was 22 when *Boyz N The Hood* came out, those lines on the screen at the end of the movie bothered me initially. They said that two weeks after Ice Cube's character "Doughboy" killed a young black man out of revenge for his own brother's death, he too was gunned down.

It bothered me because I was connected to Ice Cube through his music and he was my favorite rapper at the time. But I was old enough to understand that the artist that I revered so much wasn't being killed, it was Doughboy, the character in the movie. There was nothing left for a young man like Doughboy but death or jail. Young boys watching these movies won't be able to negotiate these things the way that adults do. Adult situations in music and film are for adults, plain and simple.

We as parents can't be a part of this deconstructing of our children. We can't go out and spend money to buy movies like *Baby Boy* for our children. Again, it's an adult film and I'm not saying that we as adults can't enjoy the film, but we can't buy it, sit our children down in front of it and walk away. Even if you have a well adjusted and intelligent teenager in your home, you should watch a movie like that *with* the child so that the message, whatever it may be, isn't lost among your child's admiration for the stars of the movies.

I know that some may see what I'm saying as going against our black filmmakers, but read my words carefully and understand what I'm saying. I think that John Singleton is a brilliant director and his heart as far as *Baby Boy* is concerned was in the right place. It's the parents that I'm speaking to. I believe that even John would tell you that young kids that aren't mentally developed yet shouldn't watch this movie without an adult to clarify some of the points that he may have made in the film. We needn't be leery of the filmmakers as much as we should be of Hollywood in general and how it views black people.

It's not lost on me that Denzel Washington had to play a crooked cop before he could win an Oscar. *Training Day* was a great film and Denzel did give an Oscar-worthy performance, no doubt. The fact that Denzel always plays a straight character in movies, and made such a wonderful turn in *Training Day* speaks to his ability as an actor and is what made it an Oscar-worthy performance. But Denzel just about always gives one of those. *Malcolm X* comes to mind. *Crimson Tide* comes to mind. But he can't get it when he's playing a progressive black leader or an intelligent naval officer. He has to be crooked, just like they see us, in order to get what he's deserved for years.

## *THAT IS THE JAM, THOUGH...*

It's hard for parents not to get hooked into watching these types of movies or listening to certain music with our children. The reason being, the generation gap isn't what it used to be. I think for the first time in history parents just about universally have music in common with their children. Because even those of us between the ages of 30 and 40 were raised on hip hop and it's still prevalent in our children's lives. We actually have music in common, unlike my generation and our parents. So because we are all listening to the same songs for the first time in history, it's hard for us to tell our children to turn that song off when it's our jam too. But just because it's hard doesn't mean that we can't do it.

I'm not stupid enough to believe that my son has never listened to any of the hardcore rap that his old man has been prone to listen to, but what's important to me is that he's not riding down the street *with me*, listening to it blaring out of my speakers. I want him to understand the same way that I did when I was growing up that even if he's gonna listen to things that I'd prefer he not listen to until he's older, he's gonna have to do it on the low, just like we did.

My older brothers introduced me to Prince and I don't know if my mother really wanted it that way. And my oldest brother, who was the biggest offender in this, started me off with *Dirty Mind*, one of Prince's raunchiest albums, as you could probably tell from the title. That album was released when I was about 11 years old and I had no business listening to it. There were things being said on there that an 11 year old wasn't supposed to hear. I'm 100% sure that my mother never had at that point or still hasn't to this day heard this album. If she had, we all would've been dealt with.

I still remember when Prince followed up his *Dirty Mind* album with *Controversy*. At that time is his career, controversy wasn't just a word to Prince, it was a description of his work. It was like a suggestion. As if someone said "Go out and create…". The last song on *Controversy* was a little ditty called "Jack U Off". That's our boy Prince, he says what he feels. That's the kind of song you want your 12 year old listening to, I'm sure.

My mother may not remember this story, but I remember one night I was playing this song aloud in the house as my mother sat on the porch watching TV with her soon-to-be husband. When my mom heard this song coming out of her living room, she just about lost it, I'm sure. I heard her yell from the porch, "Turn that off!" Thinking that my mother was just being a mother that just didn't understand or get "my music", I proceeded to turn it *down*. When she heard that it was still playing, she again yelled with a little more conviction, "I said turn that record off!" I angrily turned my record off and stormed off to my room. If Will Smith had recorded the song at that point, I would've no doubt been in my room ranting about how parents just don't understand.

The point is that I had no idea what that terminology meant, thus I was so stupid that I didn't even realize that I was offending my mother with that song. That's what a lot of our children do on a day to day basis. They listen to things over and over again, not understanding or grasping the full scope of what's being put into their minds subconsciously about any number of things. That's where we as parents have to step in, just like my mother did.

She did her job as a parent. She demanded that I respect her by turning it off. She didn't get up and come into the house and join in with me. She understood the role of parent and the role of child. There was a point when my mother listened to Millie Jackson a lot, and if you know Millie, you know that she was the pre-cursor to the 'Lil Kim's and Foxy Brown's of the world. However, my mother never blasted Millie's raunchier material all through the house for her kids to hear. She understood that it was adult music for adults, so she never included her children in any of that.

We have to understand that the artists aren't going to sensor themselves, and nor should they. If we take away their right to free speech in this country, I couldn't write this book. There's been plenty written in these pages that a lot of people will disagree with, but because we have free speech in this country, I can say what I want and these artists should have that same right. We as parents should instead sensor our children. We have to start parenting. It's a little different than it used to be, but the same principles still apply. Don't be afraid to go through their record or movie collection and take out anything that you feel shouldn't be there.

Are you gonna stop them from listening to or watching these things? Of course not. As long as there are parents out there that don't see anything wrong with their 10 year old listening to or watching whatever they please, our kids will be exposed to some of this stuff. But they must be made to understand that what they do in the streets will not be tolerated at home. If you set some of those boundaries and rules, you'll provide them with balance. Remember, they may stray from the path that we set for them, but if you give them the right tools, they can find their way back home. They may listen to a song about gunplay, drug selling or drug abuse, but they may realize that they come from a better place than the artists on these songs and though those artists may be telling their own compelling stories, it's not where all of us come from and all of us don't have to resort to such things. To quote Jay-Z from his song "Izzo": *"Hov is back/Life stories told through rap/Niggas actin' like I sold you crack/Like I told you, "Sell drugs"/ No, Hov did that/So, hopefully, you won't have to go through that"*.

Hip hop is great in the sense that it lets our children know that there's a world outside their front door. It helps them to appreciate what they have at home, because some don't have it so great and have to do some unsavory things in the streets just to survive. It makes them aware of the struggle that some of our people have to go through on a daily basis. At the same time, it will poison the mind of some of our youth because there aren't enough positives being presented these days.

There's too much emphasis placed on material things and street life in the music. It used to be a way for our people to express themselves and voice our concerns on any number of topics. It has now become a way for us to brag and boast about our material and carnal conquests, whether real or imaginary. We do this through our music and through the videos that we make. We teach our young men that life is all about big houses, cars and jewelry that make no real sense and sleeping with as many women as you possible can. We teach our young women that it's okay to put all that God has given them on the television screen, all to the glorification of some rapper and a seemingly adoring public. I wonder how some of these rappers will feel if their daughters grow up to be someone's "video hoe".

Now, on the record, some of them will tell you that they won't hate the playa, they'll hate the game. They'll say that if she allows it to happen, then it's on her. True pimps. Remember what I said, the credo is that even if you have to pimp your own mother, then you have to do what you have to do. They'll tell you that they make enough money to provide their daughters with enough so that she'll never have to do something like that. As if the mothers and fathers of these girls didn't somehow make a way for their daughters so that they wouldn't have to do some of these things. It's amazing how we still think that money is the answer to everything. You may be able to buy your daughter a lot of things, but self esteem and brains aren't two of them. Either they get those things from you or they don't get them.

If these artists think that their being rich will make their children less aware of the fact that they objectify women, then they're just as confused as the women dancing in their videos. Of course these guys are lying. We never think about how we've treated someone else's daughter until we have one of our own. And we all say things like "If she allows it to happen to her, then it's on her". But the first time your baby girl comes home crying because some loser has mistreated her, you'll get your gun (but I hope you don't use it). Hip hop has to be more responsible for the images and ideals that we put forth for our children. Like it or not, these are all our children. You may not believe that's your daughter on that video screen just because you've got money to provide her with a better life, but we all should know by now that people with money are more times than not more screwed up than us "common folk".

Both the hip hop community and parents have to come together and fix this problem. What's being spoken in hip hop these days has a lot to with what's going on in society. If we could change the conditions of what's going on in our neighborhoods, then these guys wouldn't have anything to talk about. And whether we believe it or not, there are a lot of hip hop artists that actually want it that way. Some of these guys don't want to talk about what they talk about, but they can't change the fact that it's still going on in their neighborhoods.

We still have an insane amount of drugs coming into this country through our own government. That's not the fault of the hip hop artists. We still have corrupt police departments in this country that will beat and arrest our young men just for having a better life than they do. That's not the fault of the hip hop artists. We still have liquor stores on every corner that are there to keep our people drunk, disoriented and never moving forward. That's not the fault of the hip hop artists. It's not their fault that these things exists and that some of them are byproducts of some of these things, but I applaud them for bringing them to the forefront so that we all become aware of what's happening in the black community.

What I do blame them for is their glorification of things that were designed to keep us as black people down. I do blame them for committing entertainment genocide, if you will, on their own people, all in the name of money. It's one thing to talk about your struggles in the 'hood and what you had to do to feed your family and how you had to do what was seemingly so difficult because that's the only way that you knew to survive. What I don't understand is the continued glorification of this life once you've become a multi-platinum selling rap star and have moved out of the 'hood to the suburbs, while you're still talking about the "struggle".

There is no more "struggle" when you live in a mansion. At least not the way it used to be. Now your struggle is to stay on top. Even though it's all a hustle, I think there is a difference. Now, the hip hoppers that may be reading this will say to me that I don't know what I'm talking about and I don't understand. They say that they're representing for their brothas that are still in the struggle. How 'bout this, instead of dropping half a mil on a Bentley, or $100 thousand on a chain, how 'bout starting a business or two in the 'hood and letting the brothas run it? How 'bout giving them jobs so that they don't have to exist in the "struggle" any more?

We kinda mocked MC Hammer for doing that same thing because he went broke doing it. Although he could've been smarter about it, he had the right idea. Rather than continuing to run in the same circles with the same people, he tried to give them responsibilities and real jobs. Once he got out, he came back and tried to bring them out with him. There's no doubt some of these brothas have business skills. If you think that you don't need business sense to run a neighborhood drug ring, you are sadly mistaken. These are some smart brothas, they just need their energies pointed in the right direction. You'd think that no one would understand this better than the hip hop artists. After all, the same was true about them once upon a time.

We as parents need to remember how we were brought up. Our parents were always in our business. If they saw us watching something that we had no business watching, we had to change the channel, and sometimes we had to turn the TV off completely. After my little incident with the Prince song, I became more than aware that my mother was listening, even when I thought she wasn't. It wasn't that she thought I would never listen to Prince again, and anybody who knows me knows that I was never shy about that. But she wanted me to have some respect for the position that she held. She was my mama. If I were gonna play Prince's songs around her, they'd better be the clean ones. We have to protect our children in the same way that our parents protected us. I know we'd all like to share in some of these things with our children, but sometimes it's not good for them. They don't know any better, but we should.

One the proudest moments of my life was when my son took a liking to Michael Jackson's music, another artist that I was a huge fan of growing up. After not being able to understand his fixation with the likes of N'Sync and The Backstreet Boys, it was nice to have something musically in common with my son, considering how much I love music. After that, nothing made me prouder than the day he walked into my room and said, "Dad, will you buy me a *Musicology* CD (which was Prince's latest CD at the time)?

I don't know what made me happier, the fact that my son had taken a liking to my favorite artist of all time or the fact that Prince had made a CD that I could actually buy for my son without worrying about what he might hear coming from the speakers. It's no surprise that he would learn to like Prince, as over the years, through careful filtering on my part, he has kind of grown up on his music. Contrary to popular belief, Prince has quite a few songs that are child-safe. However, I won't be dropping *Dirty Mind* in my son's lap anytime soon.

I also won't be allowing him access to my hip hop collection anytime soon. Like I said before, if he wants to hear some of that music, he'll have to do it on the low like I did. Even though my son will hear some of this music regardless, I think it's important that he didn't hear it from his dad. I think I have a little more of his respect because I didn't provide him with some of this material. I think it will matter that I waited until he was a little older and a little better prepared for some of these things. Parents have to protect their children in that same way. Our children don't understand that having exposure to some of these songs and images without any positive balance to it can be harmful.

Hip hop is a contradiction. It's a contradiction that exists in all forms of music, but I'm speaking to hip hop because that's what our children identify with the most. If you ever want to upset a 2pac fan, point out his contradictions. His fans try to elevate him above all because of his vision and due to his premature death. 2pac was a great artist, but he was bigger that just hip hop. He possessed a vision that was rare for a man not only in hip hop, but in general. But his contradictions can't be ignored.

For every "Brenda's Got A Baby", a song about teen pregnancies, something that was and still is prevalent in the black community, there was an "I Get Around", a song about a whorish man that didn't have the time to wait for you to decide whether or not you wanted to sleep with him because he had other women to hit. For every "Keep Your Head Up", a song about instilling pride in our black women and telling them to keep their heads up through all of the trials of life and absent baby daddy's that they've had to deal with, there was a "How Do You

Want It?", a song about, well, see "I Get Around". For every "Changes", there was a "Toss It Up", and so on and so on.

That's not a knock on 2pac. It's a contradiction that exists in all of us. It's just that 2pac *fans* tend to walk around as though the man wasn't human and as if he were a god. We need to be careful how we worship one another. 2pac would've told you himself that he was just a man. Check out the documentary-style film "Tupac: Resurrection" if you get a chance. He was very well aware of his contradictions, his vulnerabilities, his weaknesses, his strengths, and in a very eerie way, his own mortality. His fans will thrust that god-like status upon him, but I don't feel that he ever asked for that. He was just speaking his brilliant mind. There's no more proof that he was human that the fact that he's unfortunately no longer with us. The contradiction that existed in him was also evident in Prince. I never saw a man talk about sex and God so often in the same breath the way that he did. Considering the fact that he was single at the time, this was a contradiction.

It's even evident now in "accused" child molester R. Kelly. After "allegedly" having sex with a minor and urinating on her, he's unleashed a rash of happy, God-loves-everybody-even-if-they-are-a-child molester-type songs. I'm wondering where his god was when it was time to check ID. And, sadly enough, we've continued to support this man.

Now, I'm not saying that we shouldn't forgive our people when they do wrong, but don't they have to admit the wrongdoing first? A lot of us have thrust our forgiveness on R. Kelly when he didn't ask for it, or at least he hasn't in interview form. But in song, doesn't he seem rather apologetic for an innocent man? To quote Arsenio Hall, "Things that make you go hmmmmm". A lot of us have said to ourselves on the way to the counter to pay for our CD's, "It's no big deal. You can't stay mad forever". But I'll ask you the same question that I've ask everybody when discussing Mr. Kelly: How would you feel if that were your daughter, sister, niece or even a friend of your family that he was urinating on? It's amazing how that snaps people into reality.

The saddest thing is the fact that we selfishly only feel bad for things that happens to us, our families or people that we know. As a community, we should've been outraged, but instead we made him platinum again and again. All because he made a good ballroom song. Is it only odd to me that he calls himself the "pied piper of R & B"? Do you remember the story of the pied piper? Does it strike anyone else as odd that he'd pick a children's story? Are our children the mice that he's leading away with his magic flute or whatever that dude had in that story? But because he's good at what he does, we turn the other cheek. If he were some guy down the street that we had never benefited from knowing, we'd want him under the jail before he got our kids. But we think we're safe because he's R. Kelly. But remember folks, he goes on tour.

I'm sorry, I got lost there. Did it seem like I had convicted R. Kelly? Did it seem like I had him guilty before proven innocent? Did it seem that after over-whelming video evidence, I refused to believe his Eddie Murphy-esque assertion that "it wasn't me"? In the name of fairness, R, Kelly is innocent until proven guilty and these are only "allegations". No matter what I saw on that tape or the fact that it really, really, really, really, really looks like him on that tape, an R. Kelly look-alike could've very well broken into his house, a house that was pro-filed on BET's "How I'm Livin'", so we're sure it's his house, and made several incriminating video tapes, all in the name of framing him. It's a bigger frame job than O.J. We mustn't rush to judgment. We must allow him to pay off the jur…, I mean, have his day in court. Let us let the wheels of justice turn. Or, I guess if you're R., you don't really want "justice". You'd rather just see what happens.

I apologize for that detour. I appreciate you guys for indulging me. Getting back to the kids, we need to better monitor their intake of all these images that exist these days. We have to stop blaming the artists for what they put out. These people are entertainers, trying to earn a living. Even though I don't completely agree with all that they do and say to earn that living, I'd be a little upset if they came on my job and tried to stop me from doing what I do for a living because they didn't agree with it. What they're doing isn't illegal, it just requires us to be better at our job as parents.

Believe it or not, they do have some things to teach our children. You just have to weed through a lot to find those messages. That's what parenting is all about. Being involved enough in your own children's lives so that what they lis-ten to and what the watch isn't a surprise to you. We need to make sure that they know Algebra just as well as they know Nelly's rhymes. Strangely enough, we need to be more like Tipper. It's harder than it used to be, but if you love your children, no amount of work is too much.

Most of the artists that I've referenced throughout this chapter have my respect. I'm fans of theirs and I own a lot of their music. These are very gifted, young black men. I hate the fact that sometimes their content takes away from their gifts, but such is the life of the hip hop star. I've referenced Prince so often because he's the only mainstream artist that I've seen that's gone through some-thing similar. So often, his content overshadowed his ability. I've always noticed that parallel between Prince and hip hop. Nevermind what critics and the media say, these are some the most talented young black people that we have around (and Eminem too; didn't mean to exclude you, but, you know…).

If you've listened to a Jay-Z, a Biggie or a 2pac, you could sometimes hear some of the regrets that they have about the life that they lived before earning their millions and about some of the images that they present to our children. Artists like that, in conjunction with the likes of Common, The Roots, Talib Kweli and Mos Def, just to name a select few, gave hip hop a conscience again. When you consider that 2 of the rappers that I just mentioned are dead, and Jay has claimed he's retiring, I wonder where hip hop is headed and what will be said to our children next. Although we have a brave new soul in Kanye West (although a *little* humility would be nice), and a group like Outkast that's threatening to lead hip hop into more non-threatening and more creative places that talk about things other than how much jewelry they own or how many women they slept with last night, I can't help but wonder if anyone will be following them.

# 8

## *The mission is the message*

When I decided to write this book, I had no idea that I had so much to say. By not knowing how much I had to say, I had no idea what I would say to end it. We've gone through so many things in this book and I think that I've said as much as I could say without making this a 20 chapter book. This has been an incredible journey for me. I've often questioned myself about why I was writing this book at all. I often wondered if anyone out there would even care about what I had to say. However, there were a couple of my friends that offered me encouragement and told me to keep writing. I also felt that God required me to say something, if for no other reason, just to leave something behind for my son. I felt that I was required to leave my mark on this place in another form besides the life I helped to create.

My friends also reminded me of why I was writing it. There were some things that I was seeing in the youth of today that were disturbing. Some of these children and young adults I just happened to know, some of these things I would see on the news and, quite frankly, some of these things were within my own family. If no one but my loved ones reads these words, then it was worth it. I felt that it was time for me to at least try and create some sort of legacy for myself. I had all of these thoughts in my head about the current state of the black community, and just like a lot of us, I started to become aware of my own mortality once I reached my 30's.

Now, I don't want any of my loved ones to become concerned as I talk about death. Unfortunately, I'll be around for a little while longer to miss family meetings, react nonchalantly to things that you say and to be the last one to arrive and the first to leave at family functions. I'll still be around to be me. This is just something that most people go through when they reach their 30's. They come to the realization that they're going to die, and they start to evaluate their lives. They ask themselves, "What have I done with my life?" But in addition to that, I asked myself "What kind of legacy have I left for my son?" Not really sure up to this point, I decided to write this book.

I wondered if I could really do it, and yet here we are in the final chapter. Although I had my doubts at some points, I'm proud of the fact that I never stopped writing. There were things that just needed to be said. Sometimes, I felt that the devil didn't want me to say what I felt I had to say. But in the end, I couldn't allow myself to leave this earth with so many unspoken thoughts in my head. It's been an incredible journey and I thank God for it. I thank Him for the strength that He gave me to battle whatever demons I faced that may have caused me to question whether or not I can do this. It's been a lot of work, but it's been more of a blessing.

I feel like I've talked to everyone that I wanted to talk to, so in some ways, I don't really know what else to say. But I'll give it a try. I'll use this chapter to talk to everyone. I'll use this final hour to share my views on where we should go from here as a people. I'll use these final pages to talk directly to our youth and tell them what's expected of them, and also to tell them how much we really love them and want them to do well. I want our young people to know and understand that they are the future and that no matter how far we may have already come as a people, there's still a long, long way to go and we expect them to go further than we did.

I want to speak to the adults of the world today. I want us to understand that just because we're grown, that doesn't mean that our work is finished. We not only have the responsibility of raising our children, but we must show them how to grow old gracefully. We must leave them an inheritance, but not just in the monetary or real estate sense. We must leave them an inheritance of knowledge. We must leave them something worth continuing. We must leave them a tradition worth carrying on. We must leave them a legacy.

## "I GET IT FROM MY MAMA…"

I was raised in a single parent home by a wonderful woman, Mrs. Annie Jackson-Loritts. My mom had six children of her own, and she also raised one of my cousins. I was the last of her children to be born, and after I got here, she decided to go back to school and get her college degree. There were times when I know for a fact that it got rough on her. Rooted in God and His Word, my mother always found a way to provide for her children. All that she couldn't do on her own, she will tell you that somehow, God made a way. She would also tell you that through Him, she gained the strength to do all that she did do.

It was something that was imbedded in her from a very young age and she never forgot it. As the song says, "God is the joy and the strength of my life". That's how my mother lived then, still lives now, and that's how she wanted her children to live. Through her beliefs, she was able to lead us in wise directions. Through her beliefs, she was able to make the necessary sacrifices so that she could realize her vision of what her children were going to be. There were so many people (some within our own family) that felt that we wouldn't amount to anything because our fathers were absent. But just like a lot of people in life, we all made it on our mama's prayers.

Working to support her family while going to school so that she could better herself wasn't easy on her. Like most children, I never fully realized the sacrifices that she made for us until I was an adult. However, through all the hard work and sacrifices that she made to provide us with a roof over our heads, my mother never skimped on the necessary discipline that it took to raise her children. She never let up on the morals and values that she believed in. She never let the fact that our fathers were absent deter her from raising her children the right way. She never made excuses for herself, so that meant that she wouldn't accept any from us.

She had four boys and three girls (one girl being my cousin). Of course she had some help along the way from my uncles, but there was no doubt that my mother was doing the job of a mother and a father. She was also helped by the fact that she could count on my oldest brother to pitch in. He was the closest thing to a father that I ever had. I'm sure that my other brothers feel the same way. Armed with the word of God, my mother set out to show us the way that we were supposed to live. Though it's always difficult for a woman to raise boys on her own, my mother proved to me that it can be done if you approach it with some persistence. She showed me that if you set rules and boundaries for your children and never waver, you can most times make them into what you want them to be. Productive, law abiding members of society.

One of the most important things that my mother taught me was what a strong woman is supposed to be about. I've known many women that I would consider strong, but there has never been a woman in my life that compares to my mother. Her willingness to lay herself down in order to raise up her children is like nothing I've ever seen. I know there are a lot of you reading this book that can say the same about your mothers, so you know what a blessing they can be.

With the exception of my oldest brother, all of us went to private school at one point or another. Some of my siblings were under the impression that she had more money than she actually did, but as I stated before, once we all became adults, we realized that it wasn't so. There was a time very early on in my life when we were poor, but due to my mother's sacrifices, we never knew it. There was always food on the table and clothes on our backs. It seems as though she were some sort of budgeting guru. That was only half the story. Although my mother learned to stretch a dollar, she had something much more powerful on her side. She had God.

For as long as I can remember, I've been in church. I don't ever remember a time when I wasn't. Spirituality and the Word of God has always been something of major importance to my family. I've been a member of Zion Hill Baptist Church of Detroit, Michigan all of my life. Most of what I've written in this book as it relates to God has been from a Christian perspective. For those of you that are reading this that aren't of the Christian persuasion, it is my hope that if you choose to, you'll still be able to apply some of these things to your life. Though we may all be cut from different religious cloths, I'm pretty sure that none of us are serving a God that doesn't want us to prosper and to love one another. It's all about love of self, love for our fellow man and love of life. But these things can only be achieved if we keep God first in our lives.

When I was just a toddler, my mother was my Sunday School teacher. As a child in church, Sunday School was where you learned a lot of your fundamentals as far as church is concerned. That's the time when you can get as much of a child's undivided attention in church as possible. Expecting children to listen to the sermon once service started is pretty much wishful thinking. But if you can reach those kids during those 45 minutes or so that you have them in that Sunday School class, you could really impart some wisdom onto them. Since my mother is so good with children and possesses that wisdom, I learned a lot at an early age.

I remember us being in the back room of that small church that we had on Livingston in Detroit, and when God blessed us with another church, we were in the basement of that church. As vivid as my memories are of those churches, what's more vivid are the lessons that my mother imparted upon me in that back room and in that basement. In Sunday School class was where I first learned what God wanted us to do in relation to our fellow man. It was something that my mother had always tried to teach to her children in the home, but in church is where she brought it to me in the name of God. That's where my mother explained to me and many other wide-eyed children about The Golden Rule and how God wants us to treat one another. It's a message that we've all heard before:

*And as ye would that men should do to you, do ye also to them likewise.*
*—Luke 6:31*

Now I know these days as a society we have a different spin on this. Rather than do unto others as you would have them do unto you, we've decided that we'll do unto others as they do unto us. Of course, that's not always pretty as sometimes what's done to us isn't particularly nice. However, as you just read, that's not what God wants us to do. Though at times I've put into practice the street theory of giving it back like I got it, I've found that like everything else in life, God's way is the best way. However, what I didn't realize as a child was that my mother was trying to give me a foundation. She was trying to teach me a lesson that I could use throughout my life. She was trying to ensure that good would follow her baby boy throughout his life.

Also, having six to seven kids under one roof meant that a lesson like that was extremely important to get across. Learning to treat others as you want to be treated should always start at home. The lessons we learn, and sometimes don't learn at home are usually translated into our everyday lives as we grow up. If you've got six kids in the house and you're trying to live by the Golden Rule, they should get plenty of practice.

Treating others as we want to be treated is one of the harder things we'll have to do in our lives. One reason for that is that on a lot of occasions, it requires us to do something for someone that hasn't done anything for us. Whether you're helping a stranger on the street, helping out a local charity or maybe helping out a family member that probably never has or never would do anything for you, you have to step out on faith and do what's right. All based on the simple fact that we would want someone to do the same for us.

I can't count the number of times I've watched the news and saw some tornado or fire victim on the TV receiving help from the Red Cross. A lot of times, when interviewed, you'd find that this person has donated to the Red Cross in the past, never realizing that one day they would actually be the ones in need. People like that usually give out of the goodness of their hearts, looking to help someone else. But through their good works, they were blessed when they needed it most. That's the pretense under which we should all be giving. Out of the goodness of our hearts. You never know when that blessing will come back around. However, so many of us give only to get something in return.

Throughout my short time here on earth, I've tried to apply some of these principles to my life. Things like the joy of giving and doing it unselfishly. What's lost on a lot of us is the joy that there actually is in giving. That's supposed to be our immediate reward. The feeling that you get when you've helped someone in their time of need. The fact that you were blessed enough at the time to be able to help that person in their time of need should make you feel good. I know that message sounds very "flower power" and you're expecting me to break out into some 60's generation, Peter, Paul and Mary folk song, but those principles must be re-established in our lives today.

There are so many of us out here these days that are blessed, but would never do anything for anybody unless we could get some tangible returns for it. That feeling of knowing that you've helped someone isn't enough. The idea that our blessing is coming soon for what we have done isn't enough. Once we've done something for someone else, we want our blessing and we want it now! We're too impatient to wait on God to do His business. We check Him everyday for our return blessing like a welfare recipient checks the mail on the 1st and the 15th. And if He doesn't bless us like we feel we should be blessed, we then look to the person that we originally supplied the help to, especially if that help was in monetary form. Bottom line, somebody's gonna return this blessing the way we see fit or there's gonna be hell to pay.

It's that kind of selfishness that's torn our families, communities, our countries and this world apart. No one wants to do anything for anybody anymore. Not unless there's something besides a good feeling in it for us. There are many reasons for this. There's money, there's greed, and there's the fact that there are so many people out here these days that are users. That makes us cautious when considering helping someone. What's usually lost on us is how we would feel if the situation were reversed.

We usually lose sight of how we would feel if we needed help and we knew someone that was in the position to help us and they refused because helping you wouldn't benefit them in any way. And on other occasions, it requires us to turn the other cheek, which is very difficult for all of us to do. Like a lot of things that we do in life, it requires us to have faith. Faith is always a tough thing to have in a situation like this because we have to blindly believe that we're doing the right thing without any clear proof or evidence that we are.

To bring it all back, my mother is one of the most giving individuals I've ever known. There are any number of children that are walking this earth right now that consider my mother a mother figure to them. She always gave to others that were less fortunate than us. I think she did it because she could remember when she was in that same position. Some of us forget where we came from, but my mother not only avoided that mentality, she made sure that we remembered as well. So often we had to share our mother with other children and it wasn't always easy, especially for me because I was the baby and I was very close to my mother. But the lesson that was being taught to me was about sharing.

We had to share some of our belongings, we had to share some of our food and we had to share our mother. She had a greater mission that we sometimes didn't understand, but we were better for having to go through what we did. I don't think that any of us has ever given to the same degree that my mother has, but all of us are generous in nature because of what she passed on to us.

How we were raised has a definite impact on how we will treat others in life. One of the ways in which we can help our children succeed in future relationships and in life is by teaching them the importance of giving. By making our children understand that there is power, as well as blessings in giving to others, we teach them about sharing and we improve their ability to compromise. A lot of what I've talked about so far in this book in terms of relationships can be broken down to our inability sometimes to share with our partners, as well as compromise when it's necessary.

Something else my mother gave us was a sense of family and how important family should be to you. My mother knows just about everything there is to know about our family. If you want to know who came from what part of our family, she's the one that you wanna ask. One year, through tireless research efforts, she traced our family's history so that she could make a family tree for our reunion. Not only did she feel it was necessary to have this history on file for the reunion, she felt it was necessary so that future generations of our family would have as accurate a record as possible of our family's history.

She never told me this, but I got the sense that as a leader in our family, she felt it was important to do something like that. She had learned so many things about this family from my grandmother, my great grandmother and many of her aunts and uncles, that she felt it was worth it to preserve this knowledge and leave her imprint on this family. I guess you could say that she did it for the same reason that I wrote this book. She refused to leave here with so much history inside of her. She wanted it to be available for future generations.

There have been many before mother that has held a position of leadership in this family. For example, my grandmother was always an excellent cook and it was never on display more than it was each Thanksgiving. After my grandmother got to the point where she couldn't maintain that status at the yearly family gathering, slowly, but surely, my mother took on that role, with the assistance of my sisters.

It may not seem to some, but my mother is unquestionably the leader of our family. But it doesn't stop there for her. She's constantly trying to pass some of these things off to her children and her grandchildren. To this point, I can say that my mother has built a legacy for all of us. But she hasn't stopped there. What good is having a legacy, if it's not going to be carried on after you're gone?

Though my mother's in good health, she reminds all of us that she won't be around forever. I think for that reason, she's tried to prepare us all each day. She doesn't want the traditions of the Flowers family to go when she does. Just like the leaders that came before us, she wants us to carry this thing on. She wants the next generation to take this thing to the next level. It is my hope that we won't let her down. I've said it before in this book, and I'll say it again now: I owe everything that I am to this wonderful woman and all that she has taught me. All that has come out of me in this book is a direct result of her wisdom and her teachings. I salute you my dear mother for all that you've done for us and continue to do 'til this day. I just hope that we can all live up to the high standard that you've set for us all.

## *OUR WORK IS NEVER DONE*

Something else that my mother has done for us is showing us how we're supposed to progress in this life. In some of the previous chapters, I've talked about what kind of role models we're supposed to present to our children as they're growing up. But what I haven't touched on is what kind of role models we're supposed to be after our children have already grown up. Some of us don't realize it, but parenting goes on even after your children have grown up. There are still some areas in which they need guidance. Hopefully, our children will grow old as we all hope to do. However, we should all know by now that there's growing old, and then there's growing old gracefully.

We have to understand that everywhere that our children will go in life, we'll probably go there first. We have to continue to do our job as parents even after they've become adults and are no longer "technically" our responsibility. We have to teach our young ladies what it means to be a woman of style, dignity and grace. We must show our young men what it means to be a real and responsible man after they've achieved adulthood. As usual, there are a lot of ways in which this can be done. Some we're all aware of and some we aren't. Here's to hoping that we can put some of these things into practice.

So many times in the black community these days, we tell our children that once they reach the age of 18, they're on their own. Some of us just don't want the responsibility beyond that point, and that's sad. Others say that because that's the way that their parents did them. No matter which theory you subscribe to, if you honestly think back to when you were 18, you'll remember that you were in no way, shape or form ready for the real world. This doesn't mean only the problem children that we have in the world today that are forced out into the real world due to premature parenting. This is true with all of our children.

We must continue to be there for our children, even in their adult years. They're going to face some things as they go through their 20's and 30's that they're not prepared for, and we need to be there for that. Looking after your children does change when they become adults, but if you truly love them, it never really ends. We must continue to be on guard for our children until the day that they have to be on guard for us. Even though I'm only in my mid 30's, I can't imagine that the feeling will change even at that point. We must begin to present to them an older and more responsible figure in their lives. Even after our children become adults, they still aspire to be something that we can be proud of. In a lot of ways, they're still aspiring to be like us. We still have to give them something to aspire to, even in our older age.

We can't continue to run the streets like we used to in our younger days either. I'm not saying that you can't get out anymore, but all of that hanging out until 3 and 4am should go away at some point in you life. We need to show our young adults that there's a time and a season for everything, but when that time is up, you have to live a more sensible life. Grandparents and grandchildren shouldn't be rubbing elbows at the night club. We need to allow young people to be young people, and at the same time, stay in our place.

Again, it's not that your life ends at a certain age, but some of your activities should definitely change. You can't be young forever, and when you look at some of the things that young people go through these days, why would you wanna be? Some of the older people of today don't want to accept the fact that their time has passed and it's now time for the young people to have their moments. They just don't know how ridiculous they look in the night club at 50. We need to show these children that it's okay to bow out and do something else when you get older. Whether it's in terms of lifestyle, family, church or whatever, there comes a time when we all need to step out of the way and let the young folks have it. If you do it gracefully, they'll know how to handle it when their time comes.

Also, when these children of ours make mistakes, we can't just shake our heads and walk away. The problem that a lot of parents have is forgetting that they were once imperfect lumps of clay as well. In fact, even in our old age we still are those lumps of clay. God is never done working with us until the day He takes us home. You can't be so quick to look down your nose at your children as though you've never made mistakes in your life. I know that it's hard sometimes, especially when you've told your kids about those mistakes in hopes that they would avoid them they way that you didn't. But you must remember that somebody probably told you as well and you didn't listen. It's in a child's nature to assume that they can figure things out in a way that their parents didn't.

We've already talked about this in previous chapters. We know they're going to make some of those mistakes, and it's natural to continue parenting and tell them about themselves. But we must understand that parenting isn't all about simply telling your kids about how they've screwed up. It's also about offering them guidance and assistance in correcting the situation. We've all gone to mom and dad for advice after we were grown. If you had good parents, they never told you how you were grown and on your own and that it wasn't their problem. They gave you whatever advice was necessary to help you through a tough time, and sent you on your way. That's how were supposed to be with our children.

We have this problem in our homes, in our communities and even in our churches. We've become so holy, that we've forgotten what we were like before God saved us. Some of us have selfishly pretended that we never drank, never danced, never stayed out later than we should have, never yielded to lust and temptation and never partied on Saturday night and shouted on Sunday morning. None of those things have we ever done in our lives. So when our kids begin to do them, we pretend that we've never seen this type of thing before.

This happens a lot in church. You see the old mothers in the church that'll frown at the young ladies because of the way that they dress when they come into the sanctuary. They'll sit back and talk about them, but they'll never pull them to the side and try to teach them the right way to come into God's house. You'll see the deacons of the church that'll shake their heads at the young men that don't respect the church like they should. However, they never pull the young men aside and explain to them that God's house is sacred and should always be given the utmost respect.

Now, some of this isn't completely the fault of the elders of the church. We talked about this a while ago when discussing the fact that you can't talk to some of these children because their parents are just as childish as they are, and from time to time, you can't tell who's in charge. But there's no excuse for not trying, at the very least, to show our children a better way.

One way or another, if the streets don't claim them, our children will grow old. We can show them how to do it right by living our lives the right way. What we pass on to them will soon be passed on to our grandchildren. We don't want to ignore our children in their adult years, only to watch them turn around and do it to our grandchildren. Every family has tradition and values that they hope to pass along to the next generation. Your values and your traditions shouldn't consist of an attitude that suggests that once you're 18, you can't come back here for anything. As I stated earlier in this book, our children are in their mid to late 20's before they can adequately take care of themselves on their own. It's not always because they're lazy and can't find their way. It takes a lot more to survive these days than it did for some of us when we started out into adulthood. Sometimes they just need a little help.

Like it or not, we still have some responsibility to these children when they're at that age. I'm not telling you to pay their bills or raise them all over again. I'm saying that a little assistance to your grown-up children isn't all that bad. As long as they're moving in the right direction, I can't see where the problem is. If nothing that I've said so far works for you, then try this. Sooner or later, you may need these very same children to take care of you. Don't set a precedent by showing them that they have no responsibility to anyone other than themselves once they've reached a certain age. You wouldn't want that running through their minds while they're deciding whether or not they want to take care of you themselves or put you in a nursing home. Just something to think about.

## "*I HAVE FAITH IN THESE DESOLATE TIMES...*"

At the end of this journey, I want to speak to the youth of today. You are the main reason that I wrote this book. I know that I've spent a lot of time talking about adults and adult things, but I still wrote this book for you. You see, we as adults haven't done what we were supposed to do. We haven't shown you what we were supposed to show you. For some reason, we forgot that you were looking to us for leadership. You were looking to us to show you how to be when you grew up. A lot of us have failed you. You can thumb through the pages of what I've written and you can see some of the negatives that we actually have already shown you and continue to show you. You can see just how wrong we've been, and yet for some reason, we all wonder why you guys are the way that you are. But, I wrote this book for you.

As I've gone through my life, I've often wondered why I was sent here. I've wondered what my purpose was supposed to be in life. I'm still not completely sure of what that's supposed to be, but I now feel that I've fulfilled one of those purposes. One of my purposes in life was to deliver this message to you. I don't claim to be a prophet or anything like that and I'm sure that I've said a lot of things that have already been said, but I feel that part of my mission in this life was to reiterate some points, and to maybe put a new and different spin on some others. If you don't mind, I'd like to share a few more things with you before we close this book.

First things first, you're all beautiful in your own special way. As you probably remember from what I've written, I'm not speaking of your physical beauty because that's not the measure of you. You're beautiful from the inside. You must remember that and never let anyone take it away from you. You have so much to accomplish in your lives and the *proper* self-esteem will aide you in all that you do. If you acquire the necessary knowledge, there will be nothing that you can't do in life. The sky is the limit for you, just as it was for us. However, you guys are dealing with a much bigger sky.

There are so many more opportunities, but there are so many more dangers as well. It will be beneficial to you to be aware of both. For how will you avoid the same pitfalls in life that befell us if you have no idea what they are? Knowing what can lead you to failure in life is just as important as knowing what leads to success. These are the things that you should be aware of, and yet some of you aren't. For some of you it's because you haven't quite matured enough to really understand what life is about. For some of you, it's because some of the adults in your life have never taught you anything that will actually be of a real benefit to you in your life. Again, we have failed some of you, but I hope to help in pointing you in the right direction. Please, read on…

I could ask where we went wrong, but I think I already know. You guys started to decay mentally when the older men in your lives disappeared. I grew up without my father, who died when I was very young. However, it was later brought to my attention that he may not have been much of a father had he been here. I was fortunate enough to have a big brother that was enough years ahead of me that he could fill some of the void left by an absent father. He aided my mother in making me into a man. We lost him when I was 20, and after almost 17 years, not a day goes by that I don't think about and still miss my brother.

By the time he left here, the foundation had already been laid. I'm not in any way suggesting that my brother was perfect, as I'm sure that none of you could say that about your brothers, fathers or whatever significant male figure existed in your lives. What I am saying is that he did the best that he could to show me and my other brothers what a responsible man is supposed to be about. That, in addition to my mother's teachings, is what shaped me into the man that I am. They laid the foundation in my life, and as each day passes, I'm still trying to live up to their expectations. I'm still trying to be what they thought I could be. I'm still trying to make them proud and whether I get there or not, I'll never stop trying.

The older women have also disappeared from their rightful places. As we've already covered, instead of teaching you young ladies what it means to be women, they've regressed back to their youth, wearing clothes that by now they should've, and in some cases have (if you know what I mean), grown out of. They've become club hoppers, street runners and foolishly promiscuous in their old age. Those that haven't fallen into those traps have become holier than thou, pretending that they've never been young before. Instead of teaching you young ladies virtue and class, they've pretended that they've never been where you are and have looked down their noses at you.

If there had been more women available to teach the young women of today the right way to live, how to respect their bodies and how to be good parents to their children, a lot of you young ladies wouldn't be the way that you are, in the shape that you're in and my entire chapter on sex would be non-existent. Because those of us that are a few years older have failed you in a lot of ways, you have become less than what you were supposed to be. I don't know about my fellow parents, uncles, aunts, big brothers, big sisters or mentors, but I'm ready to assume my responsibilities. I'm ready to take my rightful place at the front of the bus.

More positive influences are missing in your lives today. As I stated a few chapters ago, some of you guys have no one to look up to beyond the people that run the streets. Some of you don't know the value of a proper education because there aren't enough educated men and women in your lives. Some of you don't know how to treat women because your fathers walked out on your mothers for other women. Some of you don't know how to treat men because your mothers told you that they were only a means for you to get money. Some of you don't know how to talk to women because your fathers called your mothers by every name besides the one that her parents gave her. Some of you don't know how to keep a man because your mothers haven't given you the proper tools to use in order to make a real man happy.

So many of you guys are the way that you are because you're hardheaded and don't want to do any better. However, the sad reality is that a lot of you are the way that you are because so many of us have never taught you to be any better than you are. Some of your fathers are still in your lives, but they aren't teaching you anything. Some of your mothers are never there because she spends more time in the club than you could ever wish to and have left grandma to raise you. Sadly enough, some of your fathers aren't there at all. Increasingly, this is becoming true with your mothers as well. The time has long since come for some of us to show you young men and young women that someone really and truly loves you and wants you to succeed in your life.

There are so many things that you guys are involved in that are counterproductive to your having a successful life. There are so many traps that have been set for years for us as blacks. Traps that were set to ensure our failure in life. So many black men and women have come before you and fought to ensure that you won't be a victim of all of these things designed to guarantee your failure. I won't give you that long list of historical black figures, as I'm sure you're all aware of a lot of them, but there have also been some within your family, I'm sure. Some of these people laid down their lives so that you might have a better one.

There are always exceptions to everything, but for the most part, as far as I can tell from your generation, you guys don't appreciate what's been done for you. Maybe it's because you're a product of parents that were unappreciative as well. Or maybe it's because you just don't appreciate the fact that you *do* have parents that love you, care for you and want nothing but the best for you. Maybe you just don't understand what your life is actually supposed to be about. Maybe you just don't realize what your true destiny is. I hope that I can say something in the next few lines that can help define where you're supposed to be headed in your life.

I'll start with education. For so many years, a proper education was denied to our people. It was denied to us because white America knew that they couldn't keep an educated people down forever. Again, some of our people died so that their children, you and me, could have the right to a proper education. They did it for the future of our people. There was a time when we as a people valued and appreciated what those before us did. I'm not suggesting that my generation was perfect. As you may remember from the intro to this book, I think I began to see the decline of our young people during my last couple of years in high school. So it started with us.

The problem that I'm having with your generation is that education seems to be dangerously low on your list of priorities, yet in order for you to succeed in life, your education level must be high. Simply put, the things that my generation could do with a high school education, your generation would need, at the very least, a two year college degree to do. We were the last generation that could've adequately taken care of itself on a high school diploma. That just won't do now.

Not only will the economy not allow it, but even the fast food jobs want more educated people these days, just to flip burgers. You have to go further into your education now just to get a *half-decent* job. The problem that I'm seeing is that the more education that is required to succeed in life, the less willing some of you are to achieve even the lowest levels of education. There are some of you that not only will not finish high school, but will even refuse to give yourself a second chance with a GED. Where will it end?

Before I write another word, I want you all to understand something before it gets twisted: I'm not speaking to all of you. I am very well aware that we have some extremely motivated young people in the world today. There are some in my own family that I believe will go on to do good things in their lives. There's really no need to speak to those of you that fit that description other than to say keep going, no matter what. You are the ones that give me the most hope for the future. You give me the hope that maybe this will all turn around soon enough.

However, if you fit the mold of the young person that I've been describing to this point, let's not kid ourselves. For some of you, not only does the shoe fit, but there's no shoe horn necessary. You are the ones that I expect to be angry about what I'm saying, mostly because I'm telling the truth. But all I ask is that you seriously think about what I'm saying right now. Where do you think you're going in your life without educating yourself at some point? Not very far, I can tell you that.

Sure, there have been many that have never finished school and have gone on to do great things in their lives, but I can tell you that they are few and far in relation to the number that fail. If they're being honest, those very same people will tell you that the road would have been a lot easier had they been educated properly. The difference between some of them and some of you is that the opportunity for education wasn't always there for our people, and in some cases, still isn't today. But it's there for a lot of you these days, and yet some of you won't take advantage of it. The only question that I have is, why? But I think I already have some answers.

Under the guise of "keepin' it real", some of you guys have not only begun to fail yourselves, but you're failing all of those people that I spoke of that gave their lives so that we might have a better one. This ties in to some of the things that I spoke about when I was discussing hip hop and its effect on you. I'm not now, nor would I ever blame hip hop for our young people failing at education.

What I did and will blame hip hop for is perpetuating the idea of fast money to you guys, while never truthfully representing to you guys how much work it takes to *legally* get rich and stay rich in this country. They don't even adequately represent to you how hard *they* had to work to get what they have or to get where they are in life. They'll mention it in an interview or two, but they don't put it in enough songs. They forget that you guys hear the songs more often than you hear or read the interviews. They're so busy telling you to "keep it real", that they're not telling you what to keep it real about. They forget that no matter how you may feel or how you may dress or how much of their language and particular slang you may learn to speak, most of us in the black community can't relate to multi-millionaires.

Instead of telling you to "represent for yo' 'hood", they need to tell you to represent for your future by educating yourself. That will be the cornerstone to any success that you have in your life. That's what's real. I'm not disrespecting my brothas in the industry because I'm proud of what they've made for us. At the same time, there are some in hip hop that do stress education to our children and they know who they are. At some point they too either had to or will have to educate themselves. Those in the industry that didn't will eventually go broke or already have.

There needs to be more of an emphasis placed on you guys' futures. Because so many of you guys aren't being educated properly, you don't know what to value and what's trivial. The movies, music and lack of education are causing you to lose sight of what really is worth your time and energy. Some of you will take another man's life over a car, a pair of shoes or, for some stupid reason, a member of the opposite sex. How dumb is that? This shows that not only do you not properly value another human being's life, but you don't value your own either. You lose sight of the fact that if you take a man's life, yours is over too. Either you'll die by the bullet yourself or you'll go to jail for life, but either way, it's all over from here on out.

I know you probably think that a lack of education has nothing to do with street life, but you couldn't be more wrong. When you're properly educated, you realize that you have more to lose by making stupid mistakes such as taking another man's life or having sex without protection and risking catching a life threatening disease or forcing yourself into the working world prematurely due to the fact that you have a child on the way. When you're properly educated, you realize that you should work to buy your own car or shoes instead of taking another's life because he won't give you his. You understand that there are more fish in the sea and if someone doesn't want you, then it's not worth anyone losing their lives over. Besides, if you catch your woman with another man or vice versa, why kill anyone? That just tells you what kind of man or woman you're dealing with and you'll be better off without them.

You guys have also become increasingly involved in drugs. However, it's not just something like crack with you guys. Although some of you unfortunately have that problem, what's more problematic for your generation is alcohol and weed. The young lady that I spoke about in Chapter 5 that I dated said to me at one point that she didn't feel like she could be with me sometimes because I don't drink. I'm aware of the fact that there's a compatibility issue there, as sad as that is, but even when she felt like she really loved me, she wondered if she'd be willing to give up alcohol for me. Is it me or is that really sad that you could love alcohol more than you could love a particular individual?

I sometimes wonder where you guys' priorities really are. When I've heard some of your parents say that they don't understand you, I've often accused them of not trying hard enough. But when something like that comes out of a person's mouth, it really is hard to understand. Now, if you've ever known an alcoholic, you know that sometimes their liquor is more important to them than loved ones. But it's alarming when I hear it coming from the mouths of people so young.

I remember reading an article in GQ Magazine and a gentleman was telling the story of his first Alcoholics Anonymous meeting. He talked about a conversation he had with another gentleman at the meeting. He said that sometimes he didn't feel like he could enjoy himself at certain functions without drinking. The other gentleman then asked him, "If you feel like you're not going to have a good time, why go?" He then said that with that question, he realized what his problem with alcohol was. He realized that what made him an alcoholic was not getting drunk when he drinks, but his dependency on alcohol to do anything. It was the fact that he felt that he couldn't have a good time without drinking that made him an alcoholic. That's how you guys seem to feel. You, along with the alcohol makers of the world, have told yourselves that a party ain't a party if ain't got Bacardi.

I've been told everything from "it lightens the mood" to "it relaxes me", but if you can't lighten the mood or relax without ingesting alcohol, then you have a problem. I'm not talking about folks that will have glass of wine here or there,

I'm talking about people that can't relax themselves with a hot bath as opposed to liquor. Having never been a drinker, I can't say for sure whether or not alcohol does any of the things that people claim it does. However, I've had a hot bath before with Miles Davis playing in the background. I've lit incense and candles. I'm sure that these things will lighten moods and relax a few folks. What I do know is that plenty of mistakes have been made by the young and the old when too much alcohol has been consumed.

Many of you reading this book, whether young or old were conceived because somebody got drunk and went too far. It doesn't mean that mommy and daddy don't love you, but they wanted you here after a little more planning as opposed to after a night of drinking and irresponsibility. There's been date rape and drunk driving, things that puts us all in danger, that comes along with irresponsible drinking.

What's happening to you young people today is that a tragedy has to occur before you realize that you're doing something irresponsible. You don't understand that drinking isn't some rite of passage or hobby, it's a responsibility. There are a lot of life altering things that can go wrong when you have no control of your faculties. You shouldn't party so hard that you're afraid of what someone will tell you about yourself when you come to the next day.

This is also an issue as it pertains to weed. There have been too many people, especially some in the entertainment industry, that have told you guys that there's nothing wrong with a little marijuana. Addictions can happen to any of us, but it usually happens to people with a weakness. The only catch to that is, those that are weak enough for addiction to take them over, usually don't find out until the addiction has taken them over. Nobody that's addicted to any drug started out with the intent of becoming an addict. They all felt that they could control it, and once it became an addiction, they all denied that it was. You guys in your youthful naïveté always forget that these people come from somewhere and these addictions start out somehow.

Most addicts were just "normal" people just like you and me at some point. A lot of them had a lot going for themselves at some points as well. For example, I've often told people that I felt that stripping was a gateway drug. Stripping to me is marijuana, and porn in cocaine and heroine. If you'd be willing to perform one sexual act for money, you'd be willing to perform another for more money.

However, a lot of the strippers that started stripping and wound up in the porn industry or prostituting didn't see that happening to themselves. But one day they looked up and it was a whole new world, they were addicted to sex and money (I'm not sure which is stronger), and they didn't know how to get out. No matter what you hear, marijuana is still a gateway drug. It still can, and most times will, lead to another addiction. Sure, there are many that have beat the odds, but why put yourself at risk? Why find out the hard way that you're one of the ones that won't? Anything that you take into your body that impairs your judgment isn't good for you, no matter what any relative, rapper, actor or street criminal tells you.

To my young ladies out there, it's time to stop a lot of what you're doing. There have been some that have read some of these chapters as I was writing them that wondered if maybe I was being a little too hard on you guys. I really don't think so. As I stated in the sections that I spoke on concerning relationships, you guys have the most to gain if we can somehow turn this thing around. You guys have begun to behave like men. It may seem like the way to be, but I'm here to tell you that you're only making things harder on yourself. Behaving like men is sometimes not even fit for a man. Why do you guys need to take on that behavior? There is a reason that men and women are fundamentally different. It's because we compliment each other in some strange way. I feel that I've explained it somewhat in this book, but I can't completely. It's all a part of God's wonderful plan.

You girls have to regain the respect that you once had for your bodies. I know we've talked about this all throughout this book, but I feel that it can't be said enough. You guys seem to have lost your mind as it pertains to sex. You've become worse than little boys when they get their first taste. As I've stated before, it seems that you guys are the aggressors nowadays and the men are being led to the bedroom by you. Though there's nothing wrong with that in theory, there's definitely something wrong with it when it's happening with multiple partners. If you don't respect yourself, no one else will.

This may seem old fashioned and even chauvinistic, but a woman shouldn't need two hands to count the number of sexual partners she's had by the time she gets married. But some of you girls have to use toes and calculators and that ain't cool. Trust me, if the number's that high, more times than not, no decent man will want you. Again, I know this seems kind of lopsided, but I speak the truth to you. When a man meets a woman that's been around, more times than not, he's more willing to be added to your list than he is to marry you. When he's ready to get married, he'll find someone that knows how to say "no". That way he knows that she'll say it to other men that may approach her. You don't need to gain a reputation, all in the name of growing up.

You also need to be aware of the blessings that God will place in your life. Don't buy into the theory that all men are dogs and your Prince Charming will always arrive later in your life. Judge each man individually because you never know how he was raised. While you may cast him off as just another dog, he may be the one. Is that a reason to rush off into marriage? Certainly not. If he's the one, he'll be there. But don't go running off into the street life because you feel you're too young to commit to anything. It may not be worth the seriousness of a marriage commitment, but you don't wanna lose something that's good for you in the name of being young and wanting to "live". Remember what I said about single people. No matter what they say, everybody wants to be with somebody. We sometimes just hide that desire behind our pride.

I'm sure you remember the young lady that I spoke about in Chapter 5. How she broke me down for another, all in the name of being young and wanting to do her own thing. Well, there's an amendment to that story. There were some other things that happened after I wrote that chapter, but before I finished this book. I left that chapter the same in order to preserve the integrity of the message that I was trying to get across. However, there was eventually more to the story. If you remember, she decided that I wasn't worth the trouble in favor of a man that admittedly didn't even treat her half as well as I did. But she felt it was okay because she didn't want to be tied down and he allowed her to be free. Eventually, that fairy tale came to an end.

Although I know the details, I won't list them here. While at one point I wanted to, and in an initial rough draft of this book I had, it never felt right within my spirit. It wasn't the right thing to do and it would have only been done in the interest of vengeance. It would've been counterproductive to what I was trying to accomplish with this book and to me as a person.

By the time I finished this book, I felt that I was healed from that situation. Telling how that situation between her and that young man ended would have been a display of the opposite. It would have been the words of someone that still harbored ill feelings and still had an axe to grind. I feel that I'm neither of those people. The only thing that I will say is that if you read and remember that chapter and you've been where she was at some point in your life, you probably have an idea of how something like that is going to end.

She eventually called me up and we began speaking again. No relationship, just friends. Eventually, she even admitted that she *may* have done me wrong. However, she still never really apologized. That may come somewhere down the road, or it may never come at all. That's why it's important to forgive for the sake of forgiving and not just when someone apologizes. The fact is that sometimes people may admit that they've done us wrong, but never actually feel sorry for doing it. So that you don't carry this type of thing around forever, you must forgive anyway and move on with your life.

Even after all of that, when she needed someone to talk to, I was still there for her. As I said in Chapter 5, I would've been justified in letting her deal with it on her own, and I'm sure that some of you reading this, as did some of my friends, feel that I should have. But it's just not in me. I stilled cared for her and even though she did me wrong and anything that happened to her was mostly her own doing, I still felt like at the very least, the Christian thing to do was to be there for her, while being sure to protect myself at the same time. Sometimes the emotion of a situation like this can lead to other things that one shouldn't be involved in.

I took no joy from that situation not working out for her. I never felt a sense of revenge or anything like that. One of the reasons that I didn't want her to treat me the way that she did was because I knew that these things have a way of coming back on you and she didn't seem to get that. At the same time, I felt no better when I found out that what I already knew would eventually happen to her had happened. This was God's business and I had turned it over to Him. So I went back on my word and allowed her to lean on me.

Once she opened up to me about what happened, I simply told her things that made her feel better. I repeated some things that I had already told her. I told her that no matter what, she deserves respect. I reminded her that she was a child of God and that she needs to carry herself that way so that guys like this won't feel comfortable with her and will take anything less than his best elsewhere. Some of us decide to change and some of us have change thrust upon on us. In order to know which is which, we need to be in touch with ourselves and in touch with God. I don't know if she knows which is which in her life, but after my dealings with her, I knew which one happened to me and I never pretended that change was my idea. This is the type of thing that happens when you disobey God's voice.

Repeating myself, it seems to me that she didn't realize what God had placed in front of her when He placed me there. I'm not saying that I'm perfect. I'm saying that I loved her unconditionally and she was either too young and inexperienced to realize what was given to her or just too selfish to appreciate it. Sometimes that kind of love only comes once in a lifetime. For her sake, I hope He gives her another shot. However, I feel that my work is done as far as she's concerned. God placed it on my heart not to shut her out and to be there for her and I was. It was as if He told me that it wasn't up to me to save her, but He still wanted me to help her through this time. I don't know if it will make a difference in her life or not, but I feel that I gave what was required of me.

With that, I've pulled myself back from her situation, allowing her to live her life, her way. I'm still willing to lend an ear, but no more advice. But this time, it's different. This time, I feet that a weight has been lifted. This time, I felt as if I've completed a mission. This time, I was smart enough to keep my heart out of the equation. I remembered what I had learned and I conducted myself accordingly. For the record, she has said to me that she sees no correlation between the way she treated me and what happened to her. As far as she's concerned, it was just some stuff that happened. I don't know if she really feels that way, but if she does, then that's her prerogative. As I said, it's time for her to live her life, her way.

To the youth, I know it seems that I'm off track again, but there is a moral here for you. The moral is that you can't treat your life as a gamble whether it's with your education, with drugs, with the relationship that you have with your family or with love. This young lady took for granted what she had with me. She felt then, and probably still feels now, that true love is everywhere and that she can find a good man around any corner. I feel now that even after what's happened, she still feels that he was the rarity and that the good men are plentiful. That's a sentiment that can only be felt by someone that hasn't been alive very long. Run that by a woman that's been married for 10 years and has been cheated on for 9.

She was like a lot of us that feel that meeting a person that's good enough for you to be with for the rest of your life won't happen at a young age. Only God in heaven knows if we would've stayed together forever had she not did what she did, but I don't think we'll ever know if it was meant to be, because it will take a lot for me to look her way again if that situation ever arose. In a situation like this, you have to win a person back and I don't know if she ever cared about me enough to do what it would take to get me back. God may not have meant for me to be her prince, but I'm sure He didn't mean for her to disregard what we had in exchange for less. I'm sure I was sent to teach her something, but I don't know if she learned anything.

You guys have to be aware and prepared for such things. It seems that something negative has surfaced within our young ladies. The more a man has to offer you and the better you're treated by that man, the worse you treat him. But the less a man has to offer you and the worse he treats you, the more likely you are to stand up to mama, daddy, grandma and grandpa about your choice. This mentality has to change for your sake and for the sake of any children that you hope to have one day. If you guys make a habit of accepting less in your lives whether it's in terms of education, behavior or in terms of a mate and the potential parents to your children, you will have children that will accept less in their lives. Even if we as adults haven't been the best role models for you guys, you have to stop that cycle and be the best role model you can for your children.

For the young ladies out there, your daughters are watching you to try and figure out what type of women they should be, so your behavior is important to monitor. More times than not, when you become parents, you'll be responsible for raising the kids, whether daddy's there or not. That's just usually the role that mom takes on. You have to teach your children the way that they should be. As for the men, the same things apply. You are a role model for your son. You can start on the role of being a positive one by not running out on him. I'm a living witness that you can be a good father to your son no matter how the relationship between you and the mother turned out. Even though my father was dead, I turned out okay. However, that wasn't a reason for me to leave the raising of my son completely up to his mother. I understood that he needed me then and still needs me now.

*Hounour thy father and thy mother: that thy days may be long upon the land which the Lord thy God giveth thee.*
*—Exodus 20:12*

Speaking of parenting, I want to touch on another subject with you guys before I close this thing out. Our last subject will be that 5th Commandment that's written above this section. Honoring your parents. This is something that has been completely lost on your generation. Most of this is your parents fault, but you share some of the blame. There's a certain amount of respect that should always be given to parents and grandparents no matter what age you may be. Your parents and grandparents are the heads of your family and should be respected as such.

So many times I hear young people (and by young people I mean those of you in your teens and those of you in your early 20's) that will talk to the elders of their families in the most disrespectful tones and manners. Some of the things that you say and how you say them are disrespectful. Most of you know that you're wrong, and you just don't care. I don't understand where this is coming from. How can you disrespect people that you're still depending on to help you through the early part of your life? How can you guys speak to people that love you so much and only want the best for you in such disrespectful manners? There are many reasons why you guys can't continue on this way.

The main reason that I feel that some of you are the way that you are is because your parents allow it. Sometimes it's because of some things that I've already discussed, like the fact that your parents have become more friends than parents. Sometimes it's because your parents have set you all on autopilot for so long, that you feel that you don't owe them or any one else any respect because you're practically raising yourselves.

Some of you have just decided that you don't have to respect your parents, and your parents either haven't been smart enough or haven't had the nerve to put you guys back in you place. This kind of behavior isn't to your benefit at all. It's up to your parents to teach you to respect your elders and authority so that you won't have that problem when you get out into the real world. It doesn't do you any good to run all over mom and dad because the rest of the world doesn't operate that way. If you haven't already, you'll soon find out that the world doesn't have to bend to your ways. You'll either find a way to adjust to the ways of the world or you'll struggle all of your life.

Even though I place the majority of the blame for this at your parent's feet, most of you guys know the difference between right and wrong. You know when you're out of line. If you've got good parents, there's no reason that you shouldn't show them the utmost respect. No matter what stages we may reach in our lives, at some point we'll need the love of a good parent to get us through a rough time. It'd be a shame if you were to miss out on that because you burned a bridge with your mom or your dad and now they won't speak to you because of the way that you've spoken to them over the years. Now granted, if you've got a great mom and dad, they'll always try to be there for you, but everyone has a breaking point.

I've seen children that will tell their parents to shut up, but when they need something, all they wanna hear their parents say is "yes". I've heard children tell their parents to stay out of their business, but when they're in a crisis and need the help of their parents, they wanna sit down and tell them all about what's going on, what kind of trouble they're in and how much it'll cost to get them out. Although mom and dad will most times take more crap off of you than anyone else, it's still not a good idea to put them to the test all the time.

Whether you guys realize it or not, these are the people that have your back, no matter what, not your so-called friends. There's only so much that friends can do for you, but there's something that your parents can give you that your friends can never give you: The love of a parent. It's a difficult thing to quantify. The love of a mother is special and can't be duplicated. The only thing that comes close is grandma's love. You'll truly be sorry if you miss out on either of those.

Another way in which you guys fail to honor your parents is through your behavior. When your parents work hard to keep a roof over your head and food on the table and you guys disrespect them by bringing home poor grades or any other problems that you may have, that's a way of dishonoring your parents. You may not think that it matters to you parents what kind of grades you get, what kind of friends you keep or how you act when you go out that door, but it does. You honor your parents by making positive decisions with your life so that they don't have to worry as much about your well being. Your parents are envisioning the day that you guys will be able to take care of yourselves.

First of all, they want you to be productive members of society. Second, they just want you out of the house. That's a little joke, but not in some cases. But even at that, they'll always be there for you and you can't take that for granted by behaving any way that you see fit. Respect where you come from. As I said, some of you are the way that you are because your parents have either not done their jobs and put you in your place or you've just decided that disrespect is the route that you'll take. But you must remember this as you go along in your life: There's nothing more important than family. There are many out there that don't have the love of a good family through no fault of their own. If you've got a good family life, they'd love to trade places with you.

We all get angry sometimes and say things to our parents and grandparents that we don't mean. We all make mistakes. But if you make a mistake, recognize your mistake and apologize for it before it's too late. There may be a reason that you make that initial mistake, but there's no excuse for not apologizing for it when you realize that you've been wrong. If all else fails, remember that what goes around comes around. Most of you will have children one day and if you're disrespectful to your parents, think about what that means for you and your children in the future.

As long as we have faith in God, we have hope. For that reason, I still have hope for the black youth of America. A lot of us as parents have walked away from God and have taken our children with us. That's why things are the way that they are and that's why a lot of you are the way that you are. If we as a people will just come back to God, a lot of our youth can still be saved. I know that you guys don't always appear to be headed in the right direction, but neither did we. I know that you guys don't always make the best decisions, but neither did the generations before you. I know that you guys have a lot of bad habits, but you're not the first to have that issue either.

It's okay to be young and to make mistakes, but there's more of a fear for your generation because times are so different for you guys and some of your mistakes are fatal. The sex that you have can kill you. The arguments that you get into can involve gunplay and can be life altering for your entire family. By simply going into the wrong chat room, your parents could potentially never see you again.

To use the example again, we fought over each other all the time. Boys fought over girls, and girls fought over boys. Sometimes we like to pretend that we didn't do that, but we did. We tell you guys how stupid stuff like that is, but not because we've never done it. It's because now that we look back on when we did it, we realize how stupid we were. However, what's scary about it when you guys do it, is the fact that sometimes people die over it. We may have been stupid enough to have the fight, but we lived to talk about it the next day.

If I could leave you guys with anything, it's the fact that life is both fragile and short. There's so much to do, and yet so little time to do it in. There needs to be a limit to the amount of time that you're willing to waste in your life. I know that a lot of you guys think that you have all the time in the world, but I'm here to tell you that it'll be gone before you know it. You have to make good use of it. I'm not suggesting that every day of your life be serious. I'm suggesting that you have balance. Don't take yourself too seriously, but don't waste a lot of time with play.

It is an absolute must that you guys learn and respect the finality of death. You're so quick to pull a trigger without really realizing and understanding how final death is. If you take a black man's life, there's no coming back from that. You affect so many lives when you do that and every time you kill a black man, you've murdered a black family because that man can no longer reproduce. Recognize the plots. I hate to see you all dying at the hands of one another over things that can simply be talked out. I hate to see you guys dying when there's so much for you to live for.

You guys need to be a little more aware of your history. So many before you have fought and died for the right to be free in this country. You can't allow that blood to be shed in vain. You guys need to understand that you'll never really arrive in the eyes of white America. This country will never really embrace us as a people and we should never forget that. So many times you guys are under the impression that money and fame equal acceptance. That couldn't be more wrong.

If people love you, they love you no matter how much you have. If you guys were more aware of what was done to us as a people over the years in this country, you'd understand these things a little better. It's not that you shouldn't want to prosper in your lives. It's not that there aren't any good white people in this country. I'm not suggesting that at all. I don't want you guys to be a victim of the same racist thinking that this country was built on. What I am suggesting is that you always remain aware. Be prosperous, yes. But never forget where you came from. Never forget that this country was built on the backs of black slaves, your ancestors. Never forget where our people have been.

We were lynched because of our pigmentation (that's skin tone for all unaware), and nothing more. Though we as a people have more rights than we've ever had before in this country, don't be fooled. It can all end tomorrow. They're still in power. Money doesn't make you equal to the powers that be in this country. We were niggers before, and we're still niggers in some of their eyes right now. They not only feel that way about blacks, they feel that way about all people of color. Do what you can to build what we can for our people, but always remember what system we're working under. So many of us are so busy trying to build big houses and drive expensive cars that we forget what America really is. It's the one of the freest countries in the world, yes, but the slavery is still here. We're mentally slaves.

By allowing us to make money in their capitalist society, they've tricked us into believing that everything is okay and we're all equal. You as the youth of today must be smarter than that. Do for your own people. Take care of your own people. Work the system, but don't let the system work you. Be aware of the fact that not only are the poor black people oppressed in this country, the rich black people are as well, whether they realize it or not. The more we've got, the more they want to bring us down. They don't want you to succeed, but that's exactly why you must.

There are a lot of you that have a lot of potential inside of you. Some of the most brilliant minds that we have today belong to the youth. Some of you guys are just caught up in some of the wrong things and some of your energies are being used in the wrong areas. Again, you aren't the first generation to have this issue. But it's not too late to do something about it. It's not too late to turn yourselves around.

In life, we have but a few true leaders. The rest are followers. I'm not just speaking of political or religious leaders. Though those are important and I do believe that there are those types of leaders among you, I'm speaking of leaders in a more ordinary sense. I'm speaking more in terms of community leadership. I'm speaking more in terms of generational leadership. I'm speaking in terms of making something more of yourselves. I'm speaking in the sense of turning around these communities that you live in. I'm speaking in terms of showing others that you guys can be more than just a generation defined by the number of you that didn't reach your 21$^{st}$ birthday.

To the leaders among our youth, it's time to take your place. Though things are different and a little tougher, I believe that you guys can do it. Other generations have survived, and I know that you can too. Young leaders, it's time to stand up and take your place. And here's to hoping that we still have followers that are willing to follow causes more worthy than promiscuity and genocide.

> *"So peace to all that hears my voice/We survive because we have no choice"*
> *—From "Epilog" by Terence Trent D'Arby*

As I close this book out, I would like to do something very special. I came up with this idea sometime during the early chapters of this book. Someone asked me why I was writing this book. I gave many reasons, but one of the main reasons that I gave was a parent's answer. I told them I was writing it for my son. As of the writing of this book, I'm a single man and I have just one child. Steffen is the single most important thing in my life.

As I've suggested that some of you single parents apply this to your life, there's no woman on the face of the earth that could separate me from my son. No matter what relationship I may find myself in, they all have to understand that nothing and no one comes before him. He's been the light of my life every since he was below my knee in stature. No matter what's happened in my life, I believe that Steffen will always love me and I realized a long time ago that sometimes, that's all that matters. Before I end this, I'll tell you a brief story that I like to tell about my son.

At one point in my life, I worked in television. I had one job doing television production for a church, I had one job where I was interning at WTVS Channel 56 here in Detroit, and I had a regular 9 to 5. My wonderful mother would keep my son for me while I pursued this dream. There were times that I would get up in the morning and go to work before my son got up and get home late at night after he had gone to bed. Those days were always hard on me because I would go a day and a half or so without seeing my son awake. I would call during the day and talk to him, but if you love your children, you know that it's not the same as seeing them.

Well, there was one night in particular that I guess even Steffen had gotten tired of this. I got up as usual to go to work one morning on one of my late days when I wouldn't get home until after he was supposed to be in the bed. On this particular night, my mom had allowed many of her many grandchildren to have a sleep over. They all slept downstairs in the living room. I came into the house at roughly 1am. I came in the back door. Knowing that the kids were downstairs sleeping, I tried to close the door quietly so that I wouldn't wake them.

All of a sudden, out of a darkened dinning room, my son walked into the kitchen. He was still half sleep and to this day, I'm not sure if he knew what he was doing, but at the same time, it seemed like he did. He walked up to me and he reached up to hug me. He never said a word, he just hugged me. But he never needed to say a word because his hug said it all. I hadn't seen him in a day, but it felt like that hug was from a boy that hadn't seen his father in years. To me, it said "I love you dad". I kissed him on his head and told him to go back to bed. He never said a word, he just turned and went back into the living room and laid down. Instantly, he was back to sleep.

It was as if God had touched him to let him know that his father was home and needed his hug. I can't lie, as I walked to my room, I had tears in my eyes. Although it all seemed so simple, it was one of the most beautiful moments that I've ever experienced in my life. Just from that moment, I can always say that I know what it feels like to have someone in my life that literally loves me for me. We should all be so lucky. So, with that, I'd like to end this book with an open letter to my son. Here it goes...

Dear Steffen,

I hope this letter finds you well and in good spirits. I'm writing this letter to let you know how much your father loves you and that he is very, very proud of the young man that you've become. I've always wanted the best for you from day one and have done my best to give it to you. Even though you seem to be progressing very well so far, I still have concerns about your future. The world that you're growing up in is very different from the one that your father grew up in. I could list all of the things that are wrong with the world today, but I can sum it all up in one simple statement: People don't love each other anymore. That's what you have to deal with in your world. That's what will be facing you as you grow into a man. The other reason that I'm writing you this letter is because I want to say something encouraging to you as you come through your teenage years into manhood. Just bear with me son, I won't be long.

I have nothing but the highest of hopes for you. I believe that you will be special and will make me very proud of you in the future as well. But there are many pitfalls that will be waiting for you as you try to make your way through this life. I know that you won't avoid them all even if I give you advice along the way. I didn't always heed your grandma's voice as she tried to guide my steps. But I want you to know that I wish that I had. I could've avoided so many mistakes in my life had I listened. But your grandma could always hang her hat on the fact that she did tell me about certain things and give me advice about others. So, I guess that's what I'm doing here. I never want it to be said that I didn't try to prepare my son for the rest of his life. I want to tell you some of these things while I can still put my arms around you and protect you from some of the evils of this world. Because I know there will come a time when I have to let you go and live your life the way that you want. But I want you to know that I'll always be there for you and I'll never let any harm come to you if I can help it

I want to tell you how important your education is. You'll never go anywhere in life without knowledge. There are so many people out here without a proper education. I never want you to be one of those people. You have so much more potential than that. I'm not saying that you have to be a doctor or a lawyer or something like that (even though that would be nice too), but you should try and be the best at whatever you choose to do. But even if you're not the best, I'll still be satisfied if you give it your best. Anything worth doing is worth doing right and to the best of your ability. Keep that with you and you'll always do well.

Don't get sidetracked by alcohol and drugs. They never have and never will add anything to what you're trying to do. I'm sure that peer pressure will come along and others will tell you that there's no harm in doing things like that. But take it from your father that's never had a drink or a smoke, a man with a clear mind is always better off. Even if some of those others have more money or better material possessions, what they're doing to their bodies at some point will catch up to them. Money and material possessions won't matter when your health is failing you because you've smoked or drank too much.

Speaking of material possessions, don't allow yourself to be defined by what you have. Always by what's in your heart. A man can have all of the possessions in the world and still be worthless on the inside because his heart isn't right. Put you faith in God and not the possessions of this world. They won't matter when you come face to face with the Father. No man has ever bought his way into heaven. Being pure of heart will get you there quicker. Now, don't get me wrong son. Dad is not suggesting that you don't try to have nice things in your life. When I say I want nothing but the best for you, I mean in every sense of the word. I just don't want you to think that what you have makes you who you are. You are beautiful whether you have it all or whether you have nothing. Keep your thoughts focused on being the best person that you can be and not driving the hottest car on the block.

Don't get sidetracked by girls. This is something that your old man struggled with a little. The most important thing to remember about girls is that there are a lot of them. What I mean by that is, don't get carried away over one girl. If you meet a girl and she's taking away from your goals in life, you can't be afraid to let her go. If it's meant to be, it'll be. They're just like buses, if you miss one, another one will be along soon enough. That's not an excuse to ride every bus, my son. Just be wise in your selection. The prettiest face isn't always the best move either. Look for a girl that's pretty on the inside as well as on the outside. If you meet a girl and you like her, take your time. Don't get carried away and don't do anything that you shouldn't be doing because someone else said that they were doing it. It's been my experience that a lot of times they're lying about what they've done. Always take things slow and always show females respect.

No matter what you may hear, it's always important to respect women. It's what they want and what they need, even though you may meet some that don't realize it. You have to be careful with females. There are a lot of them out there that don't have the best intentions. You have to learn to recognize them and steer clear of that. You may catch a bad one here and there and that's okay. There's bound to be some bad experiences in your life. But if you make sure that you learn from your mistakes, it'll go a long way in helping you to avoid them the next time.

The last thing I want to tell you son, is to keep God first in all that you do. There are a lot of things in your life that will go wrong. The one thing in your life that will never let you down or change on you is God's love for you. The Bible says that men should always pray. Remember that, son. Whenever you have trouble in your life, you take it to God in prayer. Whenever things are great in your life, remember to thank God for it. If you stick to the path that God has set for you, you're sure to have success in your life. That doesn't mean that the devil won't try to attack what you do. Satan is always busy. But if you keep God in your life, there will never be a battle with Satan that you can't win.

I wish I could protect you from all that's negative in life, but I realize that it's not possible. If it had been, there would've been many parents before me that would've done the same thing. It's been my hope that I've passed more along to you than my good looks (wink). I hope that I can pass along some sort of wisdom. But all I can do is guide you the best I can until it's time to let you go. But I want you to know that if there ever comes a time when you need me, need my advice, need someone to talk to or just need to know that you're loved, I will always be there for you. I would end this by telling you to go out and make me proud, but you already have and I'm sure that you will again. I'm looking forward to watching you grow into a man. The sky is the limit for you. Just keep your head up and stay strong. I'll be watching you from the background. Always remember, I'm your biggest fan. I would lay down my life for you, my son. I love you very, very much.

Love,
Dad

# *Endnotes*

1. Taken from "Love Will Lead You Back" by Taylor Dayne, from the album *Can't Fight Fate*

2. Taken from "Ain't No Nigga" by Jay-Z, from the album *Reasonable Doubt*

3. Taken from "Piece Of My Love" by Guy, from the album *Guy*

4. Taken from "Not Gon' Cry" by Mary J. Blige, from the *Waiting To Exhale Soundtrack* and *Share My World*

5. Taken from "Turn The Page" by Terence Trent D'Arby, from the album *Symphony Or Damn*

6. Taken from "11<sup>th</sup> Hour" by Dionne Farris, from the album *Wild Seed-Wild Flower*

7. Taken from "In This Bed I Scream" by The Artist (Prince), from the album *Emancipation*

8. Taken from "Neither One Of Us (Wants To Be The First To Say Good-bye) by Gladys Knight and the Pips, from the album *Gladys Knight and the Pips Greatest Hits*

9. Taken from "Do What I Gotta Do" by Ralph Tresvant, from the album *Ralph Tresvant*

10. Taken from "A Different Corner" by George Michael, from the albums *Wham: Music From The Edge Of Heaven* and *Ladies and Gentlemen: The Best of George Michael*

11. See 10

12. Taken from "If You Asked Me To" by Patti LaBelle, from the albums *Be Yourself, Patti LaBelle: Greatest Hits, Patti LaBelle: 20<sup>th</sup> Century Masters Collection* and *Patti LaBelle: Greatest Love Songs*

13. Taken from "My Favorite Mistake" by Sheryl Crow, from the albums *The Globe Sessions* and *The Very Best of Sheryl Crow*

14. Taken from "Can't Get You Off My Mind" by Lenny Kravitz, from the albums *Circus* and *Lenny Kravitz Greatest Hits*

15. Taken from "I Wish I Wasn't" by Heather Headley, from the album *This Is Who I Am*

16. Taken from "How Could An Angel Break My Heart?" by Toni Braxton, from the album *Secrets*

17. Taken from "I Wish It Would Rain" by The Temptations, from *The Temptations: The Ultimate Collection*

18. Taken from "Old Friends 4 Sale" by Prince, from the album *The Vault: Old Friends 4 Sale*

19. Taken from "Older" by George Michael, from the album *Older*

20. Taken from "The Heart Of The Matter" by Don Henley, from the albums *The End Of The Innocence* and *Actual Miles: Henley's Greatest Hits*

21. Taken from "Seasons" by Terence Trent D'Arby, from the album *Symphony Or Damn*

22. Taken from "In Harm's Way" by Bebe Winans, from the album *Bebe Winans*

978-0-595-41835
0-595-41835-X

Printed in the United States
63691LVS00003B/118-138